Instructor's Manual

to accompany

Interplay: The Process of Interpersonal Communication
Twelfth Edition

Ronald B. Adler
Santa Barbara City College

Lawrence B. Rosenfeld
University of North Carolina at Chapel Hill

Russell F. Proctor II
Northern Kentucky University

Prepared by

Ellen Bremen
Highline Community College

Shannon Proctor
Highline Community College

New York   Oxford
Oxford University Press
2013

Oxford University Press, Inc., publishes works that further Oxford University's
objective of excellence in research, scholarship, and education.

Oxford New York
Auckland Cape Town Dar es Salaam Hong Kong Karachi
Kuala Lumpur Madrid Melbourne Mexico City Nairobi
New Delhi Shanghai Taipei Toronto

With offices in
Argentina Austria Brazil Chile Czech Republic France Greece
Guatemala Hungary Italy Japan Poland Portugal Singapore
South Korea Switzerland Thailand Turkey Ukraine Vietnam

Copyright © 2013 by Oxford University Press, Inc.

Published by Oxford University Press, Inc.
198 Madison Avenue, New York, New York 10016
http://www.oup.com

Oxford is a registered trademark of Oxford University Press

ISBN 978-0-19-982745-9

Printing number: 9 8 7 6 5 4 3 2 1

Printed in the United States of America
on acid-free paper.

CONTENTS

PART I: GENERAL TEACHING STRATEGIES 1

THE INSTRUCTOR IS THE MAIN INGREDIENT 1

FIRST DAY OF CLASS 1

CLASSROOM ENVIRONMENT 2

THE IMPORTANCE OF EXERCISES 3

USE OF SMALL GROUPS 3

TEAM LEARNING 4
  Practical Aspects of Teaching and Learning 4
  Cooperative Learning 4
  Team Learning Methodology as a Theoretical Framework 5
  Group Dynamics and Team Learning 6
  Necessary Components of Effective Learning Teams 6
  Course Design 6
  Classroom Management 7
  Student Group Composition 8
  Team Formation 8
  Developing Performance-Oriented Group Norms 8
  Performance Evaluation 9
  References 9

GRADING SYSTEMS 11
  Traditional Examinations 11
  Open-Note Quizzes/Study Guides 11
  Group Study Exercises 11
  Unit Wind-Ups 12
  Student-Planned Examinations 12
  Student–Instructor Contracts 12
  Journal Assignments and Portfolio Entries 12
  Discussion Questions and Activities (D&A) 13
  Book Reports/Exercises 13
  Movie Analysis 13
  Communication Skills Projects 14
  Self-Assessment 14

INSTRUCTOR EVALUATION 15
  Open-Ended Specific 15
  Objective/Numerical Rating 15

GENERAL TEACHING STRATEGIES 17

PART II: COURSE ARRANGEMENT 18

INTERPERSONAL COMMUNICATION: COURSE OUTLINE 18

STANDARD INTERPERSONAL COURSE OUTLINE 18

SAMPLE INTERPERSONAL COURSE OUTLINE #1 21

SAMPLE INTERPERSONAL COURSE OUTLINE #2 27

"TEAM LEARNING" INTERPERSONAL COURSE OUTLINE...30

TEAM LEARNING FORMS 40
    Purposes of the Appeals Process...43
    Guidelines for Preparing Successful Appeals 43
    Readiness Assessment Test Appeal Forms 44
    Peer Evaluation Helping Behavior..45
    Peer Evaluation Procedures and Criteria...45
    End-of-Semester Helping Behavior Peer Evaluation 47
    Sample Readiness Assessment Test (RAT) 48

PART III: CHAPTER EXERCISES.. 50

Chapter 1: Interpersonal Process..50

Chapter 2: Interpersonal Communication in a Changing World 57

Chapter 3: Communication and the Self 65

Chapter 4: Perceiving Others 72

Chapter 5: Language 78

Chapter 6: Nonverbal Communication 85

Chapter 7: Listening..91

Chapter 8: Emotions 102

Chapter 9: Dynamics of Interpersonal Relationships 111

Chapter 10: Communication Climate...119

Chapter 11: Managing Conflict..125

Chapter 12: Interpersonal Contexts 132

The Story of Us 136

PART IV: UNIT WIND-UPS 143

**Assessment of Critical Thinking Skills Through Collaborative Testing and Case Study Analysis in the
Interpersonal Communication Course** 143

UNIT WIND-UP 1: "YOU JUST DON'T UNDERSTAND…" 148

UNIT WIND-UP 2: "I JUST NEED SOMEONE TO LISTEN" 152

UNIT WIND-UP 3: "CAN'T I PLEASE ANYONE?" 157

FINAL WIND-UP: "WHOSE LIFE IS THIS, ANYWAY?" 162

PART V: TEST QUESTIONS **168**

Chapter 1: Interpersonal Process 168

Chapter 2: Interpersonal Communication in a Changing World 179

Chapter 3: Communication and the Self 190

Chapter 4: Perceiving Others 199

Chapter 5: Language 210

Chapter 6: Nonverbal Communication 219

Chapter 7: Listening 229

Chapter 8: Emotions 238

Chapter 9: Dynamics of Interpersonal Relationships 249

Chapter 10: Communication Climate 258

Chapter 11: Managing Conflict 269

Chapter 12: Interpersonal Contexts 279

Part I: General Teaching Strategies

THE INSTRUCTOR IS THE MAIN INGREDIENT

The introductory course in interpersonal communication is unique in the college curriculum. When it is taught with the dual approach of theory and application as advocated by the authors of *Interplay*, it will lead students to an understanding of their own communication styles and those of others. Awareness and understanding are the first steps in empowering us to improve. As our students practice and acquire new expertise in daily "taken-for-granted" communication skills, they can actually *improve the quality of their lives*. This is a weighty claim for a single course!

Instructors of interpersonal communication, then, have a particularly challenging job. In addition to dealing with the various problems faced by all instructors in the classroom, the interpersonal communication teacher faces the challenge of connecting theory and daily reality as well as being a model interpersonal communicator for the class. To this end, it becomes important that interpersonal instructors be able not only to explain concepts and enhance the understanding of course materials, but actually to relate interpersonally to their students.

The single most effective way to do this is to participate actively in class exercises. While there will be many times in which the instructor must play a specialized role to facilitate an exercise, taking part on the same level as the student whenever possible pays dividends in two major ways:

1. It encourages participation from students. Sharing something of ourselves seems to increase interaction with the group. When students see that we are willing to share our experiences, they seem to be encouraged to do the same. (Remember the reciprocity factor in self-disclosure.) True to interpersonal studies that show that we are attracted to individuals who are competent but "human," it seems that we are most successful when we risk participating and making mistakes. Students seem to relate to and learn more easily from coping than from total-mastery models.
2. Our participation gives us a good perspective on the students' experience in the class. Sometimes what appears to be a simple exercise is actually quite challenging; on the other hand, activities that appear valuable in theory may prove to be dismal failures in practice.

It is also essential that we relate comfortably with our students outside of the classroom, making ourselves available during office hours and dealing with students as individuals. The first step in this process is learning students' names as early as possible in the semester. Many instructors choose to increase their rapport with students by being on a first-name basis with them.

FIRST DAY OF CLASS

The first day of class sets a tone for the remainder of the term, and, as such, it is a day on which instructors need to be most careful to create the impression of themselves and of the course that they want to remain in the students' minds. As research in impression formation indicates, the initial impression that students have of a class and of an instructor may give them an overall view of the course that endures throughout of the term. For the first class session, it is important to appear before students looking prepared, organized, and knowledgeable. Many of the people using this instructor's manual will be first-year instructors or graduate students who do not learn their teaching assignments until a day or two prior to the beginning of class. Complete preparation and organization of course lectures, exercises, and materials would be impossible only 24 hours before class starts, but strategies can be employed to make that first impression a positive one.

The first class session should include the following:

1. Introduce yourself and tell the students how you want to be addressed.
2. Distribute a course syllabus that includes the following:

a. Course Name, Number, Meeting Times, Location, Teacher Name
b. Office Location, Phone Numbers, Office Hours, E-Mail Address
c. Course Description: Catalogue description, including prerequisites, additional description as needed
d. Course Objectives
e. Course Policies:
   - Attendance
   - Assignment Format Information
   - Makeup Policy
   - Class Participation
   - Plagiarism (reference to university policy)
f. Grading Policy: Statement of how final grade will be determined, to include:
   - Grading Scale
   - Weight/Values for Various Assignments, Papers, Exams
   - Absenteeism, Extra Work, Late Work, In-Class Participation
g. Topics and Order of Coverage
h. Key Dates:
   - Exams
   - Assignment Due Dates
   - Planned Absences
i. Assignments:
   - Descriptions
   - Relative Weights
j. Course Materials:
   - Texts
   - Supplies
   - Supplemental Readings
   - Fees
k. Lab Policy (if applicable)

In addition, you may want to include the following paragraph, which is required by the North Central Accrediting Agency for Teacher Education: "(Name of your school) is an Affirmative Action Equal Opportunity Institution. Students with disabilities and other special needs should feel free to contact the professor privately if there are services or adaptations that can be made to accommodate specific needs."

3. Indicate what is expected of students before the next class meeting.
4. Introduction exercises (see activities in this manual at the end of Chapter 1 exercise section) can be used to "break the ice" and help create a supportive communication climate. (No student should leave the first class without having met at least a few new people.)

CLASSROOM ENVIRONMENT

If we expect students to interact comfortably with one another, it is important to create a conducive environment. The following suggestions have proven useful:

1. Chose a classroom with moveable chairs or desks that can be rearranged easily.
2. Arrange the classroom seating so that members of the group can see each other. If room and class size allow, a circle works best. This allows maximum face-to-face interaction and easy movement into smaller circles for group exercises and discussion. Students become more willing to discuss with one another (rather than interacting with only the instructor) when they can see each other's nonverbal reactions. The circle formation also seems to keep students generally more involved and alert. (After all, it's more embarrassing to "drift off" if everyone can see you!)

3. Sit behind different members of the class and at different spots in the circle whenever possible to enhance the perception of dealing with students at the same level and to increase the chances of active interaction.
4. Encourage class participation by asking questions and enduring the silence until you get answers. Ask questions that may have a number of possible answers, and keep soliciting answers. Call on students by name.
5. If you're fortunate enough to have a classroom specifically designed for interpersonal communication classes, personalizing the environment creates a comfortable climate in which to interact. Carpeting the floor of the classroom provides students the option of sitting there in small-group activities. This seems to increase informality and the amount of interaction that takes place. Other artifacts, such as posters, plants, and bookshelves, increase the "personalness" of a classroom environment and promote effective interpersonal communication.

THE IMPORTANCE OF EXERCISES

The unshakable belief on which this textbook and instructor's manual is based is that complete learning takes place only when the students understand a concept on an affective as well as a cognitive level. The authors would consider themselves to have failed if, by the end of a term, students could list the necessary elements of effective interpersonal communication but no longer cared about using this knowledge to improve their relationships.

This commitment to encourage readers to examine their everyday behavior explains the abundance of exercises in the textbook and instructor's manual. Participating in them should make a personal application of the subject almost inevitable. Every activity leads the reader to go beyond talking about how "people" communicate and to ask, "How do I communicate?" and "How can I make my communication more appropriate and satisfying for myself and others?"

This emphasis on self-examination necessarily involves asking students to investigate (individually and as a group) feelings and behaviors that aren't often shared in academic settings. While very little growth comes without this kind of examination, it is absolutely essential not to push too hard, not to demand more self-disclosure than the group is ready to volunteer.

USE OF SMALL GROUPS

Many of the exercises in this manual depend on the use of small groups. Instructors may choose to place students in the variety of different groups throughout the semester (chosen by proximity, "counting off," drawing names, instructor assignment, etc.), or students may remain in the same group for longer blocks of time—throughout a unit, for example, or even for the entire semester. There are benefits to each of these formats. In the first case, students will have the opportunity to work with most or all of the individuals in the class. They will experience a larger number of personality styles and will be exposed to wider variety of ideas and examples. They will leave the class feeling that they "know" everyone to a limited degree. Also, if the class is "blessed" with an individual who clearly has problems relating to others and who tends to be a negative influence, everyone will have an equal opportunity to deal with this "challenge."

On the other hand, remaining in the same group for a longer period of time fosters a sense of dedication and devotion. Students may sometimes make a special effort to attend class because they know that their group is depending on them. Group members frequently develop a real sense of group identity and attain a high degree of comfort with one another. Most importantly, members of groups that are stable are more likely to achieve the trust level necessary for self-disclosure, and the group members often maintain their relationship after the semester ends.

Interpersonal communication instructors who prefer permanent teams and are interested in a unique cooperative learning instructional strategy that can be effectively implemented in interpersonal communication classes will find the next section, on **Team Learning**, especially useful.

TEAM LEARNING[1]

Derek R. Lane, Ph.D.
Assistant Professor of Communication
University of Kentucky

Practical Aspects of Teaching and Learning

In his overview of research on teaching at the college and university level, McKeachie (1963) argues that the ultimate criteria of effective college teaching are changes in students toward the goals of higher education. These changes can be attitudinal and emotional as well as cognitive. He proposes that research evaluating the effectiveness of college instruction must consider "not only the accumulation of knowledge but the development of problem-solving skills and desirable attitudes" (p. 1118). The development of instructional strategies that contribute to learning as an outcome is key to improving the educational process. While the general principles of learning (e.g., motivation, organization, feedback) are relevant to the choice of instructional strategies, McKeachie (1994) believes,

> Much of the progress made in understanding the practical aspects of teaching and learning has come from individual faculty members who have carried out studies in their own and colleagues' classes to get empirical evidence with respect to some issue, such as the effectiveness of some teaching innovation or the student characteristics affecting response to some aspect of teaching or testing (p. 339).

Cooperative Learning

Johnson, Johnson, and Smith (1991a) discuss two paradigms of college teaching and the change that is occurring within these paradigms. First, the old paradigm involves: (a) the transferring of knowledge from faculty to students, (b) the classifying of students by grade and category, (c) conducting education within a context of impersonal relationships among students and between faculty and students, (d) maintaining a competitive organizational structure, and (e) assuming that anyone with expertise in their field can tech without training to do so. This old paradigm uses a traditional, linear model where faculty knowledge is transferred to a passive student learner.

The second, new paradigm of teaching and learning involves collaborative methodology and assumes: (a) knowledge is constructed, discovered, transformed, and extended by students; (b) students actively construct their knowledge; (c) faculty efforts are aimed at developing student's competencies and talents; (d) education is a personal transaction among students and between faculty and students as they work together; (e) the more pressure placed on students to achieve and the more difficult the material to be learned, the more important it is to provide social support within the learning situation; and (f) authentic learning takes place within a cooperative context.

Cooperative learning is not a new idea. As early as the first century Quintilian (1875) suggested that students could benefit from teaching each other. The Roman philosopher Seneca advocated cooperative learning through such statements as "Qui Docet Discet" (when you teach, you learn twice). Johnson, Johnson, and Smith (1991a) state "in the late 1700s, Joseph Lancaster and Andrew Bell made extensive use of cooperative learning groups in England and the idea was brought to America when a Lancastrian school was opened in New York City in 1806" (p. 16).

In the early 1960s, as a result of their work on cooperative learning, Johnson and F. Johnson (1991) developed the Cooperative Learning Center and the University of Minnesota. Since then, they

---

*This paper is based on ideas from an article that was originally presented at the 1997 Southern States Communication Association entitled "The Use of Permanent Learning Teams in Teaching Introductory Communication Courses: A Theoretical Framework and Rationale for Assessing the Impact of Communication on Learning."

have conducted over 85 research studies on cooperative learning and a series of meta-analyses of the last 90 years of instructional research containing a list of over 575 experimental studies and 100 correlational studies (Johnson & Johnson, 1989). The authors found that "cooperative learning promotes higher achievement than does competitive or individualistic learning" (p. 12). Other benefits of cooperative learning include: positive interpersonal relationships, higher levels of self-esteem, and the maximizing of social competencies (Johnson & Johnson, 1989). In addition, research has been compiled regarding knowledge attained through cooperative, competitive, and individualistic efforts (e.g., Johnson & Johnson, 1994; Johnson, Johnson, & Holubec, 1990).

Johnson and his colleagues (1991a) suggest that "putting students into groups to learn is not the same thing as structuring cooperation among students" (p. 18). They discern five basic elements of a cooperative learning situation: (a) positive interdependence, (b) face-to-face promotive interaction, (c) individual accountability, (d) social skills (interpersonal and small group skills), and (e) group processing and evaluation (Johnson et al., 1990). One procedure for structuring cooperative learning groups is Aronson's "jigsaw" procedure, which involves a five-step sequence for structuring cooperative learning (Aronson, Blaney, Stephan, Sikes, & Snapp, 1978).

Perhaps the most comprehensive group-based approach for harnessing the power of cooperative learning in higher education is that of Michaelsen and his colleagues (e.g., Michaelsen, 1994; Michaelsen & Black, 1994; Michaelsen, Fink, & Watson, 1994; Michaelsen, Jones, & Watson, 1993). Michaelsen, Jones, & Watson (1993) provide a distinction between Team Learning and Cooperative Learning. Both approaches make use of class time for group work and "build positive and supportive relationships between instructor and students while ensuring that students have immediate access to the instructor's task related expertise," but differences result from the "unique characteristics of the settings for which the two approaches were developed" (p. 140). Cooperative Learning was developed for elementary students with a limited degree of self-control, while Team Learning was designed for professional business students capable of exhibiting a relatively high degree of self-control.

Cooperative Learning instructors define and structure individual member roles and train students to manage group processes. On the other hand, Team Learning emphasizes the application of concepts as opposed to merely learning about them. Team Learning provides the incentives and opportunities to students because: (a) a substantial part of the course grade is based on group performance and (b) groups receive regular and immediate feedback on their performance relative to other groups. As an instructional strategy, Team Learning provides the context and method for operationalizing an experimental instructional strategy.

Team Learning Methodology as a Theoretical Framework

Team Learning has the potential to better achieve the goals and objectives of the introductory, hybrid communication course because it offers students more opportunities to develop intellectual and professional skills through course content application. Team Learning helps students enhance their ability to establish positive interpersonal relationships while increasing their self-esteem and maximizing their social competencies.

To understand how Team Learning strategies can enhance the achievement of classroom communication goals, one need only ponder the simple proverb: "I hear and I forget, I see and I remember, I DO and I understand." Instructional strategies incorporating Team Learning allow students to "do" and "understand."

The next section provides information regarding the use and utility of learning teams in instructional setting sin three parts: (a) It provides a brief discussion of the nature of group dynamics and Team Learning and examines the benefits of Team Learning in the classroom; (b) it illustrates the necessary components of effective learning teams; and (c) it identifies procedures necessary for successful integration of learning teams into the instructional environment (i.e., course design, classroom management, student group composition, and performance evaluation).

Group Dynamics and Team Learning

A group is defined as "two or more persons who are interacting with one another in such a manner that each person influences and is influence by each other. … Typically a group is composed of five or fewer members" (Shaw, 1981, p. 8). Although the essential feature that distinguishes a group from an aggregate is interaction, there are three important aspects of a group: A group must (a) endure for a reasonable period (longer than a few minutes, at least), (b) have a common goal or goals, and (c) have developed at least a rudimentary group structure (Shaw, 1981, p. 8).

Team Learning was originally designed to cope with the problems of large classes, over 120 students in an academic setting (Michaelsen, Watson, Cragin, & Fink, 1982). Team Learning primarily emphasizes learning to *use* concepts rather than merely *learning about* them. Michaelsen (1994) states: "Becoming a team is a process, not an event. Unless instructors facilitate the transformation of groups into teams, their success in using small groups is likely to be limited at best" (p. 2). The two distinctive features of instructional strategies incorporating learning teams are: (a) a redefinition of the primary roles and responsibilities in the learning process and (b) the formation of an operational learning environment that incorporates use of four new and essential operational tools (course design, classroom management, student group compositions, and performance evaluation).

Michaelsen and Black (1994) argue that instructional strategies that incorporate Team Learning require a learning model paradigm shift where the traditional model (which includes the roles (a) teacher as dispenser of knowledge and (b) students as passive receivers of information; subject mastery is determined by testing individual students) is replaced by a Team Learning model (which includes the roles of (a) instructor as course designer and manager of overall instructional process and (b) students as active participants who are accountable and responsible for their learning). Michaelsen, Watson, Cragin, and Fink (1982) identify four primary features of Team Learning: (a) permanent and purposefully heterogeneous work groups; (b) grading based on a combination of individual performance, group performance, and peer evaluation; (c) the majority of the class time devoted to small-group activities; and (d) a repetitive six-step instructional activity sequence (IAS), which assists students in developing higher level cognitive skills.

Necessary Components of Effective Learning Teams

There are five necessary and sufficient components that must be integrated into Team Learning instructional strategies. Omission of any of the components limits the ability of teams to be successful.

1. Heterogeneous composition of diverse interdependent work teams (comprised of between five and eight individuals) that minimize potential threats from cohesive subgroups.
2. Clear, specific, and widely shared group goals that encourage group cohesion.
3. Sufficiently difficult and meaningful group activities that do not allow one member of the group to accomplish the task alone.
4. Regular, descriptive, specific, relevant, timely, and usable internal peer feedback.
5. External comparisons that are emphasized through immediate and ongoing feedback about organizational performance relative to other teams.

The next four sections describe the four essential operational tools that provide the foundation for the formation of an operational learning environment: course design, classroom management, student group composition, and performance evaluation.

Course Design

Michaelsen and Black (1994) argue that successful instruction using the Team Learning model is dependent on course design in which "instructors must focus on creating two very different types of instructional activities. One type must focus on building a sound student understanding of basic concepts.

The other is to design activities that focus on building students' higher-level thinking and problem-solving skills" (p. 3). Designing activities for the classroom is perhaps the most difficult obstacle to the successful use of learning teams. Michaelsen and Black (1994) developed four questions that assist instructors when making key strategic decisions:

1. What do I want the students to be able to *do* when they have completed this unit of instruction (desired educational outcomes)?
2. What will the students have to *know* to be able to do it (course content)?
3. How can I tell what students have *already learned* on their own or from each other so I could build from there (readiness assurance/assessment/feedback)?
4. How can I tell whether or not students can effectively *use* their knowledge (application of course concepts)?

Classroom Management

When using the Team Learning model, the majority of instructor effort occurs before the course begins. Preparation and organization are key to successful incorporation of the Team Learning model. While the primary classroom management tool in the traditional learning model is lecture, classroom management in the Team Learning model is accomplished through a six-step IAS (Michaelsen, Fink, & Watson, 1994). The IAS is repeated for each major unit of instruction (typically five to seven times).

Michaelsen and Black (1994) believe "the most unique feature of the IAS is that there are no formal presentations by the instructor until the students have studied the material and completed the individual and group readiness assessment tests" (p. 5). The IAS includes working through the following six steps:

1. Individual Study
2. Individual Testing (Readiness Assurance Test—RAT)
3. Group Testing (Readiness Assurance Test—RAT)
4. Written Group Appeals
5. Instructor Feedback
6. Application-Oriented Activities

Step 1 (individual study) ensures that students prepare for class by studying assigned instructional materials. Steps 2 through 5 constitute the Readiness Assurance Process (RAP) (Michaelsen, Watson, & Schraeder, 1985; Michaelsen, Fink, & Watson, 1994). Step 2 (individual testing) provides a diagnostic tool for determining student readiness and promotes individual accountability. The individual test consists of 15–20 multiple choice and short answer questions taken from assigned readings and/or homework-type problems. To provide immediate feedback to both instructor and students for a unit of instruction, both team and individual tests are scored in class. Step 3 (group testing) ensures group accountability and peer teaching. The group test is identical to the individual test and is taken after the completion of the individual exams. Immediate scoring provides instructor and students with feedback.

Step 4 (written group appeals) increases learning and enhances group cohesiveness. Michaelsen and Black (1994) believe that written group appeals "galvanize a group's negative energy from having missed questions into a focused review of potentially troublesome concepts" (p. 6). Written appeals may come from groups—no individual written appeals are accepted. If the team appeal is granted, however, individuals in the team writing the appeal should also be given credit. Step 5 includes providing feedback to students with additional explanation prior to the application of course concepts. Instructor skills such as processing, debriefing, and facilitating discussion greatly affect the impact on student learning. These skills are similar to those required to lead discussions in a traditional instructional environment, but require more knowledge. Since the Team Learning model encourages negotiation of the learning environment, it is likely that students will challenge an instructor's knowledge more than in traditional learning situations. Therefore, an instructor must be prepared, knowledgeable, and competent. This needs to be done without damaging the positive instructional environment (graduate teaching assistants must be cautious of power plays ["I'm right, you're wrong"] with students or behaving in a condescending manner).

Step 6 requires the use of application-oriented activities to help students grow in self-confidence while developing a thorough understanding of the class concepts. This step can be problematic and even detrimental with ineffective group assignments. Michaelsen and Black (1994) believe that group assignments simultaneously accomplish four major objectives: *promote learning of essential concepts or skills, build group cohesiveness, ensure individual accountability,* and *teach students the positive value of groups.* Six characteristics of effective group assignments include:

1. Production of a *tangible output*
2. Impossible to complete without *comprehension* of course concepts
3. Sufficiently *difficult* to eliminate completion by an individual member
4. Majority of *time should be spent engaged* in activities
5. Applicable to real-world issues or problems (*pragmatic/applied*)
6. Interesting and/or *fun*

Michaelsen, Black, and Fink (in press) have recently compiled a manuscript that outlines detailed procedures for preventing group problems and developing effective assignments to be used in designing application-oriented activities. Michaelsen and Black (1994) suggest "the application activities, group projects, and exams employed should look and feel like that kinds of things you hope students would be able to do individually once they have completed the unit of instruction" (p. 6). The application of course concepts (step 6) should constitute approximately 75 percent of total class time, whereas the RAP (first five steps) should constitute no more than 25 percent of class time.

Student Group Composition

The formation and development of learning teams enable students to move from a passive role in the traditional learning model to a more active role where they are accountable and responsible for their learning. Michaelsen, Jones, and Watson (1993) report that "the development of properly managed, permanent, and purposefully heterogeneous learning teams is key to successfully increasing students' willingness to accept responsibility to ensure that learning occurs" (p. 132).

Team Formation

Three key principles have been discussed (Michaelsen & Black, 1994) for the process of forming learning teams: (a) Evenly distribute student assets among groups; (b) avoid unnecessary barriers to group cohesiveness by having teacher form the groups to eliminate students in groups with previously established relationships; and (c) make the group formation process as visible as possible.

Developing Performance-Oriented Group Norms

In order for performance-oriented group norms to be developed, students should: (a) see a clear relationship between individual member behavior and the success or failure of their team, (b) be able to monitor the extent to which members are complying with group norms, and (c) have feedback mechanisms available when individuals fail to comply with group norms. Michaelsen and Black (1994) suggest that the instructors can empower teams by: (a) providing comparisons to other teams, (b) requiring a peer evaluation, and (c) having students keep a record of attendance and performance.

Team Learning can only be successful with a substantial part of the course grade is based on group performance and the groups receive regular and immediate feedback on how they are doing in relation to other groups (which causes students to take pride in their group's success). Performance evaluation, therefore, is an important component in the Team Learning model.

Performance Evaluation

The final key procedure for the implementation of learning teams in the classroom involves three essential components related to performance evaluation: individual performance, group performance, and peer evaluation. Michaelsen, Cragin, and Watson (1981) encourage the involvement of students and teams in the development of fair and equitable grade weights. Their philosophy is that students will support a policy that they helped to create.

Essentially, the "learning teams" pedagogy includes a variety of student-centered activities both in and out of the classroom, including:

- Reading and lectures make up 25 percent of the coursework; application of the material (various forms of experiential learning) is 75 percent.
- Teams of four to five students each are formed early in the course and maintained throughout.
- A substantial portion of the course deliverables (35–45 percent) is based on team performance.
- The class takes periodic "readiness assessment tests" covering the readings and class material (first individually then immediately as a team) to ensure that they are prepared for the application portions of the course.
- The methodology ensures that students are exposed to the material at least four times before moving on to the application phase.
- The reward structure and class atmosphere are designed to facilitate cooperation *within* teams but competition *between* teams.

The Learning Teams approach to teaching requires substantial work—for the professor as well as the students—but it provides substantial rewards in terms of student learning in the interpersonal communication classroom.

References

Aronson, E., Blaney, N., Stephan, C., Sikes, J., & Snapp, M. (1978). *The jigsaw classroom.* Beverly Hills, CA: Sage.

Johnson, D. W., & Johnson, F. (1991). *Joining together: Group theory and group skills.* 4th ed. Englewood Cliffs, NJ: Prentice Hall.

Johnson, D. W., & Johnson, R. (1978). Cooperative, competitive, and individualistic learning. *Journal of Research and Development in Education, 12,* 3–15.

Johnson, D. W., & Johnson, R. (1981). Effects of cooperative and individualistic learning experiences on interethnic interaction. *Journal of Educational Psychology, 73,* 454–459.

Johnson, D. W., & Johnson, R. (1985). Classroom conflict: Controversy vs. Debate in learning groups. *American Educational Research Journal, 22,* 237–256.

Johnson, D. W., & Johnson, R. (1989). *Cooperation and competition: Theory and research.* Edina, MN: Interaction Book Company.

Johnson, D. W., & Johnson, R. (1994). *Learning together and alone: Cooperative, competitive, and individualistic learning.* 4th ed. Boston, MA: Allyn and Bacon.

Johnson, D. W., Johnson, R., & Holubec, E. (1990). *Circles of learning: Cooperation in the classroom.* Edina, MN: Interaction Book Company.

Johnson, D. W., Johnson, R. T., & Smith, K. A. (1991a). *Active learning: Cooperation in the college classroom.* Edina, MA: Interaction Books.

Johnson, D. W., Johnson, R. T., & Smith, K. A. (1991b). *Cooperative learning: Increasing college faculty instructional productivity.* Washington, DC: The George Washington University, School of Education and Human Development.

Johnson, D. W., Johnson, R., Stanne, M., & Garibaldi, A. (1990). The impact of leader and member group processing on achievement in cooperative groups. *Journal of Social Psychology, 130,* 507–516.

Lane, D. R. (1995). *Theoretical and methodological assumptions about learning: An overview of learning theory and its implications for instructional communication research.* Unpublished manuscript, University of Oklahoma, Norman.

Lane, D. R. (1996). *The use of permanent learning groups in teaching introductory communication courses: Assessing the impact of communication on human learning.* Unpublished doctoral dissertation, The University of Oklahoma, Norman.

McKeachie, W. J. (1963). Research on teaching at the college and university level. In N. L. Gage (Ed.), *Handbook of Research on Teaching* (pp. 1118–1172). Chicago: Rand McNally.

McKeachie, W. J. (Ed.). (1994). *Teaching tips: Strategies, research, and theory for college and university teachers.* 8th ed. Lexington, MA: D.C. Heath and Company.

Michaelsen, L. K. (1992). Team learning: A comprehensive approach to harnessing the power of small groups in higher education. *To Improve the Academy, 11,* 107–122

Michaelsen, L. K. (1994). Classroom organization and management: Making a case for the small-group option. In K. W. Pritchard & R. M. Sawyer (Eds.), *Handbook of college teaching: Theory and applications.* Westport, CT: Greenwood Publishing Group, Inc.

Michaelsen, L. K., & Black, R. H. (1994) Building learning teams: The key to harnessing the power of small groups in higher education, *Collaborative Learning: A Sourcebook for Higher Education* (Vol. 2,). State College, PA: National Center for Teaching, Learning & Assessment.

Michaelsen, L. K., Black, R. H., & Fink, L. D. (1995). *Problems with learning groups: An ounce of prevention.* Unpublished manuscript. University of Oklahoma.

Michaelsen, L. K., Cragin, J. P., & Watson, W. E. (1981). Grading and anxiety: A strategy for coping. *The Organizational Behavior Teaching Journal, 6,* 8–14.

Michaelsen, L. K., Fink, L.D., & Watson, W. E. (1994). Pre-instructional minitests: An efficient solution to covering content. *Journal of Management Education, 18,* 32–44.

Michaelsen, L. K., Jones, C. F., & Watson, W. E. (1993). Beyond groups and cooperation: Building high-performance learning teams. In D. L. Wright & J. P. Lunde (Eds.), *To improve the academy: Resources for faculty, instructional and organizational development* (pp. 127–145). Stillwater, OK: New Forums Press.

Michaelsen, L. K., Watson, W. E., & Black, R. H. (1989). A realistic test of individual versus group consensus decision-making. *Journal of Applied Psychology, 74,* 834–839.

Michaelsen, L. K., Watson, W. E., Cragin, J. P., & Fink, L. D. (1982). Team Learning: A potential solution to the problem of large classes. *Exchange: The Organizational Behavior Teaching Journal, 7,* 13–22.

Michaelsen, L. K., Watson, W. E., & Schraeder, C. B. (1985). Informative testing: A practical approach for tutoring with groups. *The Organizational Behavior Teaching Review, 9,* 18–33.

Quintilian (Ed.). (1875). *Institutio oratio.* London: William Heinemann.

Shaw, M. E. (1981). *Group dynamics: The psychology of small group behavior.* 3rd ed. New York: McGraw-Hill.

Slavin, R. E., & Karweit, N. L. (1984). Mastery learning and student teams: A factorial experiment in urban general mathematics classes. *American Educational Research Journal, 21,* 725–736.

Watson, W. E., Michaelsen, L. K., & Sharp, W. (1991). Member competence, group interaction, and group decision-making: A longitudinal study. *Journal of Applied Psychology, 76,* 803–809.

GRADING SYSTEMS

A good evaluation system should achieve three goals:

1. It should give students feedback on their mastery of the skills under study, to answer the question "How well do I understand the subject?"
2. It should give instructors feedback on how successful they have been in communicating the subject matter to students, to answer the question "Which areas were taught successfully and which do I need to cover more or differently?"
3. It should avoid slipping into the trap of inviting and rewarding unproductive behaviors: busywork, plagiarism, or excessive verbosity.

Several alternatives for accomplishing these goals are available and can be used singly or in combination. The systems are examined next for both advantages and disadvantages.

Traditional Examinations

The biggest advantage of traditional examinations is the likelihood that students will read and study the text with care and reflect upon the objectives of each chapter. In addition to midterm or final exams, testing prior to discussion of each chapter works well to illuminate trouble spots and clear up any misunderstandings.

The principle disadvantage is that tests may not actually measure the most important goals of the class, namely, improving the student's everyday communication behavior. For example, it is entirely possible that a student could describe in writing a number of effective behaviors for coping with criticism and never practice any of them. Thus, tests may measure skill in taking tests about communication and little else.

Open-Note Quizzes/Study Guides

In an effort to encourage reading before class discussion, an instructor may choose to incorporate open-note quizzes into the curriculum. Chapter Study Guides are included for each chapter in the Part III Chapter Exercises Section. Instruct the students to read and take notes on each chapter using the study guides. At the beginning of the class allow students to ask clarification questions related to material they did not understand. Students may then use any notes they took off the study guide to complete a short (15- to 20-question) quiz on the chapter. It is then possible to discuss the concepts using the quiz as a guide.

There are 12 chapters, so an instructor may choose to drop two to three of the lowest quiz grades. The biggest advantage is decreased lecture time. Since the students have already read the material, an instructor can spend more class time exploring how students utilize course concepts in their everyday interactions.

The Study Guides were developed by Neil Gregersen, University of Wisconsin–Waukesha.

Group Study Exercises

For each chapter in the textbook, this manual provides a matching quiz entitled "Group Study Exercise." These questions generally require students to match particular examples with the theories that the situations illustrate. Because these exercises are completed in small groups, there is usually excellent discussion about the theory, and the students are able to see more clearly how it relates to "real life." Although an answer key is provided, instructors should exercise their own judgment as to whether or not a group can offer a reasonable explanation for other responses. (The real point is that the students *think*, not that they simply identify the correct letter.) The grades on these exercises may be recorded and used as a component of the final grade. Since all members of the group receive the same grade, the students' personal investment in the group is also increased.

Unit Wind-Ups

The concept of the Unit Wind-Up is tied closely to the link between theory and application. As instructors in interpersonal communication, one of our principal goals is that our students not only know/understand theory but also begin to apply the principles of communication to their daily transactions; it does not seem adequate that we test solely on content recall. The Wind-Up presents students with a scenario of interpersonal transaction. (Ideally, they will be able both to listen to the scenario on audiotape as well as to read it in hard copy. In this case, audiotape is superior to video since video introduces too many variables into the analysis.) After they have heard the conversation, students work in small groups to answer specific questions that analyze the interaction in terms of the theory of the particular unit. All members of a group receive the same grade on this in-class project.

Part IV in this manual offers a more complete explanation of the concept, development, and use of the Unit Wind-Up as well as three Wind-Ups, one to follow each of the three units in the text. A scenario that can be used as a final exam—to be analyzed by each student individually—is also included. (The use of Unit Wind-Ups is built into the semester-course plan, which follows in Part II.)

Student-Planned Examinations

In this variation of traditional examinations, students split into small groups that submit several possible examination questions. All questions then are given to the entire class, with the understanding that the instructor will select several of them for the actual test.

While this method carries the same disadvantage as the traditional method described earlier, students study the material more intensively as they select and draw up questions; personal involvement takes on even broader dimensions.

Student–Instructor Contracts

In this system, student and instructor develop a specific program of study that the student agrees to undertake in order to return, for which he or she receives a predetermined grade. Contracts can cover work corresponding to units of study, or they can be written for term projects that may take the place of a final examination. Projects can take many forms: research papers, interviews, dramatic productions, surveys, journals.

There are two advantages to such a plan. First, it demands student initiative in proposing a course of study—a pleasant contrast to more passive types of assignments in which students play less creative roles. Second, such a format often allows students some latitude in choosing how to channel their energies. Research and experience show that the quality of work and motivation are higher when students work on subjects of personal interest.

Two disadvantages often occur in the contract method. First, some tasks that students choose may not focus on concepts that the instructor deems most important. This difficulty can be remedied by defining acceptable areas of study. Second, some students lack the ability to be self-motivated scholars.

Journal Assignments and Portfolio Entries

In place of or in addition to examinations, instructors may use assignments in which students reflect on how topics under study apply to their personal lives. The advantage of such an approach lies in extending concepts discussed beyond the classroom and into the student's everyday relationships. The value of such applications is obvious in a course designed to improve communication skills, especially since students are forced to articulate their ideas in writing, rather than just "thinking about" their behaviors.

The Journal typically asks the student to write in response to something that (s)he has read or that (s)he has experienced in class. Students may, for example, be required to write one or two pages for each class session of for two out of three sessions. Journal writing is usually fairly casual and may or may not be well focused; one potential disadvantage lies in the failure of journals to center clearly on key concepts discussed in class.

This can be remedied by using the more focused Portfolio Entries that are included for each chapter in Section III of the manual. These assignments are slightly more formal in their format and more clearly defined. These entries may ask students to examine their current behaviors, to try to solve a problem, or simply to use personal examples to illustrate the theory being studied. It is not likely that an instructor will have the time or inclination to use all of these assignments during a single semester; however, some of these assignments have had dramatic effects in improving students' interpersonal relationships.

Journal Assignments and/or Portfolio Entries should be collected periodically (perhaps at the completion of each unit) throughout the semester. It should be noted that reading these assignments takes a good deal of time, since each one is unique and needs to be responded to in a unique manner. Comments are critical—in addition to the grade. Instructors also need to assure students that anything they write will be held in total confidentiality and that the grade will be a reflection of the quality of their work, not the quality of themselves as individuals.

Discussion Questions and Activities (D&A)

These short assignments can be given to students to encourage class discussion. Many students express frustration at coming up with real-life examples "on the spot," and these assignments help them think of personal examples ahead of time that can then be shared with the class. Assignments can be adapted from longer portfolio assignments and class activities outlined in Part III or selected from the activities list at the end of each chapter in the Interplay textbook. Sample D&A assignments are provided for each chapter in Part III Activities.

Assignments should be short, generally one page in length, and students should be given credit for completion rather than graded for content. The purpose in grading is to ensure that the students thought about the concept, not necessarily whether they correctly applied it, although the instructor will have the opportunity to correct misunderstandings through discussion and written comments.

The advantage of such assignments is that students will have an example ready when asked to participate in discussion. Based on responses, an instructor will also be able to identify any troublesome concepts that need more class time.

A sample syllabus is outlined in Part II showing how the aforementioned open-note quizzes and the D&A assignments can be integrated into the curriculum.

Book Reports/Exercises

Book reports may be assigned to students to encourage more in-depth study of a particular subject area.

The greatest disadvantage of book reports as a method of evaluation is that students often prepare book reports that merely repeat what was said in the book. To overcome this disadvantage, a requirement of the assignment can be that the student develop an activity that will illustrate the book's information. The activity should be designed to teach others in the class one important thing (cognitive or affective) that the student gleaned from the book and can take the form or role-play, a questionnaire, or an exercise modeled on those in the text. Class sessions are periodically set aside for students to work out their activities with their classmates. Class members are asked to give feedback evaluating each student's exercise. The book report/exercise method seems to reinforce learning of the basic tenets of each book, and most students seem to enjoy sharing "discoveries" with their classmates.

Movie Analysis

The great thing about communication is that it permeates are lives, and popular culture often holds many examples for students to evaluate and learn from. Movies about relationships are great vehicles for course concept discussion. *The Story of Us*, starring Bruce Willis and Michelle Pfeiffer, chronicles the 15-year relationship of a couple on the verge of divorce.

It is an excellent movie to generate discussion on relational development, intimacy and distance, climate and conflict—Chapters 9–12. The movie can also be shown as a semester review for all 12 chapters. Discussion questions for all 12 chapters are included at the end of Part III of this manual.

The movie can be either shown during class or assigned as an outside exercise. Discussion questions can be reviewed during class, or the questions can be assigned as an outside analysis paper.

Communication Skills Projects

This system allows students to focus on a process for altering their communication behavior by targeting a specific aspect of their behavior that they would like to improve and then working through it in a series of steps, from self-monitoring current behaviors to specifying desired changes, to practicing the skill in real-life situations. This procedure may involve:

1. Keeping a journal of the problem behavior as it occurs verbally and nonverbally in terms of (a) the situation, (b) the actual behavior, and (c) the preferred behavior for a specified time.
2. Assessing the patterns that emerged in the journal entries.
3. Observation and recording of people whose communication in the problem area is effective.
4. Creating a specific behavioral goal, including verbal and nonverbal choices.
5. Covert rehearsal, or the imaginary practice of skills.
6. Behavior rehearsal within the classroom among peers who provide feedback on what worked and what could be improved.
7. Implementation in the actual situation followed by self-evaluation.

The Portfolio Entries for Chapters 8 and 9 are in format of Communication Skills Projects. The advantage of this method is that students learn a process for gradually and systematically altering the behaviors they self-select, one that can be repeated throughout their lives. Chapter objectives can be used to prime students' thinking about such behaviors.

The disadvantage is that students may not commit themselves to this process and turn in a fabricated project "completed" in a marathon session. Ongoing, in-class discussion of the stages of the project or draft versions will keep most students involved throughout the process.

Self-Assessment

Whether or not you choose to use it as a part of a student's grade, self-assessment is a critical element in the interpersonal communication course as well as in our daily communication interactions. It is important for students to assess their skills and weaknesses at the outset of the course and to set semester goals (see Portfolio Entry for Chapter 1). These goals should be revisited at the end of the semester when students assess their personal successes (and failures).

Some instructors may choose to use self-assessment as a factor in the final grade. This method operates on the assumption that in many respects students are in the best position to judge their own progress throughout the course. The self-assessment system asks each student to select a grade that reflects his/her effort and growth in understanding key concepts and/or progress toward meeting semester goals. This is followed by an explanation for the chosen grade based on specific criteria.

The advantage of this approach is its emphasis on self-judgment. It demonstrates that the student is responsible for his/her own growth and that whatever grade appears on his or her transcript is merely a symbol of that growth. Moreover, asking a student the question "What do you deserve?" often generates much more self-reflection about effort expended than any other system of evaluation. It also encourages the student to pay careful attention to the achievement of his/her personal goals throughout the semester.

The most obvious disadvantage is the potential for abuse. There is no guarantee that a lazy student will not give herself or himself a high grade.

No matter which grading system you choose, it is very important to delineate clearly the assignments, the due dates, and the method of grading at the outset of class. It is also important to collect work on the assigned date. These practices reinforce the seriousness of the work involved, increasing respect for the instructor and the course.

INSTRUCTOR EVALUATION

Formal evaluations are an important tool in discovering how students perceive the course. They may be used periodically during the term to allow for ongoing adjustments or at the end of the term to obtain an overall evaluation and information for developing future courses. (For a succinct and readable summary of research on student evaluation of instructors, see William E. Cahin, "Student Ratings of Teaching: A Summary of the Research," IDEA Paper No. 20, Center for Faculty Evaluation and Development, Kansas State University, September, 1988.)

Forms can be designed to fit particular classroom situations but generally fall into two types: (1) open-ended specific response and (2) objective/numerical rating. An example of each is provided next.

Open-Ended Specific

1. What expectations did you have for this course (units)? Has this course (units) met your expectations? If not, why not?
2. Do you feel the workload was too light, too heavy, or just right? Were there any specific assignments on which you would like to comment?
3. Do you think that the grading has been done fairly? If not, why not?
4. What do you think of the classroom atmosphere? How would you like to see it changed?
5. Have the readings (text and outside) been satisfactory? Please make your comments specific.
6. Is the teaching style satisfactory? What do you like about your instructor's style? What do you dislike?
7. Please make any other comments you feel might be helpful. Do you have any suggestions for improvements? Is there anything you think particularly important that we should continue doing?

Objective/Numerical Rating

Please respond by giving each item a number:

5 = excellent, 4 = good, 3 = average, 2 = fair, 1 = poor

Instructor
_____ 1. The instructor defined the course goals well.
_____ 2. The instructor met the goals.
_____ 3. The instructor was well prepared for class meetings.
_____ 4. The instructor was knowledgeable in the subject matter of the course.
_____ 5. The instructor was effective in leading and administering the class.
_____ 6. The instructor was available to meet outside of class time to assist students.
_____ 7. The instructor was enthusiastic.

Assignments
_____ 8. The effort required for the course was reasonable.
_____ 9. The amount of time given for the completion of assignments was appropriate.
_____ 10. The readings for the course were relevant to the subject matter.
_____ 11. The amount of reading expected for the course was reasonable.
_____ 12. The major text for the course was useful.

Grading and Evaluation
_____ 13. The criteria used in assigning grades were clearly defined.

_____ 14. The feedback provided by the instructor for class assignments was useful.
_____ 15. The feedback provided by the instructor for class assignments was reasonably prompt.
_____ 16. The class assignments and/or exams were appropriately difficult to challenge the student.
_____ 17. The examinations and/or assignments were fair in their scope and expectations.

Overall
_____ 18. Overall, I would rate this COURSE as (excellent, good, fair, poor).
_____ 19. Overall, I would rate this INSTRUCTOR as (excellent, good, fair, poor).

GENERAL TEACHING STRATEGIES

You may want to consider using some of the following general teaching strategies from the *Communication Teacher* (previously published as *Speech Communication Teacher*), a quarterly publication available from the Speech Communication Association, 5105 Backlick Rd., Annandale, VA 22003. Specific strategies for teaching chapter content are listed in each chapter section of this manual. **A complete index to the *Communication Teacher* is available online at** www.natcom.org.

Alexander, B. K. (1998, Spring). Generating feedback in the classroom: Three teacher- and student-based tools of assessment, 12(3), 4–5.

Boileau, D. M. (1987, Summer). A summer quiz, *1*(4), 5.

Brenner, D. (1990, Winter). Scholastic bowl exercise in the classroom, *4*(4), 6.

Burke, J. (1987, Summer). Using numbers for greater participation, *1*(4), 7.

Corey, J. (1989, Summer). Motivating students with service points, *3*(4), 1–2.

Feezel, J. D. (1992, Spring). Applications to teaching, *6*(3), 8–9.

Garrett, R. L. (1998, Fall). The interpersonal communication survey, *13*(1), 9–11.

Gozzi, R. (1989, Spring). The ten-minute study method, *3*(2), 11–12.

Gschwend, L. (2000, Spring). Every student deserves an assessment tool that teaches, *14*(3), 1–5.

Haehl, A. (1988, Winter). Adapting to non-traditional students, *2*(2), 12–13.

Hahn. D. F. (1992, Fall). To speak of many things, *7*(1), 8.

Hall, D. (1991, Spring). Join the breakfast club, *5*(3), 3.

Hauck, B. (1987, Fall). The "people pyramid": A justification for communication studies, *2*(1), 4–5.

Julian, F. D. (1991, Winter). Journal writing for the speech communication classroom, *5*(2), 3.

Kuseski, B. K. (1999, Summer). Student-led exam review, *13*(4), 5.

Langley, C. Darrell. (1989, Spring). The "thought sheet": An interpersonal communication stratagem, *3*(3), 13–14.

Lapakko, D. (1988, Fall). Sanctioned "cheating" on exams, *3*(1), 6.

Lesser, R. (1989, Fall). Lottery: Students teach the class, *4*(1), 5–6.

Macky, N. (1990, Fall). Essential pursuit: A classroom review technique, *5*(1), 8.

MacLenna, J. M. (1998, Summer). Teaching interpersonal communication: The personal icon assignment, *12*(4), 13.

McSwain, J. E. (1986, Fall). A one-minute manager of instruction, *1*(1), 13–14.

Mester, C. (1987, Fall). Peer support groups, *2*(1), 2.

Miles, P. (1988, Summer). Teacher continuous feedback technique, *2*(4), 4–6.

Noll, B. (1991, Fall). Learning through experimental research projects, *6*(1), 4–5.

Pawlowski, D. (1999, Winter). Dialoguing the gender movements, *13*(2), 4–6.

Presnell, S. (2000, Spring). BINGO: An interactive exam review exercise, *14*(3), 11–12.

Ross, C. (1989, Winter). Suggestions for teaching international students, *3*(2), 10–11.

Rumbough, T. B. (2000, Spring). 52 ways to break the ice, *14*(3), 6–8.

Schnell, J. (1999, Fall). Ideas for including African-American perspectives in selected communication courses, *14*(1), 12–13.

Schumer, Allison. (1988, Spring). Here now the news…, *2*(3), 6–7.

Smith, R. E., Jr. (2000, Spring). Communication images from art, *14*(3), 10–11.

Smithson, S. (1990, Fall). Utilizing a teaching journal to increase teaching effectiveness, *5*(1), 1.

Soller, R., and Benson, J. (1987, Summer). Using attendance sheets as feedback vehicles, *1*(4), 1.

Stevens, S. R. (2000, Winter). How to go into the lion's den and bring out a kitty cat: First-day strategies for graduate teaching assistants, *14*(2), 10–12.

Tripp, E. (1987, Fall). The oral quiz, or letting students talk more while you talk less, *2*(1), 1.

Zalewski, J. (1988, Fall). Using cartoons in test situations, *3*(1), 1.

PART II: COURSE ARRANGEMENT

Text selection, difficult task that it is, may be one of the easier steps in the development of a course. Fitting the new book into your particular program really takes some thought and time, and it is difficult to know at the beginning of a term just what emphasis and assignments will be most valuable by the end. Part II includes a semester course plan for using *Interplay* and the accompanying Instructor's Manual as the central resources for teaching the interpersonal communication course. This course outline is intended as a model the instructor can use whole, in part, or simply as a guide to organizing a particular course. The manual contains numerous teaching exercises and a bibliography for reading assignments. The textbook contains discussion questions and activities in every chapter. The following course outline is a *starting point* for constructing a syllabus for a semester course in interpersonal communication. You will need to adapt it to your own specifications and interests. For those of you interested in Team Learning, there is a complete syllabus, course outline, necessary forms, and sample readiness assessment test provided following the generic outline.

In addition to tailoring the schedule to the days/lengths of your course, here are some questions you'll want to consider when planning your own course:

1. This outline assumes three Unit Wind-Ups and a final. Do you want more or fewer exams? Do you plan to give quizzes? Will you use the Group Study Exercises? Do you plan to give assignments that will need to be explained in class?
2. This outline assumes you will cover all of the text's chapters and give them relatively equal attention. Do you want to cover every chapter? Do you want to address them in sequence? Do you want to devote more or less time to particular chapters and topics?
3. This outline assigns activity days for certain chapters. Do you want those activity days for those chapters? Do you want more or fewer activities? Which activities of the many in the manual will you choose to use? How long will they take?
4. An alternative ending to the semester might include the viewing/discussion of a feature film or student/guest presentations. Do you want to include these activities? Would you rather use speakers/films outside of class time? Would you rather use them throughout the course rather than at the end? How can you adjust the schedule to make room for these activities?

INTERPERSONAL COMMUNICATION: COURSE OUTLINE

When just the chapter and title are listed, you need to choose how the chapter materials (and other supporting materials) will be covered. How much will you lecture (as little as possible, it's hoped)? Will you use large or small group discussion? How will you involve students? What kinds of questions will you ask? What types of examples will you call for?

STANDARD INTERPERSONAL COURSE OUTLINE

Week 1

Day 1:   Introduction to the course and each other
           Reading Assignment: Chapter 1—Interpersonal Process
Day 2:   Interpersonal Process
Day 3:   Interpersonal Process

Week 2

Day 1:   Interpersonal Process Activities
           Reading Assignment: Chapter 2—Culture and Communication
Day 2:   Intercultural Communication

Day 3:	Intercultural Communication

Week 3

Day 1:	Intercultural Communication Activities
	Reading Assignment: Chapter 3—Communication and the Self
Day 2:	Self-Concept
Day 3:	Self-Concept

Week 4

Day 1:	Self-Concept Activities
	Reading Assignment: Chapter 4—Perceiving Others
Day 2:	Perception
Day 3:	Perception

Week 5

Day 1:	Perception
Day 2:	Perception Activities
Day 3:	UNIT WIND-UP 1
	Reading Assignment: Chapter 5—Language

Week 6

Day 1:	Post Wind-Up Review
	Begin Language
Day 2:	Language
Day 3:	Language

Week 7

Day 1:	Language Activities
	Reading Assignment: Chapter 6—Nonverbal Communication
Day 2:	Nonverbal Communication
Day 3:	Nonverbal Communication

Week Eight

Day 1:	Nonverbal Communication
Day 2:	Nonverbal Activities
	Reading Assignment: Chapter 7—Listening
Day 3:	Listening

Week 9

Day 1:	Listening
Day 2 :	Listening Activities
	Reading Assignment: Chapter 8—Emotions
Day 3:	Emotions

Week 10

Day 1:	Emotions
Day 2:	Emotions Activities

Day 3:   UNIT WIND-UP 2
      Reading Assignment: Chapter 9—Dynamics of Interpersonal Relationships

Week 11
Day 1:   Relationships: Attraction Variables
Day 2:   Relationships: Models
Day 3:   Dynamics Activities
      Reading Assignment: Chapter 10—Communication Climate

Week 12
Day 1:   Climate
Day 2:   Climate
Day 3:   Climate Activities
      Reading Assignment: Chapter 11—Managing Conflict

Week 13
Day 1:   Conflict
Day 2:   Conflict
Day 3:   Conflict Activities
      Reading Assignment: Chapter 12—Communication in Families and at Work

Week 14
Day 1:   Family and Work
Day 2:   Family and Work
Day 3:   Family Activities

Week 15
Day 1:   Work Activities
Day 2:   Communicating With Family and Work Activities
Day 3:   UNIT WIND-UP 3

SAMPLE INTERPERSONAL COURSE OUTLINE #1

Noreen Mysyk, EdD

Office Hours: MWF 9:30-noon and by appointment

Pfeiffer Hall Room 27

nfmysyk@noctrl.edu

Textbook: Adler, R.B., Rosenfeld, L. B., and Proctor, R. F. (2013). *Interplay: The process of interpersonal communication* (12th Ed.). New York: Oxford University Press.

Course Description: This course is designed to facilitate your understanding of the basic concepts, vocabulary, theories and processes relevant to the study of initiating, maintaining and terminating relationships through interpersonal communications. An equally important goal of this course is the development of your own interpersonal skills by increasing your repertoire of behavioral choices. Lectures, discussions, classroom activities, written and oral assignments as well as out-of-class observations will be used to aid the development of knowledge and skills relating to interpersonal communication competence. During each class we will strive to merge theory with practice.

Course Requirements:

1. **Class Attendance:** Discussion is critically important to all of our learning in this class. Therefore, your attendance is required. Attendance means both being in class on time for the full session and being fully present in the class (See #2). Your course grade will be lowered if you miss class more than three times during the term. Absences may be excused when conditions are clearly beyond the control of the student and when the instructor has been notified in advance. The instructor retains the right to judge whether documentation justifies an excused absence.

2. **Participation in class discussions and activities:** Students are expected to participate in all activities and discussions for the class. This includes being prepared to participate in discussions by reading the assigned material, bringing relevant personal experiences to class, and listening to and being respectful of the instructor and fellow students. Active participation means active contribution to the discussion, that is, opinions, questions, observations, and comments. Listening, while important, is not active participation. Students must speak up in class! Disruptive or discourteous behavior will not be tolerated.

3. **Complete all course assignments:** All assigned work must be completed to receive a grade for this class. All written assignments are to be typed, double-spaced, stapled, and reflective of college-level composition skills. This means that grammar, spelling and punctuation count on written work. Proper citation is required on all written assignments. Failure to do so is considered plagiarism, and no credit will be given for plagiarized work. All instances of suspected plagiarism will be reported to the college. Refer to the college policy on Academic Dishonesty in the Student Handbook.

4. **Complete all course assignments on their assigned days:** Late work will be reviewed by the instructor but *will not receive a grade*. Missed presentations cannot be made up except under extraordinary circumstances. Assignments and exams may be made up at the discretion of the instructor, and significant grade penalties may be assessed (up to 50 percent of the possible grade). Written assignments must be turned in no later their due dates if the student will not be attending the class. Assignments must be submitted as hard copy. No e-mail submissions will be accepted without prior approval by the instructor in response to extenuating circumstances.

Grades are earned by successful completion of the following activities:

300 points	*Exams:* There will be three exams (each contributing 100 points to your grade). These will be designed to demonstrate basic comprehension, understanding and application of selected concepts and terms introduced through the text, lecture and discussion. Exams will include multiple choice, short answer, and essay questions. The exams will not be cumulative, that is, they will cover designated concepts and will not be cumulative. However, there are concepts that will be discussed throughout the whole term and will be included in more than one exam as appropriate.
300 points	*Role Play Presentation and Analysis:* A substantial portion of your grade will involve the development of a role play presentation. Role plays provide opportunities to experience course concepts personally and to observe what theory looks like in action. Specifically this assignment includes three elements: a role play enactment, critique of role plays conducted by your fellow students, and a written analysis of your own presentation. Failure to completely cite all sources used is plagiarism and disciplinary action will be taken consistent with NCC policy. This project is scored in these categories: • A presentation of a role play, lasting approximately six minutes that accurately and clearly portrays behaviors in a specific situation. These presentations will be made the ninth week of the course and will earn a maximum of 100 points. Team members will receive the same number of credit points. All presentations will be videotaped. • As audience members for the role plays enacted by their fellow students, audience members will evaluate these presentations and will complete an evaluation form for each presentation on the day the presentations are scheduled. A maximum of 50 points (based on the number of critique forms completed) are possible. • Using the script for the role play, the videotape of the role play, and comments offered by the audience, students will critically analyze their own enactment, utilizing a minimum of seven credible reference sources. The paper is worth 150 points and is due the last regular day of class.
200 points	*Journal Assignments:* There will be eight journal assignments, approximately one journal assignment per week. Directions for the focus of your reflection and observation will be given each week for the follow week's journal, posted in the "Assignments" section of Blackboard. Each typed journal assignment is expected to be approximately 750-1000 words and will be worth 20 points (160 points for all). The remaining 40 points will be earned by a paper (Your Metajournal) due week 9 that will review all eight journal entries and identify significant connections to the objectives of this class. More detailed directions will be provided.
200 points	*Participation and Attendance:* Class participation is very important. You should read and be prepared to discuss the assigned material. All students are expected to actively participate in class discussions, cooperate with the various activities and exercises, and to be supportive of classmates. You must speak up in this communication class. The score for this category is a combination of attendance and participation, both are essential to earning maximum points.
25 points	*Extra Credit:* At several points during the term there will be opportunities to earn extra credit points through the successful completion of five spot quizzes. Subject matter for these quizzes will come from classroom discussion and required readings. Quizzes will be in the form of multiple choice questions administered on Blackboard (if you miss a spot quiz there will be no other opportunity to earn those extra credit points).

Grading

Grades are determined by total points earned.

Points	Percent	Grade
926-1000	93-100	A
895-925	90-92	A-
866-894	87-89	B+
826-865	83-86	B
795-825	80-82	B-
766-794	77-79	C+
726-765	73-76	C
695-725	70-72	C-
600-694	60-69	D
599 and below	<60	F

*Schedule**

Week 1	9/xx/20xx	Introduction	
	9/xx/20xx	Chapter 1	
	9/xx/20xx	Chapters 1 and 2	
Week 2	9/xx/20xx	Chapter 2	**Journal 1 due**
	9/xx/20xx	Chapter 3	
	9/xx/20xx	Chapter 3	**Journal 2 due**
Week 3	9/xx/20xx	Chapter 4	
	9/xx/20xx	Chapter 4	
	10/xx/20xx	Chapter 5	**Journal 3 due**
Week 4	10/xx/20xx	Chapter 5	
	10/xx/20xx		**Exam 1 (Chapters 1-5)**
	10/xx/20xx	Chapter 6	**Journal 4 due**
Week 5	10/xx/20xx	Chapter 7	
	10/xx/20xx	Chapters 7 and 8	
	10/xx/20xx	Chapter 8	**Journal 5 due**
Week 6	10/xx/20xx	Chapter 9	
	10/xx/20xx	Chapter 9	
	10/xx/20xx		**Exam 2 (Chapters 6-9)** **Journal 6 due**
Week 7	10/xx/20xx	Chapter 10	
	10/xx/20xx	Chapter 10	
	10/xx/20xx	Chapter 10	**Journal 7 due**
Week 8	11/xx/20xx	Chapter 11	
	11/xx/20xx	Chapter 11	
	11/xx/20xx	Chapter 11	**Journal 8 due**
Week 9	11/xx/20xx		**Role Play Enactments**
	11/xx/20xx		**Role Play Enactments**
	11/xx/20xx		**Role Play Enactments** **Metajournal due**
Week 10	11/xx/20xx	Chapter 12	
	11/xx/20xx	Chapter 12	
	11/xx/20xx	Chapter 12	**Role Play Analysis Paper due**
Final Exam	11/xx/20xx	(time) – (time)	**Final Exam (Chapters 10-12)**

* This schedule is flexible with the exception of assignment due dates and exams. Our schedule must be flexible enough to allow the class to develop a pace that is engaging, provides us enough time to meet our course objectives, and not overwhelming. Should any major changes in the schedule be needed, you will be notified beforehand.

Your Metajournal

The purpose of this last journal is to utilize your eight journals as a means of analyzing the basic concepts, theories and processes relevant to the study of initiating, maintaining and terminating relationships through interpersonal communications. In your journals, your reflection on course concepts and your experiences was an invitation to develop your own interpersonal skills by increasing your repertoire of behavioral choices. At this point, it's time to examine the benefits of your journals. For those of you who have taken this responsibility seriously week after week, you have a wealth of insights to draw from. If you did not, remember that this assignment is based on what you said in your journals, not what you wished you had said. In other words, missing or incomplete journals can't be made up here. What you discuss must come from your journals. Now to the details of this assignment.

The concepts of interpersonal communication do not start and stop with one chapter. The recurring themes of important concepts are the "connective tissue" that binds together the study of interpersonal communication. After reviewing all eight of your journals, identify five important concepts that were relevant for several different discussions during this term. For each recurring theme, discuss how that theme provided significant avenues for understanding other concepts. For example, we discussed the role of nonverbal communication in interpersonal communication several times. If you had chosen this theme, you would discuss how knowledge about nonverbal communication has provided you with insights into understanding cultural context, listening responses, gender differences, creating and maintaining confirming communication climates, and identity management. Find the recurring themes in your journals and describe how your understanding of a theme helped you to understand other course concepts.

The last section of this assignment asks you, one last time, to reflect on your learning experiences during this term. On the one hand, you may have learned nothing new, or on the other hand you may have encountered new perspectives on concepts with which you already had some familiarity, or you may have encountered concepts that broke new ground for you. In this section, you're not being asked to critique the course (that's for the course evaluation process). You are being asked to discuss your own management of the learning experience offered by this course. You were always in charge of your own learning so it's here in the last section of this metajournal that you discuss that management and the results of that effort in terms of your understanding of interpersonal communication, that is, how you did or did not take advantage of this opportunity to learn about the role of communication in relationships and what you're going to do with that knowledge.

24

Role Play Presentation and Analysis

Role play exercises offer a unique opportunity for behavioral learning. Taking full advantage of this learning opportunity will include both participation in the fun part of the exercise but, more importantly, application of the course concepts we have been discussing in a personal way by actually experiencing and observing the typical communication behaviors that are demonstrated. There are three parts to this assignment:

1. **The Role Play Presentation:** The first, at the same time the most enjoyable and the most challenging, will be the preparation of the role play case presentation. Choosing one of the role-playing situations made available to you (or one of your own choosing with my approval), you will prepare a presentation for the class, which will be videotaped. Each case specifies a hypothetical context for interaction, the relationship between participants, and your purpose or goal. On the day of the presentations, you and your partner(s) will enact your role play. As you are preparing the script for your role play, make sure that one or both of the characters exhibits dysfunctional communication, that is, create some communication barriers for the other partner(s) to cope with. Your task is to demonstrate the most competent, functional, or effective interpersonal communication within the situation. You should employ several of the communication skills drawn from class discussions and text material.

   Aim for quality, not quantity, in demonstrating these skills. Employ the skills that are appropriate to the situation. In a six to eight (6-8) minute role play, you may not be able to demonstrate all of these skills; but when your partner's behavior calls for you to demonstrate a certain skill, you will be expected to use that skill. In effect, this exercise asks you to be behaviorally flexible, to adapt your communication to the situation.

   To prepare for this part of the assignment, analyze your case and brainstorm all possible dysfunctional behaviors that one of the partners might exhibit. For each of these, imagine and practice how you could cope with each of these dysfunctions. Choose several of these to form the outline of your interaction. Do not allow your role play enactment to become a dramatic activity. Be yourself and focus on demonstrating dysfunctional and functional behavior in your situation. Be confident (remember the self-fulfilling prophecy) and relax. Your audience wants you to succeed and to learn from what you are doing.

   Each team will receive the same grade based on clear demonstration of behaviors, application of understanding of the concepts that form the foundations for those behaviors, and clear demonstration of the differences between functional and nonfunctional behaviors.

2. **The Role Play Critique:** The enactments of these role plays will involve all of the class. To accomplish this, each non-enacting member of the class will act as a critic of all of the role plays of which he/she is not a character. Using a check-list provided, critics will be rating the ability of the functional and the dysfunctional characters in presenting characteristics of their communication behaviors. These ratings will require the critics to provide specific examples of the behaviors and how they represent both appropriate and inappropriate communication behaviors. These critic sheets will be provided to the enactors so make sure that your comments provide constructive feedback (what went well, as well as what could have been done differently and/or other possible ways of demonstrating communication behaviors appropriate to the case).

   Grades for this section are based on the critic's ability to identify relevant behaviors and to support those selections and identifications with good examples (both those provided and those could have been provided). These will be individual grades for the critics.

3. **The Role Play Paper:** Lastly each student will prepare a detailed analysis of his/her own presentation. Using the script, videotape, and comments by the student critics, students will analyze what happened and what it meant. Answers to the following questions will be provided in this paper:

    a. What were the dysfunctional communication behaviors, how are they defined, and why could they reasonably be expected to appear in this case?

    b. What were the functional communication behaviors, how are they defined, and why were the appropriate responses to the dysfunctional behaviors? How effective were they?

    c. What alternative ways of communicating would you expect to observe in this situation (behaviors not demonstrated in your role play)?

Be specific in your critical analysis of this presentation. Anchor your analysis in credible published research, appropriately citing a minimum of **seven sources** (both within the text of your analysis and in a complete list of references at the end of your paper). Papers should average 10-12 pages in length. Your paper (each student prepares his/her own analysis), the critique sheets for your presentation prepared by your classmates, and a copy of the script are to be submitted on the due date. One copy of the script for each pair of role players should also be turned in at this time.

Student grades for this paper will be based on the quality of the critical analysis. In addition, college-level writing skills must be demonstrated, that is, organization, sentence structure, punctuation, spelling, and grammar.

SAMPLE INTERPERSONAL COURSE OUTLINE #2

Professor: Dr. Gordon Young   **Semester:**   Spring 20xx
Office: Room E327   **Phone:**
E-mail: gyoung@kingsborough.edu   **Classroom:**   M – M397
                                                   W – T4101
                                                   TH – E205

Office Hrs: Mon. 12:40 – 1:40 pm/ Tues. 10:20 – 11:20 am/ Weds. 11:30 – 12:30 pm

Text: Adler, R.B., Rosenfeld, L.B., & Proctor, R.F. (2013). *Interplay: The process of interpersonal communication* (12th ed.). New York: Oxford University Press.

Course Goals: Students will learn interpersonal concepts by actively applying them
to examples of interpersonal communication in order to solve communication problems.

- To **learn** concepts students will:
    - Provide brief summaries of the issues explored in class readings.
    - Be asked to define and give an original example of a selected concept.
    - Find the concept exemplified in real or fictional relationship dialogues.
- In **actively applying** concepts students will:
    - Read interpersonal dialogues and identify course concepts in the verbal and nonverbal behavior that is demonstrated.
    - Be able to identify examples of interpersonal concepts in everyday life.
- When **solving** communication problems students should:
    - Recognize and respond to both sides of a conflict.
    - Understand that relationships take place in diverse socio-cultural contexts.

Assignments:	Points:	Your Points:
Short writings (4)	10%	_____
Response paper (1)	10%	_____
In-class writings (4)	10%	_____
Case study paper (1)	10%	_____
Tests (best one out of 2)	20%	_____
Presentation (1)	10%	_____
Final exam (1)	20%	_____
Participation (discussion & in-class work)	10%	_____
Total →	100%	_____

Grading Policy: 100-90 points = A, 80-89 points = B, 70 – 79 points = C, 0-69 points = D. Points totals of 59 and below equal a failing grade in the course (F).

Description of Assignments:

Short writings: Students will complete several short writings during the semester. In these writings, students discuss the focus of a particular course reading.

In-class writings: This writing is completed in class. Students respond to a relationship scenario, apply a course concept, write from a specific point of view, take a position, or suggest solutions to a communication problem.

Response paper: Students apply course concepts in a short paper that either takes a position in response to a sample dialogue or that compares two readings.

Case study paper: Students examine a relationship dialogue and have to apply concepts from the course to explain all of the issues that in the dialogue.

Tests: This multiple-choice test is shows students' knowledge of course concepts. Questions may also include true/false and matching the term with its definition.

Presentation: Students will be required to do outside research on a problem related to interpersonal communications and present to the class.

Final exam: The final exam could include: true/false and multiple choice questions, questions requiring written answers, and questions relating to a short reading.

Participation: Participation means doing in-class writings, discussing and questioning during in-class discussions and activities, taking notes, being alert and awake, and on time. Attendance is key to class participation. If you are not present, you cannot participate. Missing over six (6) class meetings will deduct 10 percent (10 points) from your final grade and may result in an F in the course. Coming late to class three times will count as one absence. Using electronic devices, having personal conversations, doing homework for other classes, leaving during the class period will result in the loss of your attendance and participation points.

Guidelines For Class: Turn off any electronic devices and keep them out of sight.

Arrive on time and plan to stay for the entire class.

There are no make-ups for missed assignments.

Being absent over six times will deduct 10 percent or equal a WU. Coming late three times is one absence. Lateness is coming within the first 10 mins. of class and coming after 10 mins. is an absence.

Plagiarism: Plagiarizing is inventing, misrepresenting, falsifying information, and sharing, borrowing or purchasing assignments for this class and it will result in an F in this class.

SCHEDULE OF CLASSES:

Week starting Mon, Feb xx	Introductions/ Ch. 1: Interpersonal Process

Tues, March xx – LAST DAY TO ADD A CLASS

Week starting Mon, March xx	Ch. 2– Culture and Communication **Short writing #1**
Week starting Mon, March xx	Ch. 3 – Communication and the Self **Response paper is due/In-class writing #1**

Weds, March xx – LAST DAY TO APPLY FOR DELETION OF SPRING 2011 COURSES

Week starting Mon, March xx	Ch. 4 – Perceiving Others **Short writing #2**
Week starting Mon, March xx	Ch. 5 – Language **Test 1– Ch. 1, 2, 3, 4**
Week starting Mon, April xx	Ch. 6 – Nonverbal Communication **In-class writing #2**
Week starting Mon, April xx	Ch. 7 – Listening: Understanding & Supporting Others **Short writing #3**
Week starting Mon, April xx	Ch. 8 – Emotions

Tues., April xx to Tues, April xx – SPRING BREAK; NO CLASSES

Week starting Weds, April xx	**In-class writing #3** **Test 2– Ch. 5, 6, 7, & 8**

Thurs, April xx – LAST DAY TO APPLY FOR A "W"

Week starting Mon, May xx	Ch. 9 – Dynamics of Interpersonal Relationships
Week starting Mon, May xx	Ch. 10 – Communication Climate **In-class writing #4**
Week starting Mon, May xx	**Presentations**
Week starting Mon, May xx	Chapter 11 – Managing Conflict **Our final class for this section is Thurs, May xx** **Final case study papers due by Tuesday, May xx**

Mon, May xx – COLLEGE CLOSED – MEMORIAL DAY
Tues, May xx – LAST MEETING DAY FOR DAYTIME CLASSES
Thurs, June xx – Fri., June xx – FINAL EXAMS TO BE SCHEDULED (Ch. 9-12)

"TEAM LEARNING" INTERPERSONAL COURSE OUTLINE

COM 252
Interpersonal Communication
General Course Outline
Fall 2009
http://www.uky.edu/~drlane/interpersonal

COM 252-000 Class Meets: 8:00 a.m. to 9:15 p.m. Tuesday and Thursday EGJ 225

Instructor   Dr. Derek R. Lane *drlane@pop.uky.edu* Office: 238 Grehan Building 257-4651

Office Hours Wednesday 9:00 a.m. to 1:00 p.m. (and by appointment)

Required Course Materials
Adler, R., Rosenfeld, L., & Proctor, R. (2010). *Interplay: The process of interpersonal communication*,
Eleventh Edition, New York: Oxford University Press.

Other supplemental readings will be provided throughout the course. Required reading material
will be available in the reading room on the first flood of EGJ and/or in the W. T. Young Library of the
reserve shelves.

Students will also be expected to purchase three packages of Scantron Forms 882-ES from the
UK Bookstore.

Note: The benefits you receive in this class are directly proportional to your efforts in keeping up
with the assigned reading and actively participating in class to build trust, cooperation, support, and
mutual respect.

Course Description

Interpersonal Communication (COM 252) is designed to increase your understanding and implementation
of effective interpersonal communication behaviors and skills. Throughout the semester we will examine
basic verbal and nonverbal elements effecting communication between individuals in family, peer groups,
and work contexts. This course requires you to participate in activities designed to develop interpersonal
communication skills and will actually *improve the quality of your life* if you keep an open mind and
actively participate! Topics include: an introduction to interpersonal communication theory, strategy
development, relationship and conversation management, effective listening, conflict management,
defensive communication, communication anxiety, cultural/gender differences in communication style,
ethics in communicating, relationship development communication climate, and intercultural
communication.

Interpersonal communication introduces students to the complex interaction of social and
psychological forces operating in human communication. The course is designed with a dual approach
consisting of both theory and application that allows students opportunities to evaluate critically the
intricacies of interpersonal relationships and the communication issues surrounding human interaction in
various contexts. Theories will be considered based on relevance to empirical research and various
applied communication contexts (e.g., industry, education, medical and legal practice). There is an
important distinction between social skills/manners and the interpersonal communication skills you are
expected to develop in this course.

Course Purposes

1. The course seeks to increase student "relational sensitivity." Only as students become more socially sensitive can they recognize the various conditions that help and/or hinder the process of interpersonal communication.
2. The course seeks to increase student "behavioral flexibility." Only as students become more flexible in their behaviors can they select the appropriate behavioral responses to specific communication situations.
3. The course seeks to *motivate students* to demonstrate behaviors that facilitate competent communication and improve overall student and community life. *Enhanced communication skills create better citizens of the world.*

Competencies and Objectives[1]

Students in this course will examine the dynamics of face-to-face encounters. A number of theories of communication will be examined that describe various aspects of the communication process. Many individuals believe that "communication" is so basic that it is taken for granted and not thought about seriously. Unfortunately, this attitude tends to result in such difficulties as misunderstandings, conflict, avoidance, and stereotyping. We will examine basic concepts, theories, and research findings relevant to initiating, developing, modifying, maintaining, and terminating relationships, with an eye to the role of communication in the process. Lecture, discussion, response papers, in-class and out-of-class observations, and occasional "applied" assignments will be used to increase student knowledge and behavioral competence in interpersonal communication.

At the conclusion of the course it is expected that students will demonstrate knowledge and skills in several core areas. Specifically, students should demonstrate an increased understanding of:

1. The options and alternatives for action in a wide variety or interpersonal situations
2. Individual preferences and an increased appreciation for the differences of others
3. The dialectical tensions that can arise as students use communication to satisfy personal conflicting needs
4. How the process of perception affects communication behavior
5. The ethical dimensions of interpersonal communication
6. The importance of nonverbal communication in developing successful interpersonal interactions
7. Defensive and supportive communication climates
8. Competence and an ability to assess the appropriateness and effectiveness of interpersonal strategies used in various interpersonal situations
9. Why and how relationships develop and the role communication plays in determining the nature and quality of interpersonal relationships
10. Interpersonal communication conflict and the application of conflict management principles
11. The competencies related to communicating with individuals from other cultures and co-cultures

In addition, COM 252 addresses the following University Studies Competencies:

Writing: To communicate effectively using standard written English. (Students complete assigned written exercises designed for improved self-awareness of communication strengths and weaknesses.)

Reading: To understand, analyze, summarize, and interpret a variety of reading materials. (Class discussions and examinations cover assigned required reading.)

---

[1] A special thanks to Russell F. Proctor, Ph.D., Northern Kentucky University, for permission to reprint instructions.

Integrated Learning: To think critically and make connections in learning across the disciplines. (Students research, evaluate, and organize information in order to complete written assignments and to develop an effective oral presentation in the form of a Group Workshop.)

Creative and Critical Thinking: To elaborate on knowledge to create thoughts, processes, and/or products that are new to the students. (Students are challenged to incorporate strategies in their written assignments and oral presentations.)

Ethics/Values: To demonstrate awareness of ethical considerations in making value choices. (Students discuss value choices, personal and social ethics as related to interpersonal communication.)

Instructional Modes: Class Organization

This class will be organized into small learning teams. The majority of class time and several of the graded assignments will involve work in these teams. Class activities will include team exams, structured exercises, and workshops designed and managed by the teams. All team members will receive the same score on team exams and projects. The course combines lectures by the instructor, class discussion of assigned textbook readings, *group/team work*, audio/visual presentations emphasizing certain communication concepts and skills, oral presentations by the students, quizzes, exams, and classroom activities, all of which will contribute to your overall understanding of interpersonal communication. Out-of-class work may include written exercises (journals and communication improvement plans) and library research of communication concepts that are presented in a group workshop. Assigned chapters should be read *before* class so that you will be able to make a contribution to class discussions and activities and perform well on the quizzes and exams.

General Class Requirements

You are expected to:
- Be on time for all class meetings.
- Interact productively in class discussions and small group activities.
- Be prepared daily for discussions and quizzes by reading all assigned material BEFORE the day it is listed on the course schedule.
- Successfully deliver an instructional group presentation (workshop). FAILURE TO DO THIS ASSIGNMENT WILL RESULT IN A GRADE OF "E" FOR THE COURSE.
- Submit all written assignments, TYPED, at the BEGINNING of the class period on the designated date.

Classroom Civility

Certain basic standards of classroom civility should be adhered to, particularly in a communication course. Civility does not eliminate appropriate humor, enjoyment, or other features of a comfortable and pleasant classroom community. Classroom civility does, however, include the following:

1. Displaying respect for all members of the classroom community, both your instructor and fellow students.
2. Attentiveness to and participation in lectures, group activities, workshops, and other exercises.
3. Avoidance of unnecessary disruptions during class, such as private conversations, reading campus newspapers, and doing work for other classes.
4. Avoidance of racist, sexist, homophobic, or other negative language that may unnecessarily exclude members of our campus and classroom community.

These features of classroom civility do not comprise an exhaustive list. Rather, they represent the minimal sort of behaviors that help to make the classroom a pleasant place for all concerned.

Reasonable Accommodation

The University of Kentucky is an Affirmative Action Equal Opportunity Institution. Students with disabilities and other special needs should feel free to contact the professor privately if there are services or adaptations that can be made to accommodate specific needs. If you have a special need that may require an accommodation or assistance, please inform the instructor of the fact as soon as possible and no later than the end of the second class meeting.

Criteria for Course Completion

This course consists of several assignments, each of which must be completed. **There are no optional assignments.** Course completion is accomplished when all necessary assignments (Quizzes, Workshops, Application Journals, Communication Improvement Plans, Interpersonal Assessments, Papers, Participation, and Exams, etc.) have been completed. Failure to submit ALL assignments will result in a grade of E for the course—regardless.

Attendance Policy

ATTENDANCE IS REQUIRED. Readings, class discussions, group workshops, and in-class activities increase both your understanding of interpersonal communication theory and the development of your interpersonal communication skills. Class attendance and participation are important in accomplishing the goals of this course. If you are going to miss a class it is your responsibility to speak with the course instructor PRIOR to the class session you will be missing. In order to receive credit for attendance you must attend the ENTIRE class period. *Failure to do so will result in an absence for the given class session.*

If your class meets three times a week, you will be allowed three absences. If your class meets twice a week, you will be allowed two absences. If you class meets once a week, you will be allowed one absence (this is a total combination of excused and unexcused during the semester). However, you cannot make up work missed for unexcused absences—you simply receive a zero. **For each subsequent absence, 5 percent will be deducted from your final grade (students not attending class will not be given credit for any participation grade).**

For example, if your class meets twice a week and you finish the semester with a 91 percent average but have three absences (one more than is allowed), you will receive an 86 percent, which is a B. If you are late for your class, it is YOUR responsibility to make sure the instructor has not marked you absent for the day. This must be done on the day that you are late. Notice that you are given free absences for situations in which you are really sick or have to miss class. Do not use these "freebies" for blowing off the class and then come to the instructor later (after you have gone over the limit) when you are really sick or have an emergency and expect an excuse. The freebies *allow* for emergencies; please don't take advantage.

For any officially excused absence you are responsible for presenting official written documentation for the absence. For university-sponsored absences, this notification is to be given to the instructor prior to the absence; for other excused absences, this documentation must be presented within two weeks of the absence. Students are responsible for arranging to make up missed individual work. *Missed group work cannot be made up.* In other words: "To have an absence excused, you will need to give your instructor legitimate written proof from a recognized source explaining the absence. AND IT BETTER BE GOOD."

Please arrive to class on time. Tardiness is unprofessional and is not fair to me or to your classmates. Consequently, if you are consistently late, you can *expect to have 1 percent deducted from your final grade for EACH tardy.* Moreover, do not expect your instructor to cover any missed material.

Classroom Participation Policy

The quantity and quality of your contributions to class discussion and activities will be evaluated according to the following criteria:

1. Are you prepared for class discussions (e.g., completed reading, prepared for discussion questions)?
2. Are you able to relate your own experiences and observations to class concepts?
3. Do you respond to statements by others in an appropriate manner?
4. Do you move the discussion along, not derail it?
5. Do you ask questions and/or paraphrase when needed and appropriate?

If you do miss class, please see a classmate regarding class discussions and assignments. NO MAKEUP WORK IS AVAILABLE for oral presentations, in-class exercises, quizzes, or exams.

Course Requirements

Oral Communication Skills Work

Since this is an oral communication skills course, we want to provide you with many opportunities to develop these skills. Aside from general class participation, such opportunities may include the preparation for and performance and evaluation of role-playing activities, in-class presentations, and briefing sessions, and discussion, analysis, and critique of dyadic communication case studies, etc.

Written Work

You will be expected to use correct spelling in all written work. Use of appropriate grammatical skills in oral and written communication is also very important. Throughout the course you will expand your personal vocabulary through the study of terms related to the course. Your written work will be evaluated on both content and mechanics. Good writing should be reasonably free of mistakes and without composition errors, which are called *gross errors* (sentence fragments, run-on sentences, subject–verb disagreement, misspelled words, and typographical errors that result in such errors). All of your work **MUST BE TYPED** (using no more that 12-point type, with margins not exceeding 1 inch on the top, right, and bottom and 1.5 inches on the left) and double-spaced—unless otherwise indicated by the instructor. **You must also submit all written assignments using APA 5th Edition style guidelines.**

Reading

Your reading assignments are included in the course calendar. In addition to the textbook, you may, from time to time, be required to read other material that will be put on reserve in the Communication Reading Room in Grehan Bldg. If you do not do the reading, do not expect to benefit substantially from the course. **Class sessions are used to supplement rather that to review the reading material assigned.**

Exams and Projects

There will be 12 short, true-false, multiple-choice Readiness Assurance Tests (RATs) given during the course (approximately one at the beginning of each week). The same RATs will be given to individuals and teams. In addition, students will be expected to take a midterm exam (Chapters 1–7) and a *comprehensive final*, design a team workshop, participate in several interpersonal simulations, write a two- to four-page "I Am" reaction paper and write an eight- to ten-page interpersonal communication analysis paper that applies interpersonal communication theory and concepts to a student-selected interpersonal communication context.

Readiness Assessment Tests

You will be given 12 RATs. Each RAT will consist of multiple-choice questions addressing the reading for that day.

"I Am" Paper

We will complete a class exercise called "I Am." Following this exercise you are to try it out on friends, family, etc. and write a two- to four-page typed paper. This paper will give you the opportunity to experience the editing/grading style of the professor before completing the major interpersonal communication analysis paper.

Interpersonal Communication Analysis Paper

You will select a context from which to analyze interpersonal communication, which is to be approved by the professor. You will apply what you have learned about interpersonal communication theory to the context you have chosen. The major content and ideas of the paper will be shared in an oral presentation to your peers.

Doing Your Own Work

We expect that all of the individual assignments you complete for COM 252 (and in all your other courses) are always your own work. We find, however, that many students are not exactly sure what "your own work" means. So please read again the information on plagiarism and cheating from your UK Student Rights and Responsibilities Handbook.

The sanction or punishment for a student who has either plagiarized or cheated is a minimum of an "E" grade for the entire course, but may involve suspension, dismissal, or expulsion from the university. As you can see, these are extreme measures for academic offenses we believe are serious. If you have any questions about whether you may be plagiarizing in your work for COM 252, please be sure to contact me well in advance of the due date for your assignment.

Grading Criteria

The grades will be determined by scores in three major performance areas: *Individual Performance, Team Performance,* and *"Helping Behavior."* This course consists of several assignments, each of which must be completed. *There are no optional assignments.* Course completion is accomplished when all necessary assignments have been finished.

Grade Calculation

Individual Performance

Individual Readiness Assurance Tests		120 pts.
"I Am" Analysis Paper		50 pts.
Interpersonal Communication Analysis Paper		100 pts.
Midterm Exam (Chapters 1–7)		80 pts.
Oral Presentation of Interpersonal Analysis		50 pts.
Comprehensive Final Exam (Chapters 1–12)		120 pts.

Team Performance

Team Readiness Assessment Tests		120 pts.
Team Résumé		30 pts.
Peer Evaluation Procedures and Criteria		30 pts.
Team Workshop		200 pts.

Helping Behavior (Evaluated by Instructor and Peers)   _____100 pts.

TOTAL 1000 pts _____ / 100

Helping Behavior

Each individual will rate the helpfulness of all the other members of their teams prior to the final exam. Individual helping behavior scores will be calculated using the mean of two scores: (a) the average of the points they receive from the members of their group; and (b) the participation score they receive from the instructor. Assuming arbitrarily that (1) helping behavior is worth 10 points and (2) that there are five members in a team, an example of this procedure would be as follows: Each individual must assign a total of 40 points to the other four members in their team. Not all group members contribute equally. Some members are more motivated or more communicative than others. For this reason, raters must differentiate some in their ratings (which means that each rater would have to give at least one score of 11 or higher—with a maximum of 15—and at least one score of 9 or lower). The instructor will assign a participation grade for each of the members, and this score will be averaged with the mean score from the group members to arrive at a comprehensive helping behavior score. The helping behavior scores will produce differences in grade only **within** teams. As a result, group members can't help everyone in their group get an A by giving them a high peer evaluation score. The only way for everyone in a group to earn an A is by doing an outstanding job on the individual and team exams and projects.

Determination of Final Grades

The final grades will be determined by adding the total points in each of the three performance areas: individual performance, team performance, and maintenance (helping behavior).

Grading Scale:
The plus/minus grading system is effective for this course.

A+ = 100.00–96.45	A = 96.44–92.45	A– = 92.44–89.45	Students who attain points
B+ = 89.44–86.45	B = 86.44–82.45	B– = 82.44–79.45	that give them 59.44 percent
C+ = 79.44–76.45	C = 76.44–72.45	C– = 72.44–69.45	or less will receive a
D+ = 69.44–66.45	D = 66.44–62.45	D– = 62.44–59.45	FAILING GRADE of F.

Graded Individual Assignments

1. Individual Readiness Assurance Tests
2. "I Am" Reaction Paper
3. Interpersonal Communication Analysis Paper: Students will be presented with specific information regarding this assignment during the first two weeks of the course. The paper must be between 8 and 10 pages long, not counting the title page. Do not use a font size larger than 12 point or margins larger than 1.5 inches on the left or 1.0 inches on the top, bottom, or right.

Midterm Exam (Chapters 1–7)
Oral Presentation of Interpersonal Analysis
Comprehensive Final Exam

Graded Team Assignments

1. Team Readiness Assurance Tests
2. Design a Team Résumé

3. Develop instruments and procedures for providing performance feedback to team members that will: (1) facilitate individual growth and learning and (2) enhance the team's overall effectiveness.
4. Each team will design and manage a team workshop on specific concepts related to one of the following five major topics.

Workshop 1 Perceiving Others	Chapter 4	Thursday, September xx
Workshop 2 Language	Chapter 5	Thursday, October xx
Workshop 3 Nonverbal Communication	Chapter 6	Thursday, October xx
Workshop 4 Listening	Chapter 7	Thursday, October xx
Workshop 5 Emotions	Chapter 8	Thursday, October xx

These workshops will include: (1) a one-page synopsis of the major conceptual issues; (2) a demonstration of key concepts; (3) a brief annotated bibliography of at least ten resources not included in the textbook, which much be integrated into the workshop; and (4) the opportunity for question from the class and instructor. The grade for these presentations will be determined by an evaluation by the members of the other teams and the instructor's evaluation. Grading criteria include research component, presentation style, distribution of effort, quality of handouts, quality of activity, video usage, wrap-up/debriefing linking activities to concepts.

More on Learning Team Assignments

The importance of your membership and participation in your learning teams cannot be overstated, since this is how the majority of your efforts in class will be evaluated. The learning team in which you are a participant will function in the following ways:

1. Each of you will be responsible for supporting, encouraging, and assisting other members of your group to read the assigned material, to participate actively in class and the interpersonal exercises and meetings, and to think about the issues raised in class sessions and readings.
2. Each of you will be responsible for evaluating other members of your team in a fair, mature, and well-substantiated manner. While it is up to the individuals within the team to determine evaluation criteria, the team is ultimately responsible for explaining and defending the criteria to the instructor based on the goals the team wishes to achieve at the completion of the course. The team grading criteria will be evaluated based on comprehensiveness, rationale, and detailed substantiation.
3. Each team member will participate in <u>four major assignments</u>:
    a. The first major assignment is the active participation of all team members in the team readiness assessment tests.
    b. The second major assignment is to design a **team résumé** that will assist team members in identifying strengths of individual members, develop mutuality of concern, and build cohesion. Strengths of all individual members of the team will be integrated in order to familiarize other teams with the "competition."
    c. The third major assignment will be to develop **instruments and procedures for providing performance feedback** to team members that will: (1) facilitate individual growth and learning and (2) enhance the team's overall effectiveness. These criteria must be specific.
    d. The fourth major assignment will be a **team workshop**. Each team will present a workshop that includes the selection of a specific movie clip that will be analyzed based on all information discussed in class and covered in the textbook. Each team will present its analyses to the class.

"I Am" Paper Guidelines

The "I Am" exercise we did in class was an attempt to get you in touch with how you perceive yourself. The purpose of this assignment is to find out how *others* perceive you and to compare and contrast their perceptions with your own.

Give the slips of paper to a *minimum* of two other people who know you (the more people you ask, the more you'll learn). I recommend that you choose people who may have differing vantage points on your life (i.e., mother/boyfriend; close friend/casual friend; coworker/family member). Ask them to construct a configuration (using the format from class) that typifies *you as they see you.* Request that they be as honest as possible; then leave the room while they work on it. Upon returning, discuss with them their rationale for the rankings they made (please do so in a supportive tone; your goal is to learn, not defend!).

The purpose of your paper is to present what you learned, *applying concepts from lecture and text where appropriate.* Issues you may want to address include:

1. What were the major differences and similarities between the various configurations? How do you account for them?
2. You probably handed the slips to the respondents with some expectations of how they would rank you. Did their rankings match your expectations? (You may want to construct your expected rankings in advance and then compare and contrast).
3. What part did *meaning* and *perception* play in this assignment?

Feel free to run additional variations of this exercise. Some variations include:

"Turnabout Is Fair Play"
Construct a configuration of the people who ranked you (and see if their evaluations of you have an impact on the way you assess *them*!).

"Two Heads Are Better (or Worse) Than One"
Ask two or more people to work together on a configuration of you (and get ready for the sparks to fly!).

"Twice Removed"
Construct a configuration of how you think *another* person perceives a third person (the permutations on this are mind-boggling!).

This assignment is not so much a report or a research paper as it is a personal inventory, analysis, and reaction paper. As a result, it is appropriate (and recommended) to use first-person singular pronouns (I, me, my, mine) in describing what you experienced and learned. Avoid impersonal or collective pronouns (you, it, we)—speak for and about yourself. Please be sure to provide examples and specifics from this exercise as well as from your interactions with the people who help you to complete this assignment. Your paper will be kept confidential; feel free to be as candid as is comfortable for you.

I am expecting a two- to four-page paper (excluding title/cover page), TYPED and STAPLED. Please use double-spacing, 1-inch margins, and 10- or 12-point font, and do *not* right-justify your margins. I expect college-level writing and presentation; in other words, I want proper punctuation, spelling, and syntax, complete sentences and paragraphs, and no white-out, handwritten corrections, or typos. Failure to attend to these matters will result in a lowered grade. The assignment is due at the beginning of class on Thursday, September xx, 2010 (*Late papers will not be accepted*).

Tentative Schedule of Topics, Readings, and Labs

Thursday, August xx   Orientation to the course, expectations explored, Student Expectations/Team Formation
Interpersonal Communication Defined

Tuesday, September x   Overview of Interpersonal Communication—RAT 1, Chapter 1
Thursday, September x   Interpersonal Processes, Principles, and Preconditions
Peer Evaluation Procedures and Criteria Due

Tuesday, September x   Culture and Communication—RAT 2, Chapter 2
Thursday, September x   "I Am" Experiential Activity
Team Résumé Due

Tuesday, September xx   Communication and the Self—RAT 3, Chapter 3
Thursday, September xx   Application Workshop
"I Am" Reaction Paper Due (2–4 pages)

Tuesday, September xx   Perceiving Others—RAT 4, Chapter 4
Thursday, September xx   ***Team Workshop 1 with film clip***

Tuesday, September xx   Language—RAT 5, Chapter 5
Thursday, October x   ***Team Workshop 2 w/film clip***

Tuesday, October x   Nonverbal Communication—RAT 6, Chapter 6
Thursday, October x   ***Team Workshop 3 w/film clip***

Tuesday, October xx   Listening—RAT 7, Chapter 7
Thursday, October xx   ***Team Workshop 4 w/film clip***

Tuesday, October xx   Emotion—RAT 8, Chapter 8
Thursday, October xx   ***Team Workshop 5 w/film clip***

Tuesday, October xx   ***MIDTERM EXAMINATION*** (Chapters 1–8)
Thursday, October xx   ***Interpersonal Communication Competence***

Tuesday, November x   Dynamics of Interpersonal Relationships—RAT 9, Chapter 9
Thursday, November x   CMC Application Workshop

Tuesday, November xx   Intimacy and Distance in Relationships—RAT 10, Chapter 11
Thursday, November xx   Application

Tuesday, November xx   Managing Conflict—RAT 11, Chapter 11
Thursday, November xx   Application
Interpersonal Communication Analysis Paper Due

Tuesday, November xx   Managing Conflict—RAT 12, Chapter 11
Thursday, November xx   ***Academic Holiday: Thanksgiving***

Tuesday, December x   ***Oral Presentation of Interpersonal Communication Analysis***
Thursday, December x   ***Oral Presentation of Interpersonal Communication Analysis***

| Tuesday, December x | ***Watch Video for Final Exam***—Evaluate Helping Behavior |
| Thursday, December xx | ***Watch Video for Final Exam***—Course and Teacher Evaluation |

Comprehensive Final Examination (covering all readings, lectures, and discussion)
COM 252-000   Wednesday, December xx, 2009, 8:00 a.m.   EGJ 225

TEAM LEARNING FORMS

Teacher Expectations—"Score Points with the Professor" (to be used first day)
Guidelines for Writing Appeals
Readiness Assessment Test Team Appeal Forms
Peer Evaluation Procedures and Criteria
End-of-Semester Helping Behavior Form
Sample Readiness Assessment Test—Chapter 1

How To Score Points With Your Professor!

Some Tongue-in-Cheek Tips for Impressing the Professor[2]

1. Try to arrive in class a few minutes late each day—that way, the class (and Dr. Lane) will be sure to notice you.
2. Be sporadic in your attendance. It's not a good idea to "wear out your welcome," and Dr. Lane won't mind.
3. Class time is a good opportunity for catching up on your work in other courses. It can also be well-spent reading the newspaper, talking with a friend, or taking a nap. Dr. Lane loves to see his students using their time efficiently.
4. Avoid coming to class prepared. Reading the text in advance, for instance, means you'll lose a sense of spontaneity. You wouldn't want to "spoil" Dr. Lane's lecture, would you?
5. Dr. Lane is really flexible about his assignment due dates. If you turn in something late, don't worry—it actually helps him spread out his workload. Penalties? NEVER!
6. Only the things Dr. Lane puts on the board or the overhead are important. Keep this in mind and you'll take fewer notes.
7. Don't participate in class unless Dr. Lane calls on you. It's rude to ask questions and inappropriate to express opinions. Remember—this is education, not a talk show.
8. When someone else asks a question in class, pay no attention. Dr. Lane will be happy to answer the exact same question when you ask it a minute later.
9. Inasmuch as this is only an interpersonal communication course, don't worry about spelling, grammar, or punctuation in your written assignments—that stuff is for English classes.
10. When you make spelling errors, inform Dr. Lane it's because you don't have a computer with a spell-checker. He certainly won't expect you to use a dictionary, for heaven's sake.
11. Remember, personality is more important than performance. If Dr. Lane likes you, you're guaranteed a good grade.
12. Nobody, especially Dr. Lane, still believes "C" means "average." Simply come to class and you're guaranteed *at least* a "B."
13. If you're going to be absent, don't notify Dr. Lane in advance. Just show up several days later and ask, "Did I miss anything important?" (one of his favorite questions). Being the nice person he is, he won't hold you responsible for anything you missed while you were absent.
14. Here are some other of Dr. Lane's favorite comments:
    If you miss a question on an exam: "That's a trick question."
    If you do poorly on an assignment: "My mom (husband, dog, roommate) thought it was great."
    If you won't be in class: "I need to study for another course."

---

[2]This exercise is based on ideas from a paper written by Russell Proctor entitled "Communicating Rules With a Grin," which was originally presented at the Central States Communication Association Annual Meeting in April 1994.

15. Don't bother Dr. Lane with questions during his office hours; he has work to do. Instead, approach him one minute before class and ask him to look over the assignment you've just written.
16. Dr. Lane needs help remembering what time it is, so begin packing your books five minutes before class is over. He will appreciate the reminder and be impressed with your concern.
17. Wait until you are at the crisis point before asking for help; otherwise, he won't consider your problem important.
18. If you have a complaint or concern, don't discuss it with Dr. Lane—he won't listen or try to understand (after all, he doesn't really _believe_ in this communication stuff). Instead, talk about it with as many classmates as possible. Better yet, give Dr. Lane no clue that you are upset; then unload on him in your course evaluation. Now, _that's_ effective communication!
19. Don't drop by Dr. Lane's office to chat—he's far too busy to be concerned about you. Remember, he's not in this profession because he loves working with students; he's in it for the money.
20. Don't keep this handout or a copy of the syllabus; Dr. Lane didn't mean for you to take either of them seriously. He just made them to have something to talk about on the first day of class. Deposit them in the trash on the way out today.

Purposes of the Appeals Process

1. Clarify uncertainty about your understanding of the concepts.
2. Give additional recognition and credit when "missing" a question was caused by:
3. ambiguity in the reading material.
4. disagreement between the reading material and our choice of the "correct" answer.
5. ambiguity in the wording of the question.

Guidelines for Preparing Successful Appeals

Appeals are granted when they demonstrate that you understood the concept(s) when you answered the questions or that your lack of understanding was due to ambiguity in the reading material. As a result:

If the appeal is based on either inadequacies in the reading material or disagreement with our answer, you should:

1. state your reason(s) for disagreeing with our answer and,
2. provide specific references from the reading material to support your point of view.

If the appeal is based on ambiguity in the question, you should:

1. spell out why you thought the question was ambiguous and,
2. offer an alternative wording that would have helped you avoid the problem.

Readiness Assessment Test Appeal Forms

Readiness Assessment Test Appeal (Groups only)

Team Name _____ Test # _____ Question #_____

Proposed correct answer _____

Rationale for your appeal:

Supporting evidence:

Readiness Assessment Test Appeal (Groups only)

Team Name _____ Test # _____ Question #_____

Proposed correct answer _____

Rationale for your appeal:

Supporting evidence:

Peer Evaluation Helping Behavior

Many college students experience "group hate" because of past negative experiences working in groups. Most negative experiences, however, can be overcome by generating peer evaluation performance criteria and implementing simple evaluation procedures.

The creation of a peer evaluation process involves **two separate phases**:

Phase 1 is an *individual process* that requires each individual to generate two separate lists.

- List one contains individual goals and objectives that are to be accomplished during the semester.
- List two consists of *specific performance criteria* that are expected of all group members.

Phase 2 is a *group process* that requires the group to generate four specific products. The group must:

- Develop a list of group goals and objectives that subsumes ALL of the individual goals and objectives generated during phase 1.
- Generate a list of group performance criteria that includes ALL of the individual expectations generated during phase 1.

Produce a **well-organized document** that **best communicates** the group goals and objectives as well as group performance criteria to your instructor. *This document should be written in narrative form (using complete sentences) and be prepared using the procedure in the next section. It should be presented to the instructor in a **professional format.***

Create a **peer-grading form** that lists the specific criteria your team will use to evaluate the participation of all team members (this includes a self-evaluation) throughout the course of the semester. Your peer grading form should be created on the computer so that revisions can be easily made. *This form should also be presented to your instructor in a professional manner.*

Peer Evaluation Procedures and Criteria

Instructions:

You are to develop a system for providing performance feedback to the members of your group in this class. Your group will use this procedure to provide performance feedback within the group at regular intervals during the semester.

In order to accomplish the task, *each individual member* will:

1. Think about group experiences you have had in the past. If your experiences were negative, what made them negative? What did other group members do (or not do) that created problems? Now think about your positive experiences. What made those experiences positive?
2. Next, generate two lists. The first list should include specific INDIVIDUAL GOALS and OBJECTIVES you wish to accomplish during the course of this semester. The second list should provide specific PERFORMANCE CRITERIA you expect from every group member (e.g., attendance, preparation, motivation, positive attitude).
3. Finally, share your list with your group. Pay close attention to details and similarities between individual goals, objectives, and performance criteria.

AS A GROUP you will then:

o Develop two separate lists:
- o List 1 should contain GROUP GOALS and GROUP OBJECTIVES.
- o List 2 should contain PERFORMANCE CRITERIA.

Both lists should be generated by combining all individual lists (both group lists should reflect an integration of individual goals and individual performance criteria).

o Create a **document** that best communicates those team goals to your instructor. This document should be created in a professional format and include the following:

a. A statement of specific *team goals and objectives*. Remember, these goals should reflect an integration of individual team members' goals. *List them.* Each goal should be a separate statement, usually in one sentence. Be specific.

b. A description of how you intend to *collect the data* on which the feedback will be based. Please include copies of specific peer grading forms as examples of data collection instrument(s), and refer to these peer grading forms in your description.

c. A description of the *feedback process* you intend to use. Please specify:
- o *When feedback will be give—provide specific dates and times.*
- o *Who will give it to and to whom.*

d. An assessment of the *difficulties* you are likely to encounter in implementing your performance feedback system and *how these difficulties will be overcome* using your procedures and criteria.

e. A statement of how the system *provides input into the grading process* for the class.

Your team will create *a peer grading form* that lists the specific criteria your team will use to evaluate the participation of all team members (this will include a self-evaluation) at least twice during the semester. The purpose of this evaluation is to allow team members to make *course* corrections in their helping behaviors before the end of the semester. This *form should be presented to your instructor in a professional manner.* Your document and grading form should be created on the computer so that revisions can be made easily.

The assignment will be evaluated using the following *criteria:*

1. Is the group collecting data they will need to support the achievement of their individual and team objective(s)? Are the objectives listed clearly?
2. Will the procedures they intend to use support the achievement of their objective(s)? Do the procedures support objectives?
3. Are the procedures they intend to use practical (i.e., they meet the guidelines set forth and can be implemented effectively in the specific situation in which they will be used)? Is the assessment form consistent with guidelines and objectives?
4. Have they accurately anticipated the problems they are likely to encounter in implementing the procedures? Are anticipated problems stated clearly? Are detailed strategies included for how the problems will be overcome?

End-of-Semester Helping Behavior Peer Evaluation

Please assign scores that reflect how you really feel about the extent to which the other members of your group contributed to your learning and/or your group's performance this semester. This will be your only opportunity to reward the members of your group who actually worked hard for your group. **If you give everyone pretty much the same score, you will be hurting those who did the most and helping those who did the least.**

Instructions: In the following space, rate each of the **other** members of your group. Each member's peer evaluation score will be the average of the points he or she receives from the other members of the group. To complete the evaluation, you should:

    a. List the ***name of each of your group members in alphabetical order*** by their last names. Include your name in the list, but do not assign points to yourself.
    b. Assign a total of 50 points.
    c. Differentiate ratings among the group members so that at least one person scores 11 or higher (15 max.) and one score is 9 or lower.

Group Members	*Scores*
1._____	_____
2._____	_____
3._____	_____
4._____	_____
5._____	_____
6._____	_____

    Additional feedback. In the following space, briefly describe your reasons for your *highest* and *lowest ratings.* These comments—but not information about who provided them—will be used to provide feedback to students who wish to receive it.

    Highest ratings(s). Why did you assign this rating? (Use back side of paper if necessary.)
    Lowest rating(s). Why did you assign this rating? (Use back side of paper if necessary.)

Sample Readiness Assessment Test (RAT)

COM 252 Interpersonal Communication
The University of Kentucky

Readiness Assessment Test 1
Department of Communication

Multiple Choice Select the *best* answer. Record your answer three (3) times on the answer sheet. If you are not sure about the answer, you may "split" answers (e.g., a a c).

1–3. All of the following are valid reasons for studying communication *except*
   a. to learn new ways of viewing something already familiar.
   b. to discover weakness in others.
   c. it takes approximately 60 percent of our waking time.
   d. to be more successful in relationships.
   e. knowledge tends to increase effectiveness.

4–6. Which of the following is a limitation of the interactive view of communication?
   a. the implication that the roles of speaking and listening are done alternately
   b. the portrayal of communication as a two-way activity
   c. the emphasis on both verbal and nonverbal feedback
   d. the portrayal of misunderstandings in terms of the participants' different environments
   e. all of the above

7–9. Your first encounter at a job interview is affected by the interviewer's scowling facial expression. Which characteristic of communication best describes the situation?
   a. Communication is irreversible.
   b. Communication is a transactional process.
   c. Communication is static.
   d. Communication is dependent on personalized rules.
   e. None of the above describes it.

10–12. In a survey of personnel managers, the ability to speak and listen effectively was rated as more important than
   a. technical competence.
   b. work experience.
   c. academic background.
   d. two of the above.
   e. all of the above.

13–15. The text suggests a "qualitative" definition of an interpersonal relationships. Which of the following is NOT one of the criteria for that definition?
   a. context
   b. irreplaceability
   c. disclosure
   d. interdependence
   e. all are criteria

16–18. Two friends, Jennifer and Kristi, have developed a way of dealing with each other when they are angry. The angry person puts a note on the refrigerator indicating the problem, and the other person writes on it a time when they can talk it over. This is an example of
   a.   truncated communication.
   b.   uniqueness.
   c.   impersonal communication.
   d.   face maintenance.
   e.   unintentional communication.

19–21. Which of the following means the same thing as the statement in your text "Communication is irreversible"?
   a.   Erasing or replacing spoken words or acts is not possible.
   b.   No amount of explanation can erase the impression you have created.
   c.   It's impossible to "unreceive" a message.
   d.   Words said are irretrievable.
   e.   All mean the same as the statement.

22–24. When a religious person listens to a speaker who uses profanity, he or she would experience
   a.   external noise.
   b.   cognitive complexity.
   c.   relational noise.
   d.   physiological noise.
   e.   psychological noise.

PART III: CHAPTER EXERCISES

Chapter 1: Interpersonal Process

What Is Interpersonal Communication?

Approximate Time: 30 minutes

Purpose: To familiarize students with the definition of interpersonal communication around which *Interplay* is structured

Procedures:
1. After students have a chance to read Chapter 1, divide the class into groups of four to five.
2. Assign each group one of the following situations. Each group should decide if interpersonal communication has occurred in its assigned situation. (Where would the group members place it on a scale of 1 [interpersonal] to 7 [impersonal]?) If the group decides that the situation is impersonal, how might it be made interpersonal? The group should be able to justify its decision. Encourage the group to attempt to reach a consensus, rather than merely vote. Allow about ten minutes.

Situation 1:
While she is waiting in line at the supermarket checkout counter, a woman who is in line behind Maria comments, "Your coat looks really warm. It must be nice and cozy on these cold winter days." Maria says, "Yes, it is, thank you." Before she moves up to the clerk, Maria chats with the woman about where she got the coat and how much she has used it.

Situation 2:
Ellen and Kendrick have known each other on a surface level for a couple of years. At a party they meet and strike up a conversation about a mutual friend Kendrick would like to date. During the course of the conversation, Ellen comments, "I know your type. You think you can use my personal credibility with Sharon."

Situation 3:
"Chandra, you know we promised each other on the night that we met that we'd always be honest, no matter what. Now you can tell me what has happened."

Situation 4:
A student visits a professor to discuss an exam grade. Before the student leaves, they discover that they both grew up in northern Minnesota. For several minutes they reminisce about the cold winters there.

Situation 5:
Jim is functioning as host for his organization's fund-raising campaign dinner. He greets each member as she or he arrives and offers to take the member's coat and hat and directs the member to the bar and hors d'oeuvres trays.

3. Meet again in the large class group. Have each group present its decision and rationale on whether the group's situation fulfilled the conditions of a definition of interpersonal communication. Have members of other groups raise issues and indicate the extent to which they agree or disagree with the presenting group's decision and rationale.

4. Review the essential components of a developmental view of interpersonal communication.

Principles Illustrated:
1. Interpersonal interaction is characterized by individual regard.
2. Interpersonal relationships are characterized by the development of individualized rules.
3. Interpersonal relationships are characterized by the amount of personal information the partners share.

Communication Misconceptions

Approximate Time: 30 minutes

Purpose: To familiarize students with communication principles and misconceptions; to provide a simple, nonthreatening task for groups early in the semester. (Note: This exercise works as early as the first day of the semester.)

Procedures:
1. Type the following misconceptions about communication on an index card—one misconception per card.
   a. Communication will solve all our problems.
   b. We need more communication.
   c. Communication can break down.
   d. The more we communicate the better.
   e. Words have meaning.
   f. Communication is a verbal process.
   g. All communication is intentional.
   h. Telling is communicating
   i. Communication is natural human ability.
   j. Feeling should be communicated spontaneously, not bottled up.
2. Divide the class into groups of four to five, and give each group two index cards with a misconception printed on each. (This is assuming a class of 20–25. A good way to get interaction later is to make sure that at least one of every group's misconceptions is duplicated in another group.)
3. Do not tell the class that the statements are misconceptions. Tell them that these are statements frequently made about communication and that they have about 10 minutes to agree on a position relative to the statement. They should attempt to reach a consensus rather than use majority vote. Of course, those who have read Chapter 1 may recognize the statements, but, interestingly, some wavering usually occurs as a result of a conflict between the textbook and students' "commonsense" view of communication as impacted by peer pressure.
4. After 10 minutes, bring the groups back together. Let each group present its "consensus." Ask questions and try to get each member to speak. Encourage members of other groups to refute the conclusions of the group that is reporting. (Discussions can become rather lively if a group that had the same statement disagrees with the conclusions of the first group called on.) Write each statement and the group's consensus on the board, but do not comment on the validity of its conclusions until all groups have reported.
5. After all group have reported, point out that those who study communication say that all the statements are false, and then lead the class in a discussion of why this might be said. Provide an alternative to each statement similar to these:
   a. Communication may create or help solve problems.
   b. Quality of communication is more important than quantity.

c. One cannot not communicate.
d. Communication is a tool. It has no moral quality.
e. Meanings are in people.
f. Communication is both verbal and nonverbal.
g. Communication is both intentional and unintentional.
h. Saying something is not the same as communicating it.
i. Communication is learned.
j. Feelings need to be shared appropriately.

Communication Myth Survey

Approximate Time: 35–40 minutes

Purpose: To introduce students to a number of concepts to be covered in the course; to establish a climate conducive to interaction and discussion

Procedures:
1. Without prior discussion, distribute the Communication Principles Survey on the next page and allow students 5–7 minutes to fill it out.
2. Without collecting the surveys, go through the items and solicit answers from the class. Ask students to discuss the reasons why they responded the way they did.
3. Make the point that there are no right or wrong answers. Many who study communication do not agree on all these points, but certain perspectives will be supported in this course.

Principles Illustrated:
1. Review of Chapter 1 and overview of several concepts that will be developed in this course.
2. There are no absolute truths in communication studies.

Small Talk

Time: 30 minutes

Purposes: To illustrate the characteristics of interpersonal communication; to facilitate reflection of the effects of "small talk"; to give students an opportunity to get to know others in their class

Procedures:
1. Find another person in this class whom you don't know very well.
2. Sit down and talk with this person for the next 10 minutes or so.
3. DO NOT discuss the following topics:
    • year in school, major in school, courses you are taking, intended career
    • this class, this instructor, this department, other courses you have taken in this department.
    • hometown, other schools you have attended, your age
4. Come back together as a class and discuss the following questions:
    • Why was this difficult?
    • What kinds of things did you notice (for example difficulty, level of comfort, topics discussed, interpersonalness of conversation)?
    • Some may report their conversation was more interpersonal than it would have been had you not restricted topics; others may report it was just as impersonal or interpersonal as it would have been otherwise. Probe for their reasons behind these conclusions.

- Did this force greater levels of disclosure? Why or why not?
- To what extent were you aware of the characteristics present in your conversation? (List the characteristics on the board.)
- What did you learn?

Principles Illustrated:
1. Small talk many times is not truly interpersonal.
2. It can be difficult to have a truly interpersonal conversation.

Name Game

Approximate Time: 15 minutes, depending on the size of the class

Purposes: To learn names; to discuss the importance of names.

Procedures:

1. Arrange the class in a large circle.
2. The instructor states his/her name and says to the person on their left or right, "Now you say my name and add yours."
3. The third person must say the instructor's name, the second student's name and add their own. Eventually it will come back to the instructor who should be the last person to go and therefore have said every student's first name.
4. It may be tempting to "cheat" in this activity: the student supplies their name when someone gets stuck- don't cheat though. The act of struggling with a name is often just what we need to cement that name in our head. This activity isn't meant to be easy. If a person really cannot remember a name, have someone who hasn't gone yet help them out.

   Debrief by asking the following discussion questions:
1. Why is it so hard to remember a person's name even if they have just been introduced to you?
2. How does it feel to be in a class where the instructor doesn't know your name versus a class where the instructor calls you by name?
3. Why are names so important to people?

Principles illustrated:
1. Names are important.
2. Using someone's name sends a different message than not using the person's name.

Candy Land

Time: Approximately 20 minutes, depending on the size of the class

Purpose: For students to get to know one another

Procedures:

1. Purchase a bag of candy that has individually wrapped pieces that identify a flavor by the color of the wrapping. Starbursts work well (red, pink, yellow and orange.) Jolly Ranchers do, too.

2. Arrange the class in groups of 4-6.
3. Each student gets a piece of candy.
4. On the whiteboard or ELMO, show the class that they will introduce themselves to members of their group by saying their name, their major or what they want to study and one piece of information based on the color of the candy they received.
5. The chart showing the information to be shared could look like this:

Orange: Least favorite vegetable
Yellow: Favorite childhood memory
Red: Favorite household chose
Pink: Least favorite movie

Debrief by asking the following discussion questions:
1. What did you learn about your classmates that surprised you?
2. What if the questions had been more personal in nature? (For example, "What was last fight you had with a significant other about?") How would that have changed the interaction with the group?
3. Why are introductions important in interpersonal communication?

Principles illustrated:
1. Self-disclosure is incremental.
2. Developmental stages in relationships

What Kind of First Impression?

(Note: This activity works well after the class has met for a few times, at the end of the first week of class.)

Approximate Time: 20-30 minutes

Purpose: To identify the impression one makes

Procedures:

1. Give everyone a piece of blank white computer paper.
2. Have the students write their gender and hair color and a brief (four or five words) description of what they are wearing at the top of the paper.
3. Collect all the papers and shuffle them.
4. Give the directions: You will be getting a different person's paper back. You will be able to identify the person based on their gender, hair color and their clothing (in case you don't remember their name.) Write your first impression about the person on the paper and then pass it to your left. You may want to add a word of warning: the person will be looking at this paper, and although your first impression will be anonymous (no names on the paper) remember: Communication is irreversible: you can't take this back. Be honest, but also be mindful of the kid of communication you are using.
5. Redistribute the papers and go through 5–10 rounds of "first impressions" based upon the time constraints in the class.
6. Gather the papers and return to their original owner who reads the first impressions others had about him/her.

Debrief by asking the following discussion questions:

1. Did any of the first impressions someone wrote about you surprise you?
2. How did it feel to have to make your first impression official by writing it down knowing that the person would see it?
3. What difference would it have made in this activity if it wasn't anonymous?
4. How would this activity change if we did it at the end of the semester as opposed to the beginning?
5. How is this activity linear? What would make this activity transactional?

Principles Illustrated:
1. Impressions can be deliberate or unconscious.
2. We construct multiple identities.
3. Linear and transactional communication.

DISCUSSION FORUM PROMPT

Visit the National Association of Colleges and Employers website and review the 2011 Job Outlook Survey. http://www.naceweb.org/so12082010/college_skills/ Answer the following questions:

1. Of the top five most desirable employability skills, #1 and #3 focus on communication. Does this surprise you? Why or why not?
2. Think about three classes you've taken in college or ones that you plan to take. You can also consider on-campus clubs you've joined, work study positions, and so on. Discuss activities or assignments that you will be able to share with an employer to show that you have these particular communication skills.
3. In response to your post, ask your peers to analyze how clearly you've explained how your experiences fit the communication attributes that employers are looking for.

JOURNAL PROMPT

Review the section on competent communicators. Then, think of your current relationships that involve regular communication. Answer the following questions:

1. What do you identify as your single major strength in the area of interpersonal communication? Cite two specific personal examples where you displayed this strength. Reference characteristics of competent communicators.
2. What characteristics of communication competence do you identify as weak? Give one to two examples, discussing why these areas are challenging for you.
3. What ideas do you have for strengthening weaker areas of communication competence?

PORTFOLIO ENTRY

Interpersonal Communication: A Personal Assessment

(Note: At the end of the semester, students should be asked to reassess their skills and progress toward goals.)

Think about your current communication skills. You might consider your general communication skills (such as expressing yourself clearly, thinking before you speak, making up your mind firmly, saying "no" without feeling guilty), your self-awareness skills (such as understanding your won strengths and weaknesses, being able to identify your values, recognizing the impact of your behavior on others, setting realistic goals), and your interpersonal skills (such as listening with an open mind, being a good "people reader," expressing feeling appropriately), and so on.

In narrative (essay) form, respond to the following questions: What do you identify as your two or three most significant strengths in the area of communication? Illustrate each of these strengths by a specific personal example. What do you identify as your one or two most significant weaknesses? Illustrate (specifically) why you feel these are problem areas. Now determine three to five goals (in the area of interpersonal communication) you would like to set for yourself this semester. What is one specific thing you could do now to begin reaching one of those goals?

D & A

(This is another version of the preceding Portfolio Entry)
1. What do you identify as your single major strength in the area of interpersonal communication? Illustrate your response by giving two specific personal examples of times when you displayed this strength.
2. What do you identify as your one significant weakness? Give one example (specifically) to illustrate why you feel this is a problem area for you.
3. How do your strength and weakness relate to the communication competence section in Chapter 1? Make sure to use course terminology in your discussion.

GROUP STUDY

The following matching exercise could be used as either a group study tool or a "group quiz" exercise. (See the Introductory Essay for further information.) The following instructions should be included for each Group Study Exercise given throughout the manual:

All members of the group must decide on a single answer. When you have finished the exercise, ALL members of the group should sign off on a single copy; however, all copies must be handed in. (Groups have the right to exclude the name of any member who is unprepared and/or does not contribute to the discussion.)

Answer directly on this sheet. Begin by clarifying the terms as they have been defined in your text. When doing the exercise, pay particular attention to underlined words and phrases

TEACHING ACTIVITIES FROM THE *COMMUNICATION TEACHER*

Berko, R. (1993, Winter). Getting to know you and talking about it, *7*(2), 5–6.
Bozik, M. (1988, Summer). Who said that? *2*(4), 6.
Bozik, M and Beall, M. (1994, Winter). Modeling metaphorical thinking, *8*(3), 1–3.
Garrett R.L. (1998, Fall).The interpersonal communication survey, *13*(1), 9–11.
Gill, B. (1998, Fall). Understanding communication through popular music, *13*(1), 11–12.
Myers, S. A. (1998, Summer). Developing student awareness of interpersonal communications competence, *12*(4), 6.
Oetzel, J. G. (1994, Fall). The skills project, *9*(1), 1–2.
Phillips, T. G. (1996, Winter). Name that analogy: The communication game, *10*(2), 10–11.
Ringer, R. J. (1989, Summer). Pre-post test for interpersonal communication classes, *3*(4), 4–5.
Rumbough, T. B. (2000, Spring). 52 ways to break the ice, *14*(3), 6–8.
Wilson, W. (1989, Winter). Sex role stereotypes: What do we see in them? *3*(2), 15.

Chapter 2: Culture and Communication

Culture in Change

Approximate Time: 30–40 minutes

Purpose: To discover and discuss the impact of culture on our daily lives and to investigate how culture changes over time

Procedures:
1. Divide the students into groups of four to five members.
2. Distribute the following directions. (Students could also be given these in the class prior to the exercise and asked to complete a worksheet before coming to class.)
3. After the groups have discussed, gather for general discussion with the entire class.

Culture in Change

What we believe and value, how we behave, and how we view ourselves and others are strongly influenced by the culture in which we live. For each of the categories, discuss the following: (1) What is your own attitude toward the concept? (Your values?) (2) Give a specific example of a time when this attitude influenced your behavior. (3) How does your attitude/behavior contrast with that of your parents' generation? Your grandparents' generation? (4) How might your reactions be different if you came from another culture?

     Categories:
          Time
          Religion/Worship
          Family
     Competition
     Dating/Marriage
     Homosexuality

Discussion Points:
1. What are some of the differing attitudes toward the foregoing concepts?
2. What kinds of information do you need in order to understand the attitudes that are different from your own?
3. What are the implications for your own interpersonal communication transactions?
4. Share at least two of the particular examples you discussed in your small group.

CULTURAL SITUATIONS AND ROLES

Directions: Read the following cultural situations and respond according to the assigned cultural role. Take 5-10 minutes and respond (in written form) to the situation as a member of the assigned cultures. Bring your responses to our next class.

Situation 1
Recently you and your family have had an important discussion at the dinner table about your future. Your parents announce that they have found the "right/appropriate mate" for you to marry. While you are casual friends and have talked with this person on several occasions, you have never spent any time alone with him/her. Additionally, you have a college education and the opportunity for a good job in the business world. You feel your life is really just beginning because you are well educated and have many opportunities.

The first cultural role you must enact is that of an American female/male (depending on your gender). How would you respond to your parents' suggestion? And what are the influential factors (in terms of values, attitudes, and beliefs)?

The second cultural role you must enact is that of an East-Indian female/male (depending on your gender). How would you respond to your parents' suggestion? And what are the influential factors (in terms of values, attitudes, and beliefs)?

Situation 2
You are the owner of a construction firm. You have just received notification that one of the nearby Native American reservations is looking for a new company to build their community center. When you call the contact person at the reservation, they tell you that you must set up an appointment for a meeting with the tribal elders. The contact person at the reservation also informs you that the tribal elders will make the hiring decision for the construction job. A week later you travel to the reservation to meet with the elders in an attempt to convince them to accept your company's bid. At the meeting, the elders ask you to tell them a little about yourself and your company. Then the elders ask you to discuss what you can offer the reservation and tribal community and your qualifications for the job. You want to make sure that you win the bid and that you prove to the elders that you and your company are "right for the job."

The first culture role you must enact is that of a white business owner. What do you do and/or say to prove your worth? You responses should reflect those of the typical interview/bid situations.

The second culture role you mist enact is that of a Native American. What do you do and/or say to prove your worth to the elders? Your responses should reflect what you have learned and know of the Native American culture.

How do you think the elders respond to each person? What can make us more culturally competent in such situations?

**Side note to instructor:* The typical response of many Native American elders in such a situation would be to hire those who demonstrate collectivism and use collectivist language (i.e., talk in terms of we, team, group, and community). Typically, many Native American elders would be hesitant to hire someone who demonstrated individualism and uses individualistic language (i.e., talks in terms of I, personal achievements, personal goals, individuality) because such a person would conflict with the collectivist Native American culture.

Discussion Points:
1. How did student perceptions of the situation change based on the culture role they enacted?
2. What was the impact of each culture role on the outcome of the situation?

3. Did some of your perceptions and/or assumptions of the other culture change based on your enactment of a different culture role?
4. How might the different culture roles affect interpersonal communication?
5. Does the enactment of a cultural role encourage intercultural competency? If so, how?
6. In the first situation, how was each of the following intercultural communication concepts illustrated?
   o hard culture versus soft culture/achievement versus nurturing
   o gender as a co-culture
   o collectivist versus individualist
   o communication competency
7. In the second situation, how was each of the following intercultural communication concepts illustrated?
   o language-collectivist versus individualist
   o hard culture versus soft culture/achievement versus nurturing
   o idea of self
   o nonverbal language—eye contact
   o language and identity—how do you describe yourself?
   o high context versus low context

Principles Illustrated:
1. Cultural conditioning (collectivistic versus individualistic cultures, high context versus low context, attitudes about gender rules, etc.) affects our responses in interpersonal situations.
2. We have a tendency to respond to less familiar cultures by the use of stereotyping.

Extreme Intercultural Communication

(Note: This activity is meant to replicate an intercultural communication exchange in a concentrated way. It is a helpful activity to introduce the Intercultural Communication unit.)

Approximate Time: 10 minutes

Purposes: To recreate an intercultural communication exchange; identify some differences in intercultural communication

Procedures:

1. Identify two to three common nonverbal intercultural communication differences. (For example, the quality and consistency of eye contact, the accepted volume, proximity, etc.)
2. You will be making even numbers of opposing pairs to act out these different communication norms and then pairing the unsuspecting students together. For example, one student would be instructed to talk to their partner while "maintaining constant eye contact, standing three inches close to their partner than they normally would, etc." Their partner would be instructed to "make only fleeting eye contact, stand six inches further away from their partner than they normally would."
3. The partners cannot know the others directions, so placing quarter sheets or strips of paper face down on desks is a helpful way to keep the information private. However, you the instructor must know that the students will be pairing off and therefore provide the appropriate number of opposing pairs. On the opposite side of the quarter sheet or strip paper put a symbol or a number. When the students are given the instructions to find a partner to have a conversation with while following the instructions the instructor can say "People with

hearts on their instructions find people with diamonds on their instructions" as a way of controlling the pairs. If there is an odd number, the instructor can be in one of the pairs.
4. Very quickly the pairs will discover the awkwardness of the encounter, therefore only a minute or two of conversation is necessary.

Debrief by asking the following discussion questions:
1. Everyone choose one word to describe how they felt during that activity. (Go around the classroom and let everyone choose a word.)
2. Why do you think you felt that way?
3. In what other types of communication exchanges have you felt this way? In other words, has something like this ever happened to you?
4. What would you do if this was an actual conversation and not an activity in your Interpersonal class? How do you think you would have reacted?
5. Share with your partner the instructions you were given. (The students will want to know this, but save the reveal until the last part of debriefing.

Principles Illustrated:
1. Cultures have different communication norms.
2. Communication competence includes tolerance for ambiguity and skill.

Culture Defined

Approximate Time: 20–25 minutes

Purpose: To define culture

Procedures:

Every college student knows what culture is, but having to articulate the definition of culture is more difficult. This activity will allow students to see that even the experts disagree on what defines a culture, while trying to come up with a comprehensive definition of their own.

1. Divide the class into groups of three or four. Either distribute large sheets of newsprint or have them write their definition on a smaller piece of paper which will eventually be put on the whiteboard.
2. Each group is to come up with a comprehensive definition of culture while limiting themselves to one or two sentences.
3. Groups should get 5–10 minutes to come up with this definition and they should not use their books or the Internet, just each other.
4. Each group will present their definition of culture to the rest of the class. The instructor can ask the group for what they believe to be the strengths and weaknesses of the definition. The instructor can then ask the rest of the class for any strengths or weaknesses of the group's definition.
5. After every group has presented and briefly discussed, the instructor should show the class the textbook's definition of culture and the class can discuss the strengths and weaknesses of that definition.

Principles illustrated:
1. Defining culture is not easy.
2. Many things make up a culture.

Cultural Proverbs

Approximate Time: 20–25 minutes

Purpose: To identify cultural norms and values

Procedures:

1. Put the class into pairs.
2. After reading about cultural values and norms distribute a cultural proverb to each pair. There are a number of website that have cultural proverbs available, like these:
   "After dark all cats are leopards." Native American Proverb
   "Behind an able man there are always other able men." Chinese Proverb
   "Fish or cut bait." American Proverb
   "The country rooster does not crow in the town." African Proverb
3. Based on the proverb they were give each pair should try to determine the values of the culture that the proverb is from.
4. Tell the students, you are only speculating. If you don't know what value is being emphasized in this proverb, take a guess.
5. Each pair share their proverb with the rest of the class and what values they think the proverb refers to. Other students in the class may be from the culture and can add to the interpretation.

Debrief with the following discussion questions:

1. What are some proverbs from your culture or co-culture that you think especially indicate cultural values or norms?
2. Are cultural value and norms open to interpretation like some of these proverbs are?
3. Besides proverbs, what other ways are there to discover what a culture values or what behavioral norms are present?

Principles illustrated:
1. Culture is an integral part of daily life.
2. Culture can be identified in a number of ways.

DISCUSSION FORUM PROMPT

1. Visit the following websites:

   YouTern is an intern matching company that has been recognized in the *Wall Street Journal, Forbes,* and *USA Today.* YouTern has an associated blog that covers a host of beneficial professional topics for students:
   http://www.youtern.com/thesavvyintern/index.php/2011/08/09/using-social-media-to-leverage-your-career-the-good-the-bad-and-the-ugly/

   Avid Careerist is a blog by Donna Svei, lauded in Monster.com's "11 for 2011: Career Experts Who Can Help Your Job Search": http://www.avidcareerist.com/page/2/

2. Search the sites and read two posts that relate to finding a job through social networking.

Specifically, look for posts that discuss Facebook, GooglePlus, LinkedIn, and so on.

3. Post the links to the articles you've selected and briefly note what each article covered.

4. Based on the content, discuss three ideas that you have about changing your social network profile for a job search, finding leads via social networking, or trying social networking tools that you did not know about.

JOURNAL PROMPT

Think of a time when you have been in a situation or place where you had to interact with people you perceived as culturally different than you. Answer the following questions:

1. Define what was "different" about the other people? Religion? Socioeconomic background? Age?
2. How much experience did you have interacting with individuals from other cultures prior to this situation?
3. How would you describe your motivation and attitude toward meeting people different than yourself? Do you consider yourself open-minded?
4. How was your communication altered in this situation dealing with people who were culturally different?
5. How would the outcome of this interaction be different if you had the same experience after reading this chapter/experiencing discussion regarding intercultural communication in this class?

PORTFOLIO ENTRY

Assessing Interpersonal Communication Competence

Using the guidelines in Chapter 2, assess your own intercultural communication competence. Some considerations:
1. To which cultures do you belong? To which co-cultures?
2. How much experience do you have interacting with individuals from other cultures or co-cultures? (Remember that cultural differences are not limited to race or ethnicity.)
3. How would you describe your motivation and attitude toward meeting people different from yourself? Do you feel comfortable approaching strangers? Does their culture make a difference? Provide an example to illustrate your tolerance (or lack of tolerance) of ambiguity.
4. Do you consider yourself open-minded? Give an example of an instance in which you stereotyped. What were the results?
5. How do you respond when your find yourself in a culture (or co-culture) different from your own. Relate a specific example.

D & A

Assessing Your Intercultural Communication Competency

Think of a time when you have been in a situation or place where you had to interact with people you perceived as culturally different from you.

- Define different. Was it race, socioeconomics, education, age, religion, and so on?
- How did you feel?

- How did your emotions, attitudes, and/or lack of knowledge affect your communication?
- What were the outcomes of the interaction?
- Do you think the outcome(s) of the interaction would be different if you had the same experience now, after taking this class? How?

Keep your answers brief, but make them thorough enough to aid you in a class discussion on the topic.

GROUP STUDY

See the Introductory Essay for further information. Consult the Group Study section in Chapter 1 for additional directions to students.

TEACHING ACTIVITIES FROM THE *COMMUNICATION TEACHER*

Baldwin, J. R. (1999, Fall). Intercultural pals: A focused journal, *14*(1), 13–14.

Bollinger, L., & Sandarg, J. (1998, Winter). Dare to go where others fear to tread, *12*(2), 1–3.

Bradford, L., & Uecker, D. (1999, Spring). Intercultural simulations: Enhancing their pedagogical value, *13*(3), 1–7.

Brunson, D. A. (2000, Winter). Talking about race by talking about whiteness, *14*(2), 1–4.

Brunson, D. A. (1994, Fall). A perceptual awareness exercise in international communication, *9*(1), 2–4.

Corey, J. (1990, Fall). International bazaar, *5*(1), 4.

Dillon, R. K. (1998, Spring). The diversity board, *12*(3), 7–9.

Ekachai, d. (1996, Spring). Diversity icebreaker, *10*(3), 14–15.

Geyerman, C. B. (1996, Spring). Interpretation and the social construction of gender differences, *10*(3), 7–8.

Hankins, G. A. (1991, Summer). Don't judge a book by its cover, *5*(4) *8.*

Hart, J. L. (1999, Fall). On parachutes and knapsacks: Exploring race and gender privilege, *14*(1), 16–17.

Harvey, V. L. (1999, Fall). Cultural musical chairs, *14*(1), 6–8.

Hastings, S. O. (1998, Spring). Increasing intercultural empathy: From principle to practice, *12*(3), 9–10.

Hawkinson, K. (1991, winter). Through the eyes of Djeli Baba Sissoko: The Malian oral tradition, *5*(2), 1–2.

Hawkinson, K. (1993, Fall). Two exercises on diversity and gender, *8(1)*, 2–4.

Hochels, S. (1994, Summer). An exercise in understanding ethnocentrism, *8*(4), 10–11.

Hochels, S. (1999, Fall). Analyzing how others see the dominant U.S. culture, *14*(1), 4–5.

Jensen, M. D. (1993, Fall). Developing ways to confront hateful speech, *8*(1), 1–2.

Kinser, A. E. (1999, Fall). Diversity scrapbook, *14*(1), 1–3.

May, S. T. (2000, Winter). Proxemics: The Hula Hoop and use of personal space, *14*(2), 4–5.

Pawlowski, D. (1999, Winter). Dialoguing the gender movements, *13*(2), 4–6.

Robie, H. (1991, summer). A Native American speech text for classroom use, *5*(4), 12.

Schnell, J. (1999, Fall). Ideas for including African-American perspectives in selected communication courses, *14*(1), 12–13.

Simonds, C. J. (1999, Fall). Pennies from heaven, *14*(1), 19–20.

Souza, T. (1999, Fall). Framing equity: Examining approaches to diversity, *14*(1), 5–6.

Walter, s. (1995, Summer). Experiences in intercultural communication, *9*(4), 1–3.

Yook, E. L. (1996, Fall). An experiential approach to diversity, *11*(1), 12–13.

Chapter 3: Communication and the Self

Accentuate the Positive

(Adapted from *Games Trainers Play* by Edward E. Scannell)

Approximate time: 10 minutes

Purpose: To break down self-imposed barriers that don't allow people to "like themselves"; to enhance one's self-image by sharing comments and personal qualities

Procedures:
Most of us have been brought up to believe that it is not "right" to say nice things about one's self or, for that matter, about others. This exercise attempts to change that attitude by having teams of two persons each share some personal qualities with one another. In this exercise, each person provides his or her partner with the response to one, two, or all three of the following suggested dimensions.

1. Two *physical* attributes I like in myself.
2. Two *personality* qualities I like in myself.
3. One *talent or skill* I like in myself.

Explain that each comment must be a positive one. No negative comments are allowed. (Since most people will not have experienced such a positive encounter, it may take some gentle nudging on your part to get them started.)

Discussion Points:
1. How many of you, on hearing the assignment, smiled slightly, looked at your partner, and said, "You go first?"
2. Did you find this to be a difficult assignment to start on?
3. How do you feel about it now?

Addressing One's Self and Values

Approximate Time: 20 minutes

Purpose: To increase students' awareness of self

Procedures:
1. Have each student answer each question in point 3 spontaneously and quickly.
2. Have each student go back and reflect on and answer each question again, coming up with personal examples of what she or he did and how she or he communicated in the past under these circumstances.
3. Ask students to share answers they are comfortable sharing.
   a. I am happiest when …
   b. I am most secure when …
   c. When I am home alone I …
   d. If I could change two things about myself, I would …
   e. I believe in …
   f. I trust those who …
   g. When I choose, I …
   h. My advice to someone who wants to let her/his true self emerge or actualized would be …

Principles Illustrated:
1. Some aspects of our self-concept are revealed by analyzing our responses to questions.
2. Some aspects of our self-concept are revealed by comparing our responses to those of others.

Trace the Reflected Appraisal

Approximate Time 10–15 minutes

Purpose: To identify self concept and understand the importance of reflected appraisal

Procedures:

1. In class have everyone take out an object that they have with them (in their backpack, their purse, their pocket, etc.)
2. Ask the students to identify an adjective that they would use to describe themselves with based on the object. (As the instructor you can demonstrate: "I have an umbrella with me. You'll notice that it isn't raining, but I still carry this umbrella. That reminds me of being prepared. I would describe myself as being prepared in different circumstances.")
3. Now that the object has given them a self-describing word they are going to try to trace the origin of this self-concept. When did they start seeing themselves this way? What situations reinforce that self-concept? What situations worked against that self-concept? Who do they think of when they think of themselves in this way?
4. Some students will probably be willing to share what they have traced back, at least with a partner.

Principles Illustrated:
1. Self concept is a mirroring of judgments from those around you.
2. Self concept is relatively stable.

Unraveling Identity Management

Approximate Time: 25–30 minutes

Purpose: To become familiar with the characteristics of identity management

Procedures:

1. Briefly go over the four "Characteristics of Identity Management" on pages 79–80.
2. Divide the class into groups of two or three.
3. Using the following situations, supplementing with your own, have the students analyze the situation by applying the characteristics. Questions could include:
   - Do you think this person is constructing multiple identities? How?
   - How are others collaborating in this person's identity management?
   - Is this person managing their identity deliberately or unconsciously? How do you know?
   - How aware of the impression they are creating do you think the person is? What makes you think that?

4. After the groups have had a chance to discuss the situations come back together as a large group so the groups can share with one another. A good final question to ask the groups and individual students is: What is your take away from this exercise?

Situations:

1. A student who makes comments throughout a class as if they are in a one-on-one conversation with the instructor, not a class with many students. This student gives unasked for examples, finishes the instructor's sentences and even interrupts the instructor from time to time.
2. A person who writes a weekly blog about relationships. One post details, although anonymously, a personal argument that he had with his best friend. In writing about the argument the blogger mentions that his friend is in therapy and taking medication.
3. A person in the workplace who refuses to help a co-worker who is undergoing chemotherapy treatments to move some boxes.
4. A person who calls another person a "phony" while that person is telling about a conversion experience they recently had.
5. A person who brings an infant to a movie theater. The movie begins at 7:30 pm and is rated PG-13.

Principles illustrated:
1. We strive to construct multiple identities.
2. Identity management is collaborative.
3. Identity management can be deliberate or unconscious.
4. People differ in their degree of identity management.

Situational Self-Fulfilling Prophecies

Approximate Time: 30 minutes

Purpose: To understand the impact of the self-fulfilling prophecy

Procedures:

1. After students have an understanding of the self-fulfilling prophecy, divide the class into groups of three or four.
2. Give each group an area that they must apply the self-fulfilling prophecy to, both in a positive manner and a negative manner. For example, if the group was given "self-fulfilling prophecy and cancer treatment" they could come up with the placebo effect where a sugar pill made the patient feel better or the opposite: a sugar pill made the pain worse. Encourage the students to be as specific as possible, perhaps coming up with a situation of your own to demonstrate. Here are some possible areas:
      -Parenting a teen-ager
      -Seeing a therapist
      -Public Speaking
      -Working at a coffee shop
      -Going to court for a speeding ticket
      -Interviewing for a job
      -Going to an exercise class at the gym for the first time

-Going on blind date
-Asking the boss for a raise
-Showing an apartment you want to rent

3. After sharing their situations, debrief with the following discussion questions
    1. If the self-fulfilling prophecy has the potential to be so powerful, why don't we use it to our advantage more often?
    2. How would you alter your situation to demonstrate the second category of self-fulfilling prophecy (where another's expectations govern another's actions)?
    3. How will you use the self-fulfilling prophecy in this class this semester?

DISCUSSION FORUM PROMPT

Angela Maiers is a 20+ year educator (now educational consultant) and author of Habitudes in the Classroom and the Passion-Driven Classroom. Watch Maiers' TEDTalk about the words "You Matter" and answer the following questions:

http://www.angelamaiers.com/2011/08/new-ted-talk-you-matter.html

1. Based on Maiers' experience in the airport and her interactions with the supervisor, how could reflected appraisal impact the passengers' and supervisor's sense of self?
2. Do you believe that the message, "You matter" can alter a person's negative identity management in adulthood? Explain.
3. What are specific ways a person could tell or show another person that they matter? Give three to five examples.

JOURNAL PROMPT

Author and award-winning Southern Methodist University instructor Chris Westfall has another designation: The 2011 Elevator Pitch Champion. Westfall is a master at teaching people how to succinctly and articulately brand themselves in a brief, but impactful timeframe.

Read Westfall's blog post: The Artist and the Elevator Pitch and watch his classroom presentation located within the post. Westfall relates his elevator pitch to presentations, as well as personal branding, an instrumental concept for job candidates who must differentiate themselves from those with similar credentials.

http://moveupormoveout.com/wordpress/2011/09/artist-elevator-pitch/

Answer the following questions:

1. Based on the principles of presenting self, what attributes, characteristics, behaviors are you showing to the world to reveal your talents?
2. Based on the principles of perceived self, what aspects of your background/experiences hold you back from connecting with others or showcasing your talents?
3. Write an elevator pitch based on a talent that you feel confident about, one that could potentially be shared with an employer.

PORTFOLIO ENTRY

Understanding Myself

(NOTE: This can be a very powerful exercise. When students "lose" some of their essential characteristics, they frequently increase their owe appreciation for who they are.)

Referring to the exercise in the beginning of Chapter 3, make a list of ten words or phrases that describe the most important features of who you are. Now arrange the ten characteristics in order of their importance to your own self-image. Continue the exercise, following the directions carefully and writing your responses. Your written report should include your list of the ten fundamental items and the answer to the following questions: How do you change after *each* step? How do you feel about the "new you" that is created? (Make your descriptions *specific*. It is not enough, for example, to say, "Without my friendliness, I wouldn't have any friends, and I'd be lonely," or "Without this quality, I'd feel empty." Truly try to imagine the change that losing this characteristic would make in your basic perceived self.) What does this exercise tell you about yourself? Are there perceptions about yourself you would like to change?

D & A

Who Do You Think You Are?
1. Fill out the "Who Do You Think You Are" Survey. For the purposes of this exercise, you should include both positive and negative descriptors.
2. From each of the eight groups of terms, circle one word or phrase you think describes you best.
3. For each of the eight words or phrases, discuss how you came to believe you have that trait. Identify a specific person or event that helped develop each of the eight parts of your self-concept.
4. Be sure to include terms from the chapter to help explain your self-concept development.

WHO DO YOU THINK YOU ARE?

1. What moods or feelings best characterize you? (cheerful, considerate, optimistic, crabby, etc.)
    a._____ b_____ c_____
2. How would you describe your physical condition and/or appearance? (tall, attractive, weak, muscular, etc.)
    a._____ b_____ c_____
3. How would you describe your social traits? (friendly, shy, aloof, talkative, etc.)
    a._____ b_____ c_____
4. What talents do you possess or lack? (good artist, bad writer, great carpenter, competent swimmer, etc.)
    a._____ b_____ c_____
5. How would you describe your intellectual capacity? (curious, poor reader, good mathematician, etc.)
    a._____ b_____ c_____
6. What beliefs do you hold strongly? (vegetarian, Christian, pacifist, etc.)
    a._____ b_____ c_____
7. What social rules are the most important in your life? (brother, student, friend, bank teller, club president, etc.)
    a._____ b_____ c_____
8. What other terms haven't you listed thus far that describe other important things about you?
    a._____ b_____ c_____

*NOTE: If using the Two-Views Portfolio, an option is to ask students to refer back to this exercise when analyzing why they and their partner may have different perceptions.

GROUP STUDY

(See the Introductory Essay for further information. Consult the Group Study Section in Chapter 1 for additional direction to students.)

TEACHING ACTIVITIES FROM THE *COMMUNICATION TEACHER*

Adams, J. (1991, Summer). The mask, *5*(4), 11.

Bashore, D. (1991, Fall). The résumé as a tool for self-concept confirmation, *6*(1), 10.

Berko, R. (1985, Fall). Intra-interpersonal goal setting, 8.

Berko, R. (1996, Fall). The public "I" and the private "I," *1*(1), 6.

Crawford, L. (1993, Winter). Silence and intrapersonal observation as an initial experience, *39*(2), 11–12.

DeWitt, J., & Bozik, M. (1997, Spring). Interpersonal relationship building along the information superhighway: E-mail business across two states, *11*(3), 1–2.

Eisenberg, R. (1987, Summer). Talking to a machine, *1*(4), 12–13.

Garrett. R. L. 91992, Summer). The onion concept of self, *6*(4), 6–7.

Johnson, C. (1987, Summer). A day in the life…, *1*(4), 11.

Overton, J. (1995, Spring). On the line: A self-concept discovery activity, *9*(3), 8.

Nagel, G. (1989, Fall). "Peculiarity": An exercise in sharing, caring, and belonging, *4*(1), 3–4.

Rumbough, T. B. (2000, Spring). 52 ways to break the ice, *14*(3), 6–8.

Shumer, A. (1991, Summer). Speech communication via critical thinking—it's in the bag, *5*(4), 4.

Smith, K. A. (1997, Spring). Negotiation of self in Nickelodeon's "Rugrats," *11*(3), 9–10.

Chapter 4: Perceiving Others

Shopping List

(Developed by Kathleen Valde, University of Iowa, adapted from John R. Johnson (1989). "The Nature of Inner Speech-Instructional exercise." University of Wisconsin—Milwaukee)

Approximate Time: 15 minutes

Purpose: To introduce students to the myriad factors that may influence our perceptions
(NOTE: This is a good, quick exercise to introduce the unit on perception.)

Procedures:
1. Divide the class into dyads.
2. Place the following list on the board or on a transparency:
   milk
   toothpaste
   veggies
   bread
   detergent
   cereal
   pop
   cookies
3. Tell students to assume that this list has been given to them by their partner as items to be purchased at the store. Based on their own habits and what they may know about their partners, students are to jot down exactly which items they would buy. (e.g., a quart of whole or a gallon of skim milk)
4. Students compare lists with partners and discuss reasons for their perceptions and misperceptions.
5. A large-group discussion is held on the many factors that might influence our perceptions.

Role Reversal in Perceptual Differences

Approximate Time: 45 minutes

Purpose: To illustrate how different persons' perceptions of events may be and to identify reasons for the differences

Procedures:
1. Divide the class into groups of five. If the class works better as a large unit, this exercise can be adapted to one done by the large group.
2. Select one issue that affects everyone in the group, such as class assignments, testing, grading policy, room location, or scheduling. Note both the group's perception of the situation and the perception of another party who might see it quite differently, for example, the professor or an administrative person who schedules class times.
3. Answer the following questions, keeping in mind the group perceptions and the perspective of the other person. Give the groups 20–25 minutes to do this.
   a. What is the problem area?
   b. How is information about the "problem" selected and organized by the other party?
   c. What is the other party's interpretation of the situation?
   d. How is information about the "problem" selected and organized by you?
   e. What is your interpretation of the situation?
   f. What physical filters affect the other party's perception? What social filters affect the other

party's perception?

    g. What physical filters affect your perception of the event? What social filters affect your perception of the situation?

    h. What conclusions can you draw about different perceptions in this example?

    i. What different approaches might be taken to address the problem?

4. If you have divided into smaller groups, report to the class the basic problem on which you worked, the reasons for perceptual differences, and suggestions for action.

Principles Illustrated:
1. The same event can be perceived in different ways by different people involved in the event.
2. Physical and social perspectives influence one's selection and organization of an event.
3. Some misunderstandings are the result of differing perceptions more than differences in opinion.
4. Clear communication, "perception checking," and extensive feedback can help clarify misunderstandings.

What do you notice?

Approximate Time: 10–15 minutes

Purpose: To illustrate the importance of the perceptual process

Procedures:

1. Ask individual students to write down something that they always notice that it doesn't seem others do. You may have to prompt them with your own example, or use one of these:
   - I always notice that the tops of people's refrigerators are dirty.
   - I always notice when people say "like" a lot when they are talking.
   - I always notice the artwork on the sets of TV shows.
2. Instruct students to identify and write down the reason they always notice these things. (I'm tall and I see the tops of refrigerators. I am a speech teacher and pay attention to people's speech. I am an artist and like to look at art.)
3. Instruct the students to extend this example through the rest of the steps in the perception process (Organization: what frameworks do you often put this situation into? Interpretation: what meaning do you attach to this piece of stimuli? Negotiation: How do you influence other's interpretation of this same stimuli?)
4. Once the students have applied the thing they notice to the entire perceptual process ask a few to share with the class what they wrote.

Debrief with these discussion questions:

1. Of the people who read their perceptual process, what other options were there? Different organizational schemas, different interpretations?
2. How do we communicate when we know that there are so many different perceptual filters at work?
3. How will being aware of the perceptual process help you to become a better communicator?

Principles illustrated:
1. Perception is a process.
2. Perception is individual.
3. Perception has physiological, psychological, social and cultural influences.

Stereotypes: For and Against

Approximate Time: 20 minutes

Purpose: To recognize our use of stereotypes; to avoid excessive stereotyping

Procedures:

Do this activity in stages.

Stage 1:
1. Have student identify and write down a stereotype that they use. You may have to give an example, if so, give one that is not positive. Blondes are dumb, redheads have tempers, jocks are stupid, etc.
2. Remind the students that you want them to be honest, but that you are still in a classroom environment. (How comfortable you and the students feel about sharing will dictate the degree of the caution you give.)
3. Ask students to share some of their stereotypes.
4. Follow up with this comment/question: "When talk turns to stereotypes and the problems they cause, usually a few people defend the use of the stereotype. What kinds of things do you imagine they say?"

Stage 2:
1. Have students identify and write down a stereotype that has been used against them.
2. Ask students to share some of those stereotypes.
3. Follow with this comment: Is anyone willing to defend the person who used that stereotype against them?
4. You may conclude the activity with a reminder about what differentiates stereotypes from reasonable generalizations (found on pages 123–124.)

Principles Illustrated:
1. We all use stereotypes.
2. Stereotypes can harm interpersonal communication.

"Empatherapy"

Approximate Time: 20–25 minutes

Purpose: To get students accustomed to empathizing in difficult situations

Procedures:

1. Tell students that it is easy to empathize with people we like and agree with, but the real test of the ability to empathize is with someone we don't like or disagree with.
2. Tell students that they need to think of a real interpersonal conflict that they are having or have had. They won't be asked to share the conflict unless they want to, but it must be real. The instructor will be leading the class through a forced empathy exercise.
3. Have the students write or distribute a handout with the following prompts regarding their personal conflict:
    a. I am right about _____
    b. You are wrong about _____

    c. You are right about _____

    d. I am wrong about _____

    e. I'm glad we are having this conflict because _____

    f. I'm upset we are having this conflict because _____

    g. In one year this conflict _____

4. Lead the students through the seven prompts, giving further explanation, examples, and encouragement (many will say there is nothing the other person is right about, remind them this is a forced empathy exercise.)

5. Once they are done with the seven prompts and every blank has been filled in ask them write how they feel about the conflict now versus how they felt about the conflict before they did the seven prompts. Tell the students it doesn't matter how small (or how big) the change is, just the slightest difference in the conflict should be documented.

6. Some students will have major breakthroughs "I never realized they thought..." or "This conflict is so dumb, I'm going to let it go..." or "I didn't know how much this was bothering me."

7. If anyone would like to share their change/observation about the conflict they can, without giving the details of the conflict.

Principles illustrated:

1. Empathy has value.

2. Empathy requires open-mindedness.

DISCUSSION FORUM PROMPT

In 1961 Marshall McLuhan wrote that the medium is the message. By this McLuhan meant that the medium by which communication occurs, such as the telephone, the television, or handwriting, is more influential in shaping one's understanding of a message than the content of the message itself. McLuhan concluded that the same message content communicated over different media, such as television, radio, and printed material, would be interpreted differently by message receivers.

Remember that during the early 1960s, when McLuhan explained the relationship between media and their effects on understanding, television itself was a new medium whose effects were not fully understood. McLuhan believed that understanding the effects of a medium and the public's ability to adopt to a new medium or technology took 20 years.

We are now facing new communication and, particularly, social media technologies whose effects we do not yet know. You have likely already felt the impact of increasing communication technologies in your own life. Answer the following questions:

1. How have your relationships developed differently via use of social media, such as Facebook? What are the benefits of Facebook and other social media tools for relationship management? What are the drawbacks?

2. What impact does Facebook have on self-disclosure? How does increased or decreased self-disclosure impact your relationships with those on Facebook?

3. Given that Facebook is largely image-driven, what impact does Facebook have on your perception of the way that others live their lives? Do you perceive others as relating to you in the same way as before? Or do you believe others' lives are very different than yours?

JOURNAL PROMPT

Go on a technology fast for three days with two people in your life. No e-mail, Facebook, Twitter, or texting. You may call or visit each other in person. If possible, do not tell the person your intentions. Simply change your mode of communication with them. Answer the following questions:

1. How did your communication change when you altered your usual mode of technologically mediated communication?
2. What was the other person's reaction to the change in communication? Positive? Negative? Explain.
3. Did you feel more satisfied or dissatisfied with the relationship, based on the increased face-to-face or phone interaction? Why or why not?
4. Do you believe you will permanently change the way you communicate with this person? Why or why not?

PORTFOLIO ENTRY

(Based on an assignment in Ron Adler and Neil Towne, *Looking Out/Looking In*, 5th ed.)

Two Views
1. Choose a disagreement you presently have with another person or group. The disagreement might be a personal one, such as an argument about how to settle a financial problem or why you should not have a curfew, or it might be a dispute over a contemporary public issue, such as the right of women to obtain abortions on demand or the treatment of AIDS patients.
2. Describe the background of the situation sufficiently so that the instructor will be able to understand the remainder of the exercise. (This section will vary in length according to the complexity of the problem.)
3. Write a personal letter *to your "opponent"* stating your arguments and why you take the position you take. Your letter should be long enough to develop your ides—approximately 300–350 words.
4. Now put yourself in the other person's position. Write a letter *to you*, as if written by your "opponent," in which you present his/her side of the issue. This letter should also be 300–350 words in length.
5. Now show the description you wrote in step 4 to your "partner," the person whose beliefs are different from yours. Have that person read your account and correct any statements that don't reflect his/her position accurately. Remember, you're doing this so that you can more clearly understand how the issue looks to the other person. (Of course, you may also share your view with him/her.)
6. Make any necessary corrections in the account you wrote in step 4, and again show it to your partner. Unless there are major problems, it is not necessary to rewrite the entire letter. If you do choose to write a new letter, please include your first attempt with the assignment. When (s)he agrees that you understand his/her position, have her/him *sign* your paper to indicate this.
7. *Now record your conclusion to this experiment. Has this perceptual shift made any difference in how you view the issue or how you feel about your partner?
* This is the single most important assignment in the first journal. BE SURE TO COMPLETE *ALL* PHASES OF THE ASSIGNMENT!

D & A

Review the "Common Tendencies in Perception" section in the chapter, and choose three to discuss. Think of a time when you have experienced each one. What were the outcomes? Would they have been different if the common tendency hadn't played a part in your perception?

GROUP STUDY

(See the Introductory Essay for further information. Consult the Group Study section for Chapter 1 for additional directions for students.)

TEACHING ACTIVITIES FROM THE *COMMUNICATION TEACHER*

Anderson, J. (1986, Fall). Communication crossword puzzle, *1*(1), 4.

Blythin, E. (1988, Winter). Communication crosswords, *2*(2), 15–16.

Bozik, M. (1988, Summer). Who said that?, *1*(1), 6.

Cohen, M. (1986, Fall). A grin-and-bear-it quiz, 5.

Hall, D. (1987, Fall). Interpersonal messages in music, *2*(1), 7.

Hankins, G. (1991, Summer). Don't judge a book by its cover, *5*(4), 8.

Hochel, S. (1999, Fall). Analyzing how others see the dominant U.S. culture, *14*(1), 4–5.

Jensen, M. (1989, Summer). Listening with the third ear: An experience in empathy, *3*(4), 10–11.

Johnson, C. (1989, Summer). Empathy interview, *3*(4), 4.

Kassing, J. W. (1994, Summer). The color of perception, *8*(4), 4–5.

Lau, J. (1988, Winter). Women and men, men and women, *5*(2), 9.

Litterst, J. (1988, Winter). Observation project, *2*(2), 10–11.

Patterson, B. R. (1994, Fall). An experiential vehicle for instructor on human perception, *9*(1), 7–8.

Ross, R. (1991, Spring). What is in the shoe box?, *5*(3), 12.

Schnell, J. (1992, Winter). The china protests as a perception case study, *6*(2), 13.

Schrader, D. (1992, Winter). A demonstration of the impression formation process, *6*(2), 6–7.

Wakefield, B. (1990, Fall). Are we aware?, *5*(1), 5.

Walters, K. (1987, Spring). Perception assignment: Moving beyond biases, *1*(3), 4–5.

Zalewski, I., and Waters, L. (1989, Spring). Using popular games to teach communication, *3*(3), 13.

Chapter 5: Language

How Often Is Often?

Approximate Time: 20–30 minutes

Purpose: To demonstrate that words can mean different things to different people

Procedures:
1. Distribute a handout similar to the one that follows.
2. Discuss differences in responses. Even on words that sound fairly precise, people have diverse interpretations. Encourage students to give reasons for their choices.

HOW OFTEN IS OFTEN?

Given here is a group of words often used to indicate degrees of frequency with which events tend to happen. The words mean different things to different people.

Beside each word, specify how many times out of 100 you think the word indicates an act is likely to happen. For example, if "seldom" indicates to you that a thing should happen about 10 times out of 100, you should mark a 10 in the space before the expression. If it means about 2 times in 100, then mark 2.

_____ 1. almost never   _____ 11. hardly ever
_____ 2. very often   _____ 12. seldom
_____ 3. always   _____ 13. never
_____ 4. very seldom   _____ 14. rather often
_____ 5. about as often as not _____ 15. not often
_____ 6. usually not   _____ 16. rarely
_____ 7. frequently   _____ 17. now and then
_____ 8. usually   _____ 18. once in a while
_____ 9. generally   _____ 19. occasionally
_____ 10. sometimes   _____ 20. often

How many are:
A. _____ a few?
B. _____ several?
C. _____ many?
D. _____ not many?
E. _____ a lot?

Principles Illustrated:
1. Meanings are in people, not in words.
2. Even words that sound precise may have different interpretations for different people.
3. Use words as precisely as possible when clarity is your goal.

Overused Language

Approximate time: 10 minutes

Purpose: To attune students to the importance of language

Procedures:

1. Ask students to write down a few words they think are overused in everyday conversation. (See the results of an unscientific poll below.)
2. Ask students to write a sentence or describe a situation in which they have heard the particular word used in a tired way.
3. Ask students to write a sentence of describe a situation in which it would be okay to use this word.
4. Pair students up and have them share what they came up with. Individuals or pairs can share with the rest of the class time permitting.

   Some overused words:
   Brilliant
   Amazing
   Interesting
   Cool
   Awesome

Debrief with the following discussion questions:
1. Do you agree that the words we have heard are overused? Why or why not?
2. Why do you think these words are overused?
3. What's wrong with using a word a lot?

Principles illustrated:
1. Language is subjective.
2. Language can be powerful or not.
3. Language can be ambiguous.

Guess the Real Meaning

Approximate time: 10 minutes

Purpose: To acquaint students with the frequency of euphemisms in everyday speech

Procedures:

1. Collect euphemisms from different areas of life (politics, health, teaching, etc.). You'll find a sample list below.
2. Show the class one euphemism at a time and have each person write down what they think the euphemism is really referring to in plain speech.
3. After going through 10 (or however many time permits) have students read their guesses.
4. If no one guesses correctly, supply the class with the correct answer.

Sample euphemisms:

1. "put to sleep" means euthanizing an animal
2. "Garden of Honor" is a veteran's graveyard
3. "undocumented worker" used to be called illegal alien or illegal
4. Mark Sanford used "soul mate" to refer to his mistress
5. "collateral damage" is the killing of civilians
6. "Information Commons" is used to refer to a library
7. "relaxed attitude" can mean lazy
8. "substance abuse" is overusing alcohol and drugs
9. "between jobs" means unemployed
10. "freedom fighter" has been used to refer to terrorists

Debrief with the following questions:
1. Which euphemisms did you find the most acceptable for use in everyday life?
2. Which euphemisms did you find the biggest stretch for what it really meant?
3. What euphemisms do you use in your daily communication?

Principles illustrated:
1. Euphemisms are used in all walks of life.
2. Euphemisms are used to soften the impact of unpleasant information.
3. Euphemisms can obstruct clear communication.

Race Labels

Approximate Time: 20–25 minutes

Purpose: to allow students to discuss the practice of race labels and the implications of these labels

Procedures:

1. There are numerous articles and blogs that discuss the use of the terms "African American" and "black" and also the use of the term "person of color." Or the terms "Hispanic" or "Latino" Below is a partial list.
2. Divide the class into as many groups as you have articles/blogs. Have each group read the article and report a summary of the author's thoughts to the rest of the class.
3. After all of the summaries are complete, on the whiteboard draw a table with the following categories: "African American" "black" "person of color" "Doesn't matter" and have the students give reasons for each based on the reading of the articles.

Articles dealing with race labels:
       http://www.gallup.com/poll/28816/black-african-american.aspx
       http://www.manhattan-institute.org/html/_latimes-why_im_black.htm
       http://itre.cis.upenn.edu/~myl/languagelog/archives/004055.html
       http://www.lasculturas.com/aa/aa070501a.htm

Debrief with the following questions:
1. What are the labels used for?
2. How do you feel using one of these race labels versus another one?
3. What does it feel like to have a label attached to a race?
4. What other labels are used by and for people of other races?

Principles illustrated:
1. Language is powerful.
2. Language is dynamic.
3. There is diversity over the use of race labels.

Twitter and 140 Characters

Approximate Time: 15–20 minutes; up to 30 minutes if students create their own tweets

Purpose: to allow students to identify word choice when communication constraints are imposed.

Procedures:

Note to Instructor: You can do this exercise as a collective experience in the classroom, or have students set up their own Twitter accounts and assign this project as homework. You will need to set up your own Twitter account.

1. Log on to Twitter.com and sign in to your Twitter account.
2. Do a search for people who have interests/expertise in the class subject, or ask students for tweets on subjects that students select (i.e., sports, a particular celebrity, etc.).
3. Ask students to analyze how the message is impacted when limited to 140 characters. Why did the tweeter select the words that they did?
4. How does the word usage of tweets differ when information is shared versus marketed?
5. What about celebrities who tweet? Do students perceive that they "know" the celebrity better based on the information shared on Twitter?
6. Find a college- or subject-related article on the web and have students come up with a tweet to share. (Remind students that they have to account for the URL characters). Have students discuss the ease or difficulty staying within Twitter's 140 character parameters.

DISCUSSION FORUM PROMPT

Lisa Braithwaite is a public speaking coach from Santa Barbara, California, interviewed by the *Los Angeles Times* and *Chicago Tribune* as an expert in her craft. Braithwaite's blog, "Speak Schmeak" covers all aspects of the public speaking process, though much of her content also relates to interpersonal communication.

Read the entry "What's Your Crutch Phrase?"
http://coachlisab.blogspot.com/2008/09/whats-your-crutch-phrase.html

Answer the following questions:
1. Monitor your conversations for one to two days and try to catch any "crutch phrases" that you use. Ask others to help you as you speak with them. What do you say repetitively?
2. Why do you believe you use the "crutch phrase" that you do? Do you perceive your "crutch phrase" impacting your ability to clearly communicate?
3. Devise up to three strategies that you can use to, as Braithwaite puts it, "eradicate your crutch phrase."

JOURNAL PROMPT

Word choice is critical when saying "I'm sorry." Depending on the composition of a message, apologizing can sound empty or can achieve tremendous repair. Read:

> Achieved Strategies: When Leaders Say Sorry, authored by Shawn Murphy, CEO, Change/Transition Strategist
>
> http://achievedstrategies.com/blog/when-leaders-say-sorry/

and watch:

> Randy Pausch, late Carnegie Mellon professor and author of The Last Lecture: Condensed Version of The Last Lecture on Oprah Winfrey, specifically the three-part apology
>
> http://www.youtube.com/watch?v=Wn9L4CxAaQY

Answer the following questions:

1. Describe a time that you either apologized or someone apologized to you and did **not** follow the ideas noted in Shawn Murphy's blog post or Randy Pausch's lecture. What message did the person send by the words they chose?
2. Describe how the person who delivered the problematic apology could have better phrased their remorse?
3. Do you have someone to whom you need to say "I'm sorry"? Write an apology encompassing Murphy's advice and Pausch's three elements.

PORTFOLIO ENTRY

The Language Key

Identify three (3) specific personal examples of times when choice of language led to positive or negative results in your own interpersonal relationships. For each situation, cite the person(s) involved, the place of the occurrence, the situation, and the language used. Then identify the type of language problem (ambiguous language, relative words, euphemism, static evaluation, fact/inference problems, etc.) and note the results of each incident. How did language play a pivotal role in these experiences? (Each example should illustrate a different type of language problem.)

D & A

The Language Key just outlined.

GROUP STUDY

(See the Introductory Essay for further information. Consult the Group Study section for Chapter 1 for additional directions for students.)

TEACHING ACTIVITIES FROM THE *COMMUNICATION TEACHER*

Bollinger, L., and Sandarg, J. (1998, Winter). Dare to go where others fear to tread, *12*(2), 1–3.
Bozik, M. (1985, Fall). Words and gender, 6.
Hochel, S. (1990, Winter). Language awareness and assessment, *4*(2), 4–5.
Hopson, C. (1986, Fall). What am I describing?, *1*(1), 5.
Jensen, M. (1988, Summer). Revising speech style, *2*(4), 3–4.
McGrath, R. (1987, Fall). The slang game, *2*(1), 5.

Phillips, T. G. (1997, Summer). Introducing gender-biased language: Much ado about something, *11*(4), 3–4.

Rockwell, P. (1988, Winter). Wheel of phonemes, *2*(2), 5.

Rowley, E. N. (1992, Fall). More than mere words, *7*(1), 5.

Weaver, R. L. II. (1995, Winter). Responsible communicators own their messages, *9*(2), 8–9.

Young, K. S. (1999, Summer). Proving the importance of inclusive language in the basic course, *13*(4), 7–8.

Zizik, C. H. (1995, Summer). Powerspeak: Avoiding ambiguous language, *9*(4), 8–9.

Chapter 6: Nonverbal Communication

Analyzing Communication of Clothing

Approximate Time: 50 minutes

Purpose: To acquaint students with "object language": personal artifacts and clothing

Procedures:
1. Hold a general discussion of the communicative nature of clothing and artifacts (rings, etc.); then direct each student to categorize his or her own clothing as:
   a. formal wear
   b. informal
   c. intimate
   d. private
   e. functional
2. Have each student describe articles of clothing he or she would never wear to church, to work, in a locker room, in front of his or her parents.
3. Catalogue each item of clothing with regard to why it was purchased in terms of:
   a. function
   b. sexiness
   c. daring
   d. role-fulfillment
   e. outrageousness
   f. expense
   g. fashionableness
   h. funkiness
4. Finally, have students design a hypothetical wardrobe by having them name ten items they would love to own, regardless of price, and identify what is communicated by each item of clothing.

Principles Illustrated:
1. How we dress communicates.
2. There is a relationship between personality type and clothing choice.

Space Invasion

Approximate Time: 20 minutes

Purpose: To experience how the four proxemic distances identified by Hall affect communication

Procedures:
1. Have students pair off into dyads. Be sure there both mixed-sex and same-sex dyads.
2. Tell the students they will be carrying on a conversation. They can talk about what they did last weekend or will do next weekend as a starting point or anything else they choose. (The topic is not important.)
3. Have one member of each dyad come to the center of the room and turn out to face his/her partner. The partner should place him-/herself as far away from the partner as possible within the confines of the room. (Public Distance)
4. The conversation begins and continues for approximately two minutes.

5. Stop the conversation (a whistle is helpful), and have the partners move in toward one another until they are just touching fingertips. They drop their arms and continue the conversation at this distance. (Social Distance)
6. After a few minutes, again stop the conversation and have the students move in so that they can place a hand on their partner's shoulder. They drop their arms and continue the conversation at the distance. (Personal Distance)
7. Finally, have the students move toward one another until the tips of their shoes are touching. The conversation continues. (Intimate Distance) BOTH feet should be touching; this needs to be monitored by the instructor.
8   After a maximum of two minutes at this close proximity, have students return to their seats and discuss the experience.
    a. What were your reactions to conversing at Public Distance? How did the distance make a difference in your conversation (degree of intimacy, vocal volume, number of exchanges)?
    b. How did this change when you moved in to the Social Distance? For how many of you was this the most comfortable distance?
    c. What changes occurred as you moved in to the Personal Distance? For how many was this the most comfortable?
    d. How did you respond to the Intimate Distance? How might you have reacted had this exercise been done on the first day of class? How did your posture change at this distance? Did you do anything to compensate for the closeness? (limited eye contact, change in posture, folding arms)
    e. How well do you know your partner? To what extent did this make a difference in your level of comfort? (Male/female dyads, male/male dyads, female/female dyads will have varying responses.) How might culture make a difference?

Principles Illustrated:
1. The use of varying proxemic distances has an impact on the intimacy and comfortability of conversation.
2. Different people will be most comfortable at different distances.
3. When individuals are forced into uncomfortably close proximity, they will do something to compensate for the lack of physical distance.

"Shh ... We're Playing Cards!"

Approximate Time: 15–25 minutes

Purpose: To demonstrate the functions of nonverbal communication

Procedures:

1. Bring five or six decks of cards to class, depending on the size of your class.
2. Teach the students, perhaps by playing an open hand, a very easy card game like "Go Fish," "Gin" or "War." (This activity could also be done with easy board games like "Chutes and Ladders" or "Uncle Wiggly.")
3. In groups of two, three, or four, have students play the game *without talking*. There must be absolutely no talking during the games.
4. After a hand or two of playing the games with no talking (although there will almost certainly be giggling) come back as a big group to discuss.

Use the following questions to debrief:

1. What was the most difficult part of playing the game without speaking?
2. How did you manage to play the game without being able to speak?
3. What specific nonverbal behaviors helped you accomplish the functions of nonverbal communication outlined in your textbook:
   -Create and Maintain the relationship
   -Regulating Interaction
   -Influencing Others
   -Concealing/Deceiving
   -Managing Identities

Principles Illustrated:
1. Nonverbal communication has communicative value.
2. The functions of nonverbal communication.

The Overdone Standing Ovation

Approximate Time: 10–15 minutes

Purpose: To demonstrate the wide variety of nonverbal communication with a specific example

Procedures:

1. Google "overdone standing ovation" and you will find many articles and postings regarding the once rare, but now common, standing ovation. (For example, "In defense of the overdone standing O" *Seattle Times*, September 14, 2008.)
2. As a class read one or two of the articles.
3. Use the following questions to lead a discussion:
   -What does a standing ovation signify?
   -What criteria would have to be met in order for you to give a standing ovation?
   -Is there something to be said for keeping standing ovations rare?
   -Are there problems if standing ovations are overdone? What are they?
   -Are there other nonverbal ways an audience can let performers know that they have appreciated the performance?

Principles illustrated:
1. Nonverbal communication is primarily relational.
2. Nonverbal communication is powerful.

These are the Rules

Approximate Time: 20–25 minutes

Purpose: To have students brainstorm about the intricacies of nonverbal communication in daily communication exchanges

Procedures:

1. Tell your class that they will be coming up with a nonverbal rule book for visitors from another planet.

2. Divide the students into groups of three or four. Assign each group one of the types of nonverbal communication (e.g., "face and eyes," "posture," "gestures," "touch," etc.).
3. Each group should come up with three or four rules to include in the rulebook for visitors from another planet. The groups will find this easy at first, but in thinking about context (parent-child, boyfriend-girlfriend), people involved (different genders, different cultures), the rules will become more involved.
4. Each group shares their rules with the rest of the class.

Debrief with the following questions:
1. How many rules do you think you could have come up with if you had more time?
2. How do the rules change depending on who and how many are involved in the communication exchange?
3. How did you know these were rules? Were the disagreements on the rules you came up with in your group?

Principles Illustrated:
1. Nonverbal communication is primarily relational.
2. Nonverbal communication can be ambiguous.
3. Nonverbal communication is influenced by gender and culture.

DISCUSSION FORUM PROMPT

Select one nonverbal taboo to use with another person, either on campus or with a family member or friend:

-Stand too close
-Fail to make eye contact
-Change your facial expression so it vastly differs from your message
-Speak too loudly or too softly
-Or come up with your own

Answer the following questions:
1. Which nonverbal taboo did you select? Why did you select that particular taboo?
2. What was the outcome of your experiment? Did you feel that you achieved the intended effect? Why or why not?
3. If you selected a family member or friend, how did your relational involvement impact the experiment? Do you perceive that your attempt would have differed with someone you did not know well? How?

JOURNAL PROMPT

Tim Tyrell-Smith, marketing coach and career strategist writes for *US News and World Reports* Career blog, as well as his own blog, http://www.timsstrategy.com. Read his piece on the top 10 interview mistakes to avoid and select one other blog post about interviewing. Then, answer the following questions:

http://money.usnews.com/money/blogs/outside-voices-careers/2011/05/24/10-job-interview-mistakes-to-avoid

http://timsstrategy.com/how-to-promote-a-conversational-job-interview

1. Tyrell-Smith writes about both verbal and nonverbal mistakes that job candidates make in interviews. Select two nonverbal mistakes from the list and discuss the underlying message that an employer might receive from a candidate making these errors.
2. Do you believe that you could commit any of these nonverbal mistakes in interviews? Which ones?
3. Based on the additional blog post that you selected, what strategies can you take to avoid nonverbal mistakes when you interview? What new nonverbal strategies will you use in job interviews?
4. What nonverbal mistakes would you add to Tyrell-Smith's list?

Note to faculty: You can also modify this prompt to encompass telephone interviewing. Blogs to reference:

CNN Money: "Don't Wear Pajamas to a Phone Interview"

The Chatty Professor: "A Suit for a Phone Interview?"

PORTFOLIO ENTRY

Nonverbals I Have Known

Give a personal example (a total of 10 examples) of how you have used each of the types of nonverbal communication discussed in Chapter 6: face and eyes, kinesics, touch, paralanguage, proxemics (personal space), territory, chronemics, physical attractiveness, clothing, and environment. Note that these examples should reflect *specific incidents*, not just general tendencies. Based on these examples, personal reflection, and comments made to you by others, how do you rate yourself as a nonverbal communicator in terms of frequency, awareness, and accuracy of decoding messages? Again, be specific.

D & A

Nonverbals I Have Known just outlined. An instructor may choose to shorten this to ask students to select five of the ten to discuss.

GROUP STUDY

(See the Introductory Essay for further information. Consult the Group study Section for Chapter 1 for additional directions for students.)

TEACHING ACTIVITIES FROM THE *COMMUNICATION TEACHER*

Booth-Butterfield, M. (1992, Summer). Analysis of an audiotaped conversation with a friend, *6*(4), 14–15.
Bozik, M. (1984, Winter). A picture's worth a thousand words, *1*(2), 5.

Coakley, C. (1991, Spring). Getting acquainted nonverbally, *5*(2), 15.

Demo, N. (1991, Spring). The game of twister—an exercise in proxemic interaction, *5*(3), 2.

Johnson, C. (1987, Fall). People's Court comes to the classroom, *2*(1), 10.

May, S. T. (2000, Winter). Proxemics: The Hula Hoop and use of personal space, *14*(2), 4–5.

Overton, J. (1993, Summer). Look and learn: Using field observation in the nonverbal course, *7*(4), 4.

Parker, R. G., and Leathers, D. G. (1992, Fall).You be the judge: Impression management in the courtroom, *7*(1), 4.

Rollman, S. (1988, Spring). Classroom exercises for teaching nonverbal communication, *2*(3), 13.

Schnell, J. (1988, Summer). Experimental learning of nonverbal communication in popular magazine advertising, *2*(4), 1–2.

Schreier, H. N. (2000, Winter). Experiencing persuasion and the persuader, *14*(2), 7–9.

Siddens, P. J. III. (1996, Spring). Touch, territoriality and nonverbal communication, *10*(3), 2–4.

Sims, A. (1987, Winter). Survey research on projected impressions, *1*(2), 7.

Spicer, K. L. (1988, Summer). Developing nonverbal skills through finger-plays, *2*(4), 14.

Valentine, C. A., and Arnold, W. E. (1992, Summer). Nonverbal scavenger hunt, *6*(2), 14–15.

Chapter 7: Listening: Understanding and Supporting Others

Becoming an Effective Listener

(Created by Gregory Lamp, University of Wisconsin Center—Rock County)

Approximate Time: 40–50 minutes or two 25-minute segments

Purpose: To afford students the opportunity to practice the skills of listening for information and listening for feelings in a positive environment

Procedures:
1. Divide the class into groups of three. Designate the students as A, B, and C. They will rotate roles as the speaker, the listener, and the observer.
2. Give each student the information that follows on Listening for Facts and Listening for Feelings as well as the two checklists.
3. Begin by having student A serve as the speaker and Student B as the listener. Student A begins to speak, discussing one of his/her "beefs" about school, work, social life, or home (or any other topic of the student's or instructor's choice). Speakers converse for at least one minute without any substantive verbal feedback from the listener. Student C serves as the observer, using the "Observer's Checklist" form.
4. When the speaker has finished, the listener provides feedback in the form of a paraphrase.
5. The observer offers his or her comments to the listener.
6. Students rotate positions so that each has an opportunity to be the speaker and the listener and the observer.
7. Large-group discussion may follow at this point, or the triads may be instructed to continue with Part II of the assignment, Listening for Feelings.
8. Follow a similar format for Part II of the exercise, Listening for Feelings, being sure to choose a topic that will arouse emotional reactions in the students. This time, the listeners and the observers will focus beyond what the speaker is saying to what (s)he is feeling. Some suggested topics are:
   > your most embarrassing moment
   > your most meaningful/significant relationship
   > the most exciting event in your life
   > the saddest event in your life
   > your feelings toward the opposite sex
9. Continue with steps 4, 5, and 6. Follow with a large-group discussion.

Discussion Points:
1. How effectively did you find that people listened?
2. Did you find yourself listening differently in this situation that you ordinarily do?
3. Which role was the most difficult (speaker, listener/paraphraser, observer)? Why?
4. Did it make a difference to you as a speaker knowing that your words and behaviors were being carefully attended to?
5. What applications and ramifications does the exercise have for you as a "real life" listener?

Principles Illustrated:
1. We use different techniques for listening in different ways.
2. Listening is an active a process and takes effort and concentration.
3. Our listening abilities can be improved with practice.
4. Effective listening requires a commitment to understanding the other person.

PART I: PARAPHRASING—LISTENING FOR FACTS

Objectives: Restatements are used:
1. To indicate your desire to understand the speaker's thoughts and to think with the speaker.
2. To check your listening accuracy and to encourage further discussion.
3. To let the speaker know you are committed to grasping the facts.

Method:
Focus on the content of the speaker's message.
Identify key ideas.
Listen until you experience the speaker's point of view.
Wait for a natural "break" in the conversation.
Briefly restate the speaker's ideas, emphasizing the facts.
State the essence of the speaker's content.
Respond with your own words to what the speaker has said.
Request feedback.

Listener Response Format:
"As I understand it, you are saying that ... Is that what you intended?"
"What I think you said was ... Is that right?"
"Let me see if I have this right ... Is that what you said?"

Message Communicated from the Listener to the Speaker:
"I'm interested in you as a person, and I think that what you feel is important. I respect your thoughts, and even if I don't agree with them, I know they are valid for you. I want to understand you. I think you're worth listening to, and I want you to know that I'm the kind of person you can talk to." (Carl R. Rogers)

Procedure for Paraphrasing:
- Make the decision to listen.
- Reduce any outside interference.
- Distance your emotions.
- Temporarily set aside your own opinion.
- Take a listening posture:
    Face the speaker.
    Make eye to eye contact.
    Lean forward.
    Have an open, receptive posture.
    Establish a close, but not uncomfortably close, interactional distance.
    Maintain responsive facial expressions.
- Listen for facts.
- Verbalize brief and encouraging expressives (mm-hmmm; uh huh, I see, right).
- Withhold judgment. (Do NOT evaluate; do NOT agree or disagree.)
- If necessary, ask for clarification, examples, or more helpful detail.
- Speak in a warm and pleasant voice tone.
- Feed back the message as you understand it to see if that is what the speaker intended.
- Request feedback to check your perceptions.

OBSERVER'S CHECKLIST: LISTENING FOR FACTS
In the spaces provided, put a "+" if the listener demonstrated the behavior and a "−" if the listener did not.

Did the listener…
_____ face the speaker?
_____ make eye-to-eye contact?
_____ lean forward?
_____ have an open, receptive posture?
_____ establish a close, but not uncomfortably close, interactional distance?
_____ maintain responsive facial expressions?
_____ listen for understanding first?
_____ verbalize brief and encouraging expressives?
_____ withhold judgment (did not evaluate; did not agree or disagree)?
_____ wait for a natural "break" in the conversation before asking questions or restating the speaker's idea?
_____ if necessary, ask for clarification, examples, or more helpful detail?
_____ briefly restate the speaker's ideas, emphasizing the facts to see if that was what the speaker intended?
_____ state the essence of the speaker's content.?
_____ respond in his/her own words to what the speaker has said?
_____ speak in a warm and pleasant voice tone?
_____ request feedback?

Additional Comments:

PART II: LISTENING FOR FEELINGS

Objective: Responding in a way to show that you have listened for feelings is used to...
1. Show your desire to feel with the sender.
2. Reduce anxiety, anger, or other negative feelings.
3. Verify the listener's perception of the sender's feelings.
4. Let the other person know you are working to understand how s/he feels.

Method:
1. Reflect the other persons' feelings.
2. Observe body language.
3. Note the general content of the speaker's message.
4. Focus on the feeling words and nonverbals.
5. Match the speaker's depth of meaning, whether light or serious.
6. Ensure accurate communication of feelings by matching the speaker's meaning.

Listener Response Format:
"You feel that you didn't receive the proper treatment, is that right?"
"It was unjust as you perceived it, is that it?"
"I sense that you like doing the job but not sure how to go about is, right?"
"It's frustrating to have this happen to you, right?"

Procedure for Listening for Feelings:
Follow the foregoing pointers, plus:
   a. Focus on the feeling words.
   b. Reflect the speaker's feelings nonverbally.
   c. Feedback the feelings as you understand them to see if that is what the speaker intended.

OBSERVER'S CHECKLIST: LISTENING FOR FEELINGS
In the spaces provided, put a "+" if the listener demonstrated the behavior and a "–"if the listener did not.

Did the listener…
_____ face the speaker?
_____ make eye-to-eye contact?
_____ lean forward?
_____ have an open, receptive posture?
_____ establish a close, but not uncomfortably close, interactional distance?
_____ maintain responsive facial expressions?
_____ observe the speaker's body language?
_____ reflect the speaker's feelings nonverbally?
_____ verbalize brief and encouraging expressives?
_____ withhold judgment (did not evaluate; did not agree or disagree)?
_____ wait for a natural "break" in the conversation before asking questions or reflecting the speaker's feelings?
_____ if necessary, ask for clarification, examples, or more helpful details?
_____ briefly restate/reflect the speaker's feelings?
_____ speak in a warm and pleasant voice tone?
_____ request feedback?

Additional Comments:

Listening Challenge

Approximate Time: 30 minutes

Purpose: To illustrate how people fail to listen to others because they often prepare their next statements while others are talking

Procedures:
1. Divide the class into dyads.
2. Write several controversial topics on the board, such as abortion, gun control, the President's budget. Ask the students to take opposite sides on the issue, even if they disagree with the position they will have to argue.
3. Direct the dyads to begin debating the issues. After three to five minutes of debate, tell them to switch sides. After a period of time, tell them to switch sides again.
4. Discuss what happened. What feelings were generated? Hostility? Frustration? Empathy?
5. Ask the same dyads to select a different topic. This time, each person has to restate the other's position before he or she can speak for his or her own position. Let this discussion proceed for five to eight minutes.
6. Contrast the second situation with the first. Was it equally (or more) frustrating? What were the merits of each approach? Problems?

Principles Illustrated:
1. We often fail to listen effectively because we are preparing our statements in advance.
2. Effective listening is challenging; it is difficult and tiring.
3. Listening effectiveness can be improved with effort.

What's next?

This activity is similar to the acting exercise "Freeze."
1. The students will be giving a group impromptu speech. They can stand and give their part, come to the front of the room or stay seated where they are.
2. Give the students a topic that anyone can talk about: best vacation spots, campus issues, gender wars, etc.
3. One person will start the impromptu speech (this activity is not about speaking, rather about listening, but it is best not to announce that purpose.)
4. At an arbitrary point in the student's speech the instructor says "Freeze" or "Stop" followed by "Thank you, what's next?" and picks another student to continue to the speech. Do not ask for volunteers, pick a random student.
5. The next student must carry on the speech until the instructor says "Freeze" and the replacement student continues the speech. (The activity must be a speech because there needs to be logical continuity between the speakers to demonstrate they were listening. If it is a story, speakers can make up crazy additions for the sake of creativity.)
6. Continue the activity for as long as it takes to demonstrate how important listening is in order to competently carry on a conversation.

Debrief with the following discussion questions:
1. Was it easy or difficult to listen to the students who went before you?
2. What was your motivation for listening?
3. What interfered with your ability to listen?

Listening on the Job

Approximate Time: 10–15 minutes

Purpose: To have students think about the kind of listening they will be doing in their future careers

Procedures:

1. Ask students to write down in the most specific terms possible the career they want to get when they are done with college. Some students will say they don't know or haven't picked a major, assure them that you won't hold them to this career and they can pick something that they may not do, but they do need to be as specific as possible. For example: nurse at a high school, financial planner, interior decorator, hotel manager, and so on.
2. Showing the students a list of the types of listening discussed in the text (silent listening, questioning, paraphrasing, empathizing, supporting, analyzing, evaluating and advising.) assign each individual one of these types.
3. Students must come up with a situation in which they would use this type of listening and describe the situation. For example, if "questioning" is assigned you might say: "As a communication studies teacher a student from my class comes to me to tell me he is having a hard time in his math class and feels he is being picked on by the instructor. If I was going to use the questioning type of listening I would use a question that clarified meanings. I would ask the student what he meant by 'having a hard time'? Poor grades, not understanding or feeling embarrassed in class? I would also ask what form the 'being picked on' is taking.
4. Once the students have completed the situation, have them share with a partner.
5. A few of the pairs or individuals may want to share with the whole class.

Debrief with the following discussion questions:
1. What was the most difficult part of the type of listening you were assigned?
2. What other type of listening would have been effective in this situation?
3. What type of listening would you expect the other person(s) to demonstrate?

Activity could be concluded by going over the principles of "Which style to use?" that ends Chapter 7.

Principles Illustrated:
1. Effective listening occurs in many different forms.

Poor Listening Skits

Approximate Time: 15–25 minutes

Purpose: To show that we all listening ineffectively

Procedures:

1. Divide the class into seven groups.
2. Tell the class that they are going to demonstrate one of the poor listening habits from the chapter, and the other groups are going to guess which habit they are demonstrating.
3. Go to each group and secretly assign them one of the poor listening habits (e.g., "pseudolistening," "filling in gaps," "stage hogging," etc.).

4. Each group should come up with a short skit that demonstrates the poor listening habit without using the term they were assigned.
5. After each group demonstrates and the rest of the class guesses correctly a spokesperson for the group should give a definition of the poor listening habit.

Debrief with the following discussion questions:
1. Which of the poor listening habits do you find yourself engaged in the most?
2. What can you do to overcome this habit?
3. Which of the poor listening habits is completely new to you?

Principles Illustrated:
1. Listening is not easy.
2. We all engage in poor listening.
3. Listening is a mindful activity.

DISCUSSION FORUM PROMPT

Listening is a skill taught the least and used the most, particularly at work. For those who wish to become leaders, assertive, engaged, and proactive listening is absolutely critical. In reviewing career experts' blogs, listening is identified in both blatant and subtle themes.

One such blogger, Meghan M. Biro, is a serial entrepreneur, leader and globally recognized career expert in talent acquisition, creative personal and corporate branding. As the CEO of TalentCulture, Meghan blogs about professional issues, particularly characteristics of employees/employers in today's workforce. Read her piece from 12most.com on the 12 Essential Leadership Traits **http://12most.com/2011/09/22/12-essential-leadership-traits/**.

Answer the following questions:

1. Although Biro notes listening as a key leadership trait in the 12most.com post, note three other traits and describe how listening is key to those leadership qualities.
2. Do you agree that "Everyone listens to the first half of a sentence and then starts talking?" Explain. How does the chapter discuss this habit and what solutions does it recommend for remedying it?

JOURNAL PROMPT

Listening does not just happen face-to-face, but also when we respond to another person in writing. Use your favorite social media outlet (Facebook, Twitter, Google+. You may also use a text discussion) and follow a couple of conversations. The conversations can be yours or interactions that others are having. Answer the following questions:

1. How is the listening process (hearing through responding) noted in the text impacted by conversations held via social media?
2. Copy an example of an original comment and another person's response to the comment. What did the respondent say to indicate that they "heard" the other person's message?
3. Copy an example of an original comment and response where you perceived that the other person wasn't "listening" to what the original poster said. What did the respondent say to make you believe that the original poster was not heard?

4. Do you feel that other people are listening to you when you interact with them via social media? Why or why not?

PORTFOLIO ENTRY

Listening Diary

(Based on an exercise in Mary O. Wiemann's Activities Manual for *Looking Out/Looking In*, 8th ed.)

Nobody's a perfect listener. Here's a chance for you to see how often you truly listen and how much of the time you just pretend.

Purpose:
1. To help you to identify the styles of listening/nonlistening you use in your interpersonal relationships
2. To help you to identify your response styles
3. To help you to discover the consequences of the listening styles you use

Background:
Your text discusses several types of listening/nonlistening and styles of feedback:

Listening	Nonlistening	Response Styles
To Understand and Retain Information	Pseudolistening	Passive
	Stage Hogging	Active-
To Build and Maintain Relationships	Selective Listening	Questioning
To Evaluate Messages	Filling in the Gaps	Paraphrasing
	Insulated Listening	Empathizing
To Appreciate and Enjoy	Defensive Listening	Directive-
(This is another reason, less clearly	Ambushing	Supporting
related to interpersonal communication,	Analyzing	
why we might listen.)	Advising	
	Evaluating	

Instructions:
1. Before beginning your diary, circle the three listening/nonlistening styles and three response styles you think use most frequently.
2. For the next five days, pay attention to your listening behavior. Don't try to change the way you act; just observe the times when you're really trying to understand someone and the times you're behaving in one of the nonlistening ways listed in the foregoing table.
3. Using the entry sheets provided, note FIVE listening experiences for each of the five days (a total of 25 entries). Be sure to include a weekend in your survey. Each entry should include the following information:
   a. Time and place
   b. People involved
   c. Situation
   d. Emotions—mood/atmosphere (yours? your parent's? expressed or not?)
   e. Style of listening used (See foregoing table.)
   f. Response style (yours and/or your partner's)
   g. Outcome (Did your listening and responses bring the situation to a satisfactory conclusion?)

While your entry sheets will be handed in with your Portfolio, the notes are for your benefit, not the instructor's. Be sure you include enough information so that you will be able to draw conclusions and support your conclusions with specific examples.

4. Using the information your recorded over the five days, analyze your listening behavior. Create a cohesive essay in which you discuss the following points. (Be sure to use specific examples from your data sheets to support and illustrate your points. Your essay should be approximately three typed, double-spaced pages.

   a. Did you anticipate the results of the diary? Why or why not? Did you find that the styles you used most frequently were the ones you circled prior to collecting the data?

   b. Which listening/nonlistening and response styles did you use most frequently? Do you see any patterns in your listening behaviors? (Do particular situations or people or times of day regularly correlate with certain listening/nonlistening behaviors or response styles?)

   c. What conclusions can you draw about your listening behavior?

   d. How effective are your listening patterns? How satisfied are you with your listening behavior? *Explain why you are satisfied or dissatisfied.* How would you wish to change? How can you begin to change?

Date: _____

Results	Response Style	Listening/ Nonlistening	Situation	Emotion(s)	Time/Place/ People

D & A

Review the poor listening habits discussed in the chapter. Describe an experience where you have either used or been subjected to four of the seven habits. What was the outcome of each?

GROUP STUDY

(See the Introductory Essay for further information. Consult the Group Study section in Chapter 1 for additional directions to students.)

TEACHING ACTIVITIES FROM THE *COMMUNICATION TEACHER*

Bohlken, B. (1994, Winter). Learning to listen as you listen to learn, *8*(2), 8–9.

Bohlken, B. (1996, Spring). Think about listening, *10*(3), 5–6.

Forestieri, M. (1987, Spring). Listening instruction, *1*(3), 14–15.

Garvin, J. A. (1990, Spring). Where is it and how do we get there?, *4*(3), 15.

Hyde, R. B. (1993, Winter). Council: Using a talking stick to teach listening, *7*(2), 1–2.

Jensen, M. (1989, Summer). Listening with the third ear: An experience in empathy, *3*(4), 10–11.

Johnson, M. (1991, Winter). Student listening tests, *5*(2), 5.

Kaye, T. (1990, Spring). Respecting others' point of view, *4*(3), 12.

Lamoureux, E. L. (1990, Summer). Practice creative word choice with dialogic listening, *4*(4), 4–5.

Loesch, R. (1987, Summer). Three nonverbal listening styles: A demonstration, *1*(4), 4.

Mallard, K. S. (1998, Winter). The listening box, *12*(2), 9.

McPeak, J. (1994, Spring). Listening activities, *8*(3), 15–16.

Mino, M. (1997, Fall). Creating listening rules, *12*(1), 8.

Potnoy, E. (1989, Spring). Activities to promote students' speaking and listening abilities, *3*(3), 14–16.

Rausch, R. (1985, Fall). On-the-job listening, 6.

Schneider, V. (1987, Fall). A three-step process for better speaking and listening, *2*(1), 10–11.

Starnell, B. (1986, Fall). Critic's corner, *1*(1), 1–2.

Wallace, J. D. (1996, Fall. The rumor game revisited, *10*(1), 6–7.

Wirkus, T. E. (1993, Winter). Creating student-generated listening activities, *7*(2), 3–4.

Chapter 8: Emotions

Thinking Things Through

Approximate time: 45–50 minutes

Purpose: To focus group discussion on the ways in which assumptions affect our interpretations and how we feel

Procedures:
1. In your small group, consider the following ten episodes and discuss these questions:
   a. What irrational assumptions is the person making? What fallacies are present?
   b. How do these assumptions cause the person to feel the way she does?
   c. What rational assumptions does the person need in order to change her feelings into more positive feelings?
2. In your group, discuss assumptions each of you has and that influence your feelings of depression, anger, frustration, distress, and worry. When you are experiencing each of these feelings, what assumptions are causing you to feel that way? How can you change these assumptions to make your life happier?

Episodes

1. Sally likes to have here coworkers place their work neatly in a pile on her desk so that she can add her work to the pile, staple it all together, and give it to their supervisor. Her coworkers, however, throw their work into the supervisor's basket in a very disorderly and messy fashion. Sally then becomes very worried and upset. "I can't stand it," Sally says to herself. "It's terrible what they are doing. And it isn't fair to me or our supervisor!"
2. Jill has been given responsibility for planning next year's budget for her department. This amount of responsibility scares her. For several weeks she has done nothing on the budget. "I'll do it next week," she keeps thinking.
3. John went to the office one morning and in the hallway passed a person he had never met. He said, "Hello," and the person just looked at him and walked on without saying a word. John became depressed. "I'm really not a very attractive person," he thought to himself. "No one seems to like me."
4. Dan is an intensive-care paramedic technician and is constantly depressed and worried about whether he can do his job competently. For every decision that has to be made, he asks his supervisor what he should do. One day he came into work and found that his supervisor had quit. "What will I do now?" he thought. "I can't handle the job without her."
5. Jane went to her desk and found a note from her supervisor that she had made an error in the report she had worked on the day before. The note told her to correct the error and continue working on the report. Jane became depressed. "Why am I so dumb and stupid?" she thought to herself. "I can't seem to do anything right. That supervisor must think I'm terrible at my job."
6. Heidi has a knack for insulting people. She insults her coworkers, her boss, customers, and passersby who ask for directions. Her boss has repeatedly told Heidi that if she doesn't change she will be fired. This depresses Heidi and makes her very angry with her boss. "How can I change?" Heidi says. "I've been this way ever since I could talk. It's too late for me to change now."
7. Tim was checking the repairs another technician had made on a television set. He found a mistake and became very angry. "I have to punish him," he thought. "He made a mistake and he has to suffer the consequences for it."
8. Bonnie doesn't like to fill out forms. She gets furious every day because her job as a legal secretary requires her to fill out form after form after form. "Every time I see a form my stomach

102

ties itself into knots" she says. "I hate forms! I know they have to be done in order for the work to be filed with the courts, but I still hate them!"

9. Bob is very anxious about keeping his job. "What if the company goes out of business?" he thinks. "What if my boss gets angry with me? What if the secretary I yelled at is the boss's daughter?" All day he worries about whether he will have a job tomorrow.

10. Jack is a very friendly person who listens quite well. All his coworkers tell their problems to Jack. He listens sympathetically. Then he goes home deeply depressed. "Life is so terrible for the people I work with," he thinks. "They have such severe problems and such sad lives."

Principles Illustrated:
1. The assumptions we make greatly influence our interpretations of the meaning of events in our life. These interpretations determine our feelings.
2. The same event can be depressing or amusing, depending on the assumptions and interpretations we make.

Rational Thinking

Approximate Time: 30 minutes

Purpose: To sharpen students' skills at thinking rationally on the spot

Procedures:
1. Before class, generate a list of four or five "scenes" that are interpersonal in nature and are likely to have anxiety connected to them for anyone experiencing a similar situation in real life.
2. Possible scenes are:
   a. A potential employee just beginning a job interview
   b. A couple just beginning their first date
   c. A teacher or boss criticizing a student or employee for showing up late
3. Ask for three volunteers from the class to act out each scene: a "subject," a second person, and the subject's "little voice"—his or her thoughts.
4. Have the students play out each scene by having the subject and the second party interact, while the "little voice" stands just behind the subject and speaks the thoughts that the subject probably is having. For example, in a scene where the subject is asking an instructor to reconsider a low grade, the voice might say, "I hope I haven't made things worse by bring this up. Maybe he'll lower the grade after rereading the test. Maybe he'll see something else wrong that he missed before. I'm such an idiot! Why didn't I keep my mouth shut?"
5. Whenever the voice expresses an irrational thought, the observers watching the skit should call out "foul." At this point the action is stopped while the group discusses the irrational thought and suggests a more rational line of self-talk. The players then replay the scene, with the voice speaking in a more rational way.

Principles Illustrated:
1. Often what we think about an event causes us to have negative feeling about it.
2. Irrational self-talk can be overcome and replaced with rational internal monologues.

Emotional Script

Approximate Time: 30–40 minutes

Purpose: To reflect on the existence and role of emotions in a conflict

Procedures:

1. Have students come up with a real conflict they are having or have had. Tell them they won't be sharing this conflict with anyone unless they want to, so they should feel free to be honest.
2. Students will be writing a script about this conflict. They will be writing so they can reflect upon the emotions associated with the conflict. It is important for them to see what they have written; therefore just thinking about the script should be discouraged.
3. While the students are thinking about a real conflict they are having or have had, briefly go over the Guidelines for Expressing Emotions found in the chapter 8.
4. After revisiting the guidelines either have the students label parts on their own paper or give them a handout with space for them to write under each of the following headings:
    i. Recognize your feelings
    ii. Choose the best language
    iii. Share multiple feelings
    iv. Recognize the difference between feeling and acting
    v. Accept responsibility for your feelings
    vi. Choose the best time and place to express your feelings

5. Give the students 10–15 minutes to complete the exercise to the best of their ability. Remind them that this is an exercise to help them understand the emotions surrounding the conflict and you are not asking them to act, merely to reflect and what they do with that reflection is up to them.
6. Depending on the class, students may be willing to discuss some of what they wrote with a partner, but this is not mandatory. Also, depending on the class students may be willing to discuss what they wrote with the rest of the class; again, not mandatory.

Debrief with the following discussion questions:
1. Of the six guidelines, which was the most difficult and why?
2. Of the six guidelines, which was the easiest and why?
3. If you chose to use this script in attempting to resolve the actual conflict, what would be some of the challenges and opportunities in that conversation?

Principles Illustrated:
1. Expressing emotions takes time and careful thought.
2. Communication is transactional.
3. Emotions can be communicated in a positive way.

Emotions at Work

Approximate Time: 20–25 minutes

Purpose: To understand that social conventions influence emotional expression

Procedures:

1. Make and distribute a handout with a list of occupations on one side (see sample below) and space for writing under these categories on the other side:

    Best Emotion:

    Worst Emotion:

    Why best?

    Why worst?

    Activating event:

    Thought for best:

    Thought for worst:

2. Divide the students into groups of three or four.
3. Have the students discuss and write the best and worst emotion that could be displayed by each of these professions.
4. Have the groups pick one of the professions to share with the class. In addition to listing the "best" and "worst" emotions have the students answer the question why: "Why would this be the best?" "Why would this be the worst emotion to express?"
5. As a class review the section of Chapter 8 entitled "Thoughts Cause Feelings."
6. Have each group take the profession that they shared and come up with *one* situation where it was a thought or belief that caused the best emotion to be expressed and how the thought/belief could activate the worse emotion in that person.

    Sample list of professions:
    Receptionist
    Writer
    College professor
    Funeral director
    Architect
    Computer repair person
    Real estate agent
    Nurse
    Elementary school principal
    Financial advisor
    Restaurant manager
    Costume designer
    Librarian
    Personal trainer
    Criminal defense attorney

    Sample best/worst emotion:
    Profession: Preschool teacher

    Best emotion: Joyful Why? Taking pride in his/her young students may be why they went into preschool teaching in the first place.

Worst emotion: Depressed

Why? When you are depressed you may be despondent and not care about the children when they need most to feel cared for, plus you may not recognize when they are in trouble.

Activating event: Child asks the preschool teacher to teach him how to tie his shoelaces.

Joyful because: The child is curious—a sign of intelligence and the teacher can do what they are meant to do: teach!

Depressed because: Everyone will want to learn how to tie their shoelaces and the teacher will have to demonstrate and correct it over and over again.

Principles illustrated:
1. Social conventions and emotions.
2. Thoughts/beliefs cause emotions rather than activating events.

Emotional Contagion

Approximate Time: 5–10 minutes at the beginning and end of the class session

Purpose: To demonstrate that emotions can be contagious

Procedures:

1. At the beginning of the class, without referring to Chapter 8 or emotions, tell the class you are going to conduct a little unscientific experiment and would like their help.
2. Ask half of the students to leave the room (you may need to explain that they can't know what the experiment is about, but that it will not embarrass them or hurt them in any way.) It is best if the half that leaves the room will be sitting next to or close to one of the students who didn't leave the room.
3. With the remaining students go over the section of Chapter 8 entitled "Emotional Contagion."
4. Instruct the students that they are going to demonstrate an emotion throughout the class to see if one of the students who left the class would "catch" that emotion by the end of the class. Tell the students to be subtle (reminding them that researchers "have demonstrated that this process can occur quickly and with little or no verbal communication" p. 302.) Tell the students that in the last 5–10 minutes of class you are going to have them pair off with the missing students and they can demonstrate their emotion a little more forcefully then if they would like.
5. Invite the other students to come back to the class. Conduct class as you normally would without mentioning the experiment again.
6. With 10–15 minutes left in the class have the students pair off. Ask them to discuss some concept from the class. Give the students five minutes.

Debrief with the following questions:
1. Everyone give one word for how you feel right now (go around the room.)
2. Depending on the responses, why do you feel this way?
3. Explain the experiment to those who left the room and ask them if they felt at all that they "caught" an emotion from anyone in the class?

Note: It's important to remember that if the experiment does not end with the anticipated results the experiment is not a failure- it is still ripe for discussion. Why didn't the students catch the emotion? What other variables were involved?

Principles Illustrated:
1. Emotional contagion.

DISCUSSION FORUM PROMPT

Do a web search for "emotions" and "work". Find a credible article on the subject and answer the following questions:

1. Post a link to the article that you found and write a brief summary of the information covered.
2. Did the article focus mostly on women showing emotions at work? Or both genders?
3. Write three recommendations that the article gave and discuss whether or not you agree with the tips given to manage emotions in the workplace.

JOURNAL PROMPT

Read the CNN piece "Don't Let Others Stress You Out"

http://thechart.blogs.cnn.com/2011/09/07/dont-let-others-stress-you-out/

Answer the following questions:

1. Do you agree that "emotions are contagious"? Why or why not?
2. Have you experienced a time when others' emotions "rubbed off" on you? Explain.

If you find your own mood changing due to others' emotions, how does the article recommend that you avoid this? Do you agree or disagree? Explain. What strategies do you use to control your emotions, despite what others around you are feeling?

PORTFOLIO ENTRY

Emotions: Thinking, Feeling, and Acting

We all experience emotions, but we identify them and express them with varying degrees of expertise. The purpose of this exercise is to have you focus on the role emotions play within your daily life.

1. Complete the three-day survey by filling out the entry sheets. You should note **five** different experiences for each of the three days. (While you will be asked to hand in your entry sheets, the notes are for your benefit, not the instructor's. be sure to include enough information so that you will be able to draw conclusions and support your conclusions with specific examples. You may use any kind of personal shorthand that is meaningful for you.)
2. Using the data on your entry sheets, analyze the role of emotions in your life during this three-day period and in general.
   a. How easy was it for you to identify the emotions? Which methods did you use for the purpose of identification: proprioceptive stimuli (physical reactions)? nonverbal manifestations? cognitive interpretations? Illustrate your response with two *specific* examples.
   b. Analyze the types of emotions you experienced. How wide a range of emotions? Are they mainly primary or mixed? Are most of them facilitative or debilitative? Illustrate by giving specific examples.

c. Do you think this three-day period provides a "typical" sample of your emotions? If not, explain why not.
d. Did you find evidence that you subscribe to any of the fallacies given in your text? Give two examples of incidents when you did subscribe to a fallacy. (You may go outside of the three-day period if you wish.)
e. How freely do you express your emotions? With whom do you express yourself most freely? Least freely? Why?
f. How comfortable are you with your emotions? What is the impact of emotions on your daily interpersonal relationships?
g. Make any other observations you'd like based on your entry sheets or other thinking that you have done on this topic.

Date: _____

Results	How Expressed?	How Recognized?	Facilitative/ Debilitative	Situation	Primary/ Mixed	Emotion(s)	Time/Place/ People

D & A

Complete the Invitation to Insight 1 (emotions in one particular relationship), at the end of the chapter (p. 272).

GROUP STUDY

(See the Introductory Essay for further information. Consult the Group Study section in Chapter 1 for additional directions to students.)

TEACHING ACTIVITIES FROM THE *COMMUNICATION TEACHER*

Coakley, C. (1986, Fall). Feelings, *1*(1) 16.
Hutchinson, J. A. (1988, Winter). The love debate, *2*(2), 13–14.
Lane, S. D. (1997, Spring). Communicating emotions, *11*(3), 2–4.

Chapter 9: Dynamics of Interpersonal Relationships

Wanted: Relationships

Approximate Time: 30 minutes

Purpose: To have each student assess the type of person he or she prefers in various situations; to demonstrate that relationship needs differ from situation to situation

Procedures:
1. Have each student write and bring into class three "want ads" (of the singles magazine or online variety) advertising for people to fill three different types of relationship "vacancies" in their lives. The student should also describe him-/herself in each of the ads.
   a. Advertise for a person with whom you wish to establish a working relationship.
   b. Advertise for a person with whom you wish to have a friendship.
   c. Advertise for a person with whom you would like to develop a long-term spousal relationship.
2. Divide the students into groups of about five members. Give them the following instructions: In your small group, share the ads that have been written by each member. For each person, compile two lists, one showing the characteristics that are uniform in all three ads and one showing those that are distinct from one ad to another.
   a. Are there strong similarities among the members of the group?
   b. What might account for the differences between the members?
   c. How do the ads reflect your goals for each of these relationships?
   d. What role does impression management play in these ads? Do you present the same "self" for each of the ads?
   e. What does the exercise tell you about yourself? About others in the group?
   Choose a number of ads and insights from your group to share.
3. Conduct a large-group discussion based on the foregoing questions.

Principles Illustrated:
1. There are situational elements in relationship needs.
2. People have an "implicit" personality theory that informs them of the type of person they need, or want, in a relationship.

Considering Friendship

Approximate Time: 30–40 minutes

Purpose: To allow students to discover and discuss the dimensions of friendship

Procedures:
1. Divide the students into groups of five to seven.
2. Distribute the following discussion sheet. Be sure that someone from each group takes notes to report back to the large group. (If time is short, different groups can be assigned to discuss different questions.)
3. After a prescribed amount to time, meet back in the large group to share responses.

CONSIDERING FRIENDSHIP

Some questions for discussion:
- How would you define the word *friends*?

- What are the most important characteristics of a friend? Brainstorm to come up with at least 15 characteristics. Then try to come to consensus on rank-ordering the top five characteristics.
- What role does honesty play in your friendships? Is absolute honesty necessary? possible? desirable? What are the potential advantages and dangers of honesty in interpersonal situations? Is there a form of "pure" honesty that people can determine for themselves and always depend on using, or does what is "honest" sometimes vary with the situation or with how much information is available? Is there a difference between lying and not telling the whole truth? Discuss some situation is which "complete" honesty either strengthened or harmed an interpersonal relationship.
- What is necessary in order to foster a friendship? Do you spend time on your friends? How many is "enough" friends? How/when do friendships deteriorate? Have you ever had to "break off" a relationship? How did you do it? How did you feel about it?
- Do you see differences between male/male, female/female, and male/female relationships? Does it make a difference whether or not you are "attached (regularly dating, living with someone, married)?

Relationship Dynamics

Time: 20 minutes; with discussion 50 minutes.

Purpose: To give you experience in identifying relational dialectics in everyday situations

Procedures:
1. Reread the text information on relational dialectics.
2. Listed on the next page are six descriptions of common dynamics in personal relationships. Identify which relational dialectic is most prominent in each. Record your answers in the blanks.

This activity works nicely along with the lecture of relational dialectics in Chapter 9. The idea of relational dialectics is foreign to many college students; therefore addressing the subject matter with a hands-on activity is a good way to solidify this information to the familiar so that they can use that information to analyze their own relationships.

Principle Illustrated:
1. How the different relational dialectics play out in interpersonal situations.

Relational Dialectic	Description of Dynamics

Example:
Novelty/predictability

Erin and Mike want to take a vacation and are undecided whether to return to a place they know and like or to go somewhere new and different.

Jen wants to tell her friend Ann about her problems with school, but Jen also wants to keep her academic difficulties private.

Ty and Dave have gotten together to watch football games every weekend for two years. They really enjoy this pattern in their friendship, yet they are also feeling that it is getting stale.

Mary likes the fact that her boyfriend, Jim, respects her right not to tell him about certain aspects of her life. At the same time, she sometimes feels that what they don't know about each other creates a barrier between them.

Robert feels that he and Navita would be closer if they did more things together, yet he also likes the fact that each of them has independent interests.

Dan feels he and Kate have fallen into routines in how they spend time together. On one hand, he likes the steady rhythm they have; on the other hand, it seems boring.

After spending a week together on a backpacking trip, Mike and Ed get back to campus and don't call or see each other for several days.

Come to Order

Approximate Time: 20 minutes

Purpose: To familiarize students with Knapp's model of relational development.

Procedures:

1. This is an activity to do before beginning the unit that includes chapter 9 (which includes Knapp's model.)
2. On 8 ½ x 11 sheets of paper print the 10 stages of Knapp's model in large point type.
3. Divide the class into 10 groups. Without using their books or other sources ask the groups to put the stages in order from coming together, through relational maintenance to coming apart.
4. A few will be easy (initiating, terminating, for example) but other terms will be unfamiliar. Tell the students to do their best.
5. Once the attempt at putting the stages in order is complete (taping to a wall or whiteboard helps) go through the stages and ask the students for a definition or example. If there is a stage that the group doesn't know, help them out. (For example, circumscribing means restricting or limiting. It comes from "circum" to circle or "scribe" to write, so when you draw a circle you are limiting or restricting space.)
6. Now, open the book to page 337 to see Knapp's model in its correct order.

Debrief the activity with the following discussion questions:
1. What are the similarities and differences in what we came up with and Knapp's model?
2. In your experience is Knapp's model of relational development accurate? Has there been a time when the model we put together was more accurate?
3. What are some strengths of this model? Weaknesses?

Principles illustrated:
1. Knapp's model is sometimes an accurate model of relational development.
2. Not all relationships develop in a linear fashion.

"Meta" Lives

Approximate time: 10 minutes

Purpose: To familiarize students with the concept of metacommunication

Procedures:

1. Come up with examples of "meta" in areas other than interpersonal communication (see partial list below.)
2. Define the concept of "meta" and share the examples with students. (If you can play portions of the songs or the movies, that's even better!)
3. Ask the students for a few examples of their own.
4. Introduce the concept of metacommunication. Give a few examples.

5. Have pairs come up with an example of verbal and an example of nonverbal metacommunication to share with the rest of the class.

"Meta" Examples

Songs about songs
"Killing Me Softly" Roberta Flack
"Sad Songs Say So Much" Elton John
"When Smokey Sings" ABC

Movies about movies
Paranormal Activity (2007)
The Player (1992)
Tropic Thunder (2008)

Books about books
"Great Books" by David Denby
"The Eyre Affair" by Jasper Fforde
"Reading Lolita in Tehran" by Azar Nafisi

Learning about learning
Learning about learning styles
Learning about education
A lesson plan about making lesson plans

Principles illustrated:
1. Relational dimension of communication.
2. Metacommunication can be nonverbal.

DISCUSSION FORUM PROMPT

Dr. John Gottman is one of the foremost scientific researchers on marital relationships, particularly relational satisfaction and marriage dissolution. He is affiliated with the University of Washington and has authored numerous books, including *The Seven Principles for Making Marriage Work*. Watch any of the brief videos featuring Dr. Gottman from the Gottman Institute and answer the following questions:

1. Briefly summarize Gottman's message in the video you selected.
2. Based on Gottman's message, what would you tell your adult children or a good friend about what you learned from viewing Gottman's advice?

JOURNAL PROMPT

There are numerous websites that have steps to take in forgiving someone.
1. Access one of these types of websites and review the steps. For example:
   http://www.beyondaffairs.com/articles/12_steps_to_forgiveness.htm
   http://learningtoforgive.com/9-steps/
2. Pick a situation in your life where forgiveness is an option.
3. Apply the steps to forgiveness in the article to your situation.
4. Do you feel this is a realistic way to forgive someone? Would you recommend this

strategy or use it yourself? Why or why not?

5. What are other ways to forgive someone?

PORTFOLIO ENTRY

Analyzing a Relationship

This entry covers the theory found in Chapter 9.

Using an essay format, analyze one of your most important relationships. Begin by identifying the individual and briefly describing the relationship. Then use the principles in the chapters to analyze this relationship.

1. Consider the variables of why we form relationships (attraction, similarity, complementarity, proximity, etc.). How did these variables function in the beginning of your relationships? How do the variables function now that you have a more established relationship?
2. Discuss your relationship in terms of Knapp's Stages of Coming Together/Apart. How did you move from one sage to another? Where are you now? What tells you this?
3. How do the dialectical tensions function in this relationship? Give at least two specific examples, and describe how you managed the tension.
4. What types of compliance-gaining strategies do you use in this relationship? What kind does your friend use? Give at least two specific examples of the use of these strategies.
5. What role does self-disclosure play in this relationship? Why do you self-disclose (see Chapter 10). What benefits have you found in self-disclosure in this relationship? How important is honesty in this relationship? Do you ever use "alternatives" to self-disclosure (lies, "white lies," equivocation, hinting)? What are the results of such behavior? Give a specific example.
6. What role does metacommunication play in this relationship?
7. How would you describe the "social penetration" of this relationship?
8. What is your level of satisfaction in the relationship? What could/should be changed? What is your prediction for the future?

D & A

Consider the reasons we form relationships outlined in the chapter. Choose a relationship and discuss each variable and its role in your relational development. How do they affect your relationship differently now that it is established?

MOVIE ANALYSIS

See the movie analysis of *The Story of Us* at the end of Part III.

GROUP STUDY

(See the Introductory Essay for further information. Consult the Group Study section in Chapter 1 for additional directions to students.)

TEACHING ACTIVITIES FROM THE *COMMUNICATION TEACHER*

Ayres, J. (1990, Spring). How to use relationship to get more out of theory, *4*(3), 13–14.
DeVito, J. (1987, Winter). Interpersonal relationships related in card and songs, *1*(2), 4.
DeWitt, J., & Bozik, M. (1997, Spring). Interpersonal relationship building along the information superhighway: E-mail buddies across two states, *11*(3), 1–2.

Kassing, J. W. (1996, Winter). Can you hear what else I'm saying?, *10*(1), 4–5.

Masten, R. (1989, Winter). Conversation, *3*(2), 12–13.

Rivers, M. J. (1994, Fall). Friendship network, *9*(1), 12–13.

Rozema, H. (1988, Summer). Using literature to teach interpersonal communication concepts, *2*(4), 10–11.

Stahle, R. B. (1991, Spring). What's the attraction?, *5*(3), 6.

Tolar, D. L. (1989, Fall). Carl Rogers' three characteristics of a growth-promoting relationship, *4*(1), 4–5.

Chapter 10: Communication Climate

Communicating Levels of Confirmation

Approximate Time: 50 minutes. Instructor may decide to assign this as overnight homework to be used for the next class meeting group discussion.

Purpose: To give practice in creating communication that expresses different levels of confirmation of another person

Procedures:
1. If the students do not recall the levels of confirmation and the communication that creates them, go over this information again.
2. Listed shortly are four situations. For each one, write a statement that expresses each of the three levels of confirmation: recognition, acknowledgment, and endorsement.

Principles Illustrated:
1. Different levels of confirmation mean different responses in language and nonverbal behavior.
2. While all levels of confirmation are positive, the effect of each level is different.

Example:
A five-year-old child runs to you and says, "Look, look, I found a four-leaf clover!"

    a. recognition: "Hello (smile)"

    b. acknowledgment "So you are pretty excited, aren't you?"

    c. endorsement "Wow! You are right. You did find a four-leaf clover!"

1. Your best friend comes to your place without having mentioned she/he was coming by. Your friend walks in and says, "I'm really worried about what is happening with my parents. They seem angry with each other all the time, and I believe they may be thinking about a separation or divorce.
   a. recognition:

   b. acknowledgment

   c. endorsement:

2. At a meeting of a political group, someone whom you know only casually says to you, "All we ever do in this group is talk. We never really do anything. I am very frustrated by the lack of action."
   a. recognition:

   b. acknowledgment

c. endorsement

3. While you are home over winter break, one of your parents says to you, "I'm worried about your uncle. His health is failing, and I think maybe we need to move him into a nursing home."
   a. recognition:

   b. acknowledgment

   c. endorsement

4. The person whom you have been dating steadily for about four months tells you, "I don't like the way we handle conflict. Whenever we disagree it seems that each of us digs our heels in and refuses to listen to the other or to even try to understand the other's point of view."
   a. recognition:

   b. acknowledgment

   c. endorsement

Defensiveness Makeover

Approximate time: 30 minutes

Purpose: To become familiar with Gibb's Categories of Supportive and Defensive Behaviors

Procedures:

1. After the students have read about Gibb's categories or after a lecture on the same topic divide the class into six groups.
2. Each group will be assigned one of Gibb's six pairs of behaviors.
3. The group must come up with a situation (a skit works well) in which they demonstrate the defensive behavior.
4. Using the *same situation*, the group will demonstrate the supportive behavior.

5. If groups are having difficulty thinking of a situation, give them prompts: planning a surprise party, going to talk to a professor about an unsatisfactory grade or a supervisor giving an employee a performance review.
6. As the instructor you may need to help the students keep the situation the same, just alter the Gibb behavior.

Debrief the activity with the following discussion questions:
1. How did the tone of the situation change from the before to the after?
2. What would be difficult about using the supportive behavior in a real communication exchange?
3. Can you think of a communication exchange you have had in the recent past and how you might "make it over" with one of Gibb's categories?

Principle's Illustrated:
1. Defensive and supportive behaviors both create/affect the tone of a relationship.
2. It is possible to alter the tone with supportive behaviors.

Critic's Corner

Approximate Time: depending on the length of the clip 10–15 minutes

Purpose: To practice offering constructive criticism

Procedures:

1. Sitcoms abound in characters who possess less than competent communication skills, and are therefore perfect opportunities for students to practice giving constructive criticism.
2. Play a clip of a character in a situation that needs constructive criticism. (For example, a clip with any of the characters from *The Big Bang Theory*, Barney (Neil Patrick Harris) from *How I Met Your Mother*, Russell (David Spade) from *Rules of Engagement* or any of the characters from *The Office*.)
3. Ask the students to imagine the character in question asking for advice on this situation.
4. Using the guidelines found in Chapter 10 have the students either write a script as an individual or in pairs including
   i. Check your motives
   ii. Choose a good time
   iii. Buffer negatives with positives
   iv. Follow up
5. Have individuals or pairs share with the rest of the group how they would offer the constructive criticism.

Debrief the activity with the following discussion questions:
1. Are there any parallels between this obviously manufactured exercise done in class and a real situation where you would offer constructive criticism?
2. How would the situation change if the person had not asked for advice?
3. When was the last time someone offered you constructive criticism? How did frame it and how did you take it?

Principles illustrated:
1. Constructive criticism requires the appropriate attitude as well as communication skills.

Agree with the Critic

Approximate Time: 15–20 minutes

Purpose: To give students an opportunity to practice agreeing with criticism

Procedures:

1. Go over the four types of agreement discussed in Chapter 10 (agree with the truth, agree with the odds, agree with the principle, agree with the critics' perception) having the definitions of each on the board on screen where they can be accessed easily by students.
2. Students should get into pairs.
3. Students are going to critique several things about their partners. These critiques may or may not be what partners actually think about each other. The critiques are less important than the response to the critiques.
4. Direct students to critique their partners in the following categories using this phrasing: "I think…" For example, "I think your lipstick is too dark." Both partners should critique and both partners should agree with the critic.
     i. Attendance in class
    ii. Sense of humor
   iii. Taste in movies
    iv. Clothing
     v. Friends

5. The student who is agreeing with the critic will choose the category of agreement that is most appropriate given the criticism by identifying the category and give a specific example of that category in agreeing with the critic.

Debrief with the following discussion questions:
1. What was the most difficult part of agreeing with the critic? Be specific.
2. When would be a time you would not want to agree with the critic?
3. What are the strengths and weaknesses of "agree with the critic" as you think about using this strategy in a real communication exchange?

Principles illustrated:
1. Agree with the critic when one doesn't believe the criticism is valid.

DISCUSSION FORUM PROMPT

Blogs/online articles are prime targets of both productive and downright nasty comments. Review the following three blogs, which contain easily challenged subjects and discuss whether you felt the comments are respectful, defensive, or downright malicious. Comment on one of these articles and copy what you've written in your discussion forum post.

Quincy Tutoring: Do Learning Styles Even Exist?

http://quincytutoring.com/2011/09/do-learning-styles-even-exist/

Chronicle of Higher Education: Community College Students Perform Worse Online than Face-to-Face

http://chronicle.com/article/Community-College-Students/128281/

USA Today College What I Wish Someone Had Told Me Freshman Year

http://www.usatodayeducate.com/staging/index.php/blog/what-i-wish-someone-had-told-me-freshman-year

JOURNAL PROMPT

Not surprisingly, positive communication climates and sales go hand-in-hand. Many professional bloggers capture this concept as they discuss how to improve productivity, relationships, and, of course, numbers. Anthony Iannarino, President and Chief Sales Officer of Solutions Staffing, and adjunct faculty for graduate and undergraduate studies at Capital University (Ohio), is one such blogger who covers numerous communication tips within his posts.

In the following entries, Iannarino covers two aspects of communication climate-building: Delivering bad news and acknowledging and validating others. Read his posts and answer the following questions:

http://thesalesblog.com/2011/09/be-the-bearer-of-bad-news/?utm_source=feedburner&utm_medium=feed&utm_campaign=Feed%3A+typepad%2Fiannarino%2Fthesalesblog+%28TheSalesBlog%29

http://thesalesblog.com/2011/09/acknowledging-and-validating-others/

1. Think of a time that you had to deliver bad news or when someone had to deliver bad news to you. Discuss the timing and environment when the conversation took place. Did you feel like the discussion occurred in a proper time and location? What would you have changed?
2. Based on Gibb's confirming and disconfirming statements, what type of communication climate was created in the above situation? What words were used that were acknowledging and validating? (If the content was completely negative, discuss how the conversation could have had more face-saving, positive overtones).
3. Do you consider constructive criticism as bad news? Why or why not? What elements of Iannarino's discussions would you use to offer constructive criticism in the future?

PORTFOLIO ENTRY

Analyzing Defensiveness

Defensiveness implies protecting ourselves from a perceived threat. The universal tendency is to try to "save face" by defending our presenting self when we perceive that it has been attacked by what social scientists call *face-threatening acts*. Frequently, this creates a climate that leads to a negative defensive spiral. For this assignment, you will do the following:

1. Identify three different times when you perceived that you were under attack and responded by using one of the Gibb defensive categories. Briefly describe each situation and your response.
2. Identify the Gibb category you used.
3. Describe how you might have otherwise responded in order to create a more positive and supportive climate.
4. Analyze your defensive behavior. In general, do you consider yourself a "defensive" person? Why or why not? Are there certain topics that tend to trigger your defensiveness? Are there certain people with whom you are more defensive than normal?

D & A

Analyzing Defensiveness just outlined. Instructors may choose to have students cite only two examples.

MOVIE ANALYSIS

See the movie analysis of *The Story of Us* at the end of Part III of this manual.

GROUP STUDY

(See the Introductory Essay for further information. Consult the Group Study section in Chapter 1 for additional directions to students.)

TEACHING ACTIVITIES FROM THE *COMMUNICATION TEACHER*

Nagel, G. (1989, Fall). 'Peculiarity': An exercise in sharing, caring, and belonging, *4*(1), 3–4.
Weaver II, R. L., and Cotrell, H. W. (1990, Winter). Role playing assertiveness scenes, *4*(2), 13–14.

Chapter 11: Managing Conflict

Perception of Conflict

Approximate Time: 20 minutes

Purpose: To identify common perceptions of conflict

Procedures:
1. Write the word *CONFLICT* on the board.
2. Ask students to write down the first word that comes to mind when they see the word *CONFLICT*. Write their words on the board.
3. Ask students to write down three or four things about which they believe it is worth having a conflict, that is, things worth fighting for.
4. Have them jot down one or two things over which others seem to have conflicts but that they believe are silly to "fight about."
5. Go around the class and write all the words (from step 2) on the board.
6. Ask what the words (at least most of them) have in common. (Most are likely to be negative.) Discuss the implications of this perception for conflict and conflict management.
7. Ask for student responses to the other two questions. Note that some topics (typically money, curfew, siblings) appear on both lists. What are the implications of this on conflict resolution?
8. Discuss how conflict can be a beneficial force. Relate this discussion to the textbook identification of types of conflict resolution.

Principles Illustrated:
1. Conflict has a negative connotation for many.
2. Negative perceptions of conflict make us reluctant to welcome it for its positive value.
3. Conflict is inevitable.
4. Conflict can be a helpful, dynamic force in communication.
5. Perceptions of what is "important enough" to warrant conflict can differ from one person to another.

Conflict Styles Survey

Approximate Time: 20 minutes

Purpose: To heighten students' awareness of their patterns of conflict style and to launch the discussion of the variety of styles that they and others employ

Procedures:
1. Without prior discussion, distribute the Conflict Styles Survey to class members and tell them to respond to the items. There are no right or wrong answers.
2. When students are finished, tell them the categories for each column and briefly discuss their findings. Use this exercise to lead into a lecture on the various conflict styles.

CONFLICT STYLES SURVEY

Instructions: Indicate your opinion of each of the following short proverbs as a conflict strategy. In each case, ask the question: How desirable is this strategy as a method for resolving conflict?

Using the key, write the appropriate number in the blank to the left of each proverb.

1 = completely undesirable   4 = desirable
2 = undesirable   5 = very desirable
3 = neither desirable nor undesirable

_____ 1. You scratch my back; I'll scratch yours.

_____ 2. When two quarrel, he who keeps silent first is the most praiseworthy.

_____ 3. Soft words win hard hearts.

_____ 4. A person who will not flee will make his foe flee.

_____ 5. Come and let us reason together.

_____ 6. It is easier to refrain than to retreat from a quarrel.

_____ 7. Half a load is better than none.

_____ 8. A question must be answered by knowledge, not by numbers, if it's to have a right decision.

_____ 9. When someone hits you with a stone, hit him with a piece of cotton.

_____ 10. The arguments of the strongest always have the weight.

_____ 11. By digging and digging, the truth is discovered.

_____ 12. Smooth words make smooth ways.

_____ 13. If you cannot make a man think as you do, make him do as you do.

_____ 14. He who fights and runs away lives to fight another day.

_____ 15. A fair exchange brings no quarrel.

_____ 16. Might overcomes right.

_____ 17. Tit for tat is fair play.

_____ 18. Kind words are worth much and cost little.

_____ 19. Seek 'til you find, and you'll not lose your labor.

_____ 20. Kill your enemies with kindness.

_____ 21. He loses least in a quarrel who keeps his tongue in cheek.

_____ 22. Try, and trust will move mountains.

_____ 23. Put your foot down where you mean to stand.

_____ 24. One gift for another makes good friends.

_____ 25. Don't stir up a hornet's nest.

Transfer your rating numbers to the following blanks. The numbers correspond to the proverb numbers. Total each column.

5 ____	4 ____	1 ____	2 ____	3 ____
8 ____	10 ____	7 ____	6 ____	12 ____
11 ____	13 ____	15 ____	9 ____	18 ____
19 ____	16 ____	17 ____	14 ____	20 ____
22 ____	23 ____	24 ____	21 ____	25 ____

Total ____ ____ ____ ____ ____

Here are the interpretations for the various columns:

1—Problem Solving; Assertive
2—Forcing; Aggressive
3—Compromising
4—Withdrawing; Nonassertive
5—Smoothing; Accommodating

Principles Illustrated:
1. Different individuals have different perceptions about conflict.
2. Different individuals approach conflict in different ways.

Conflict Resolution Script

Approximate Time: 30–40 minutes

Purpose: To give students a chance to practice win-win conflict management

Procedures:

1. Tell students to think of a conflict they are currently having or have had that wasn't resolved to the involved parties satisfaction. They need to use a real conflict, and won't be asked to share the conflict unless they want to.
2. While the students are coming up with the conflict discuss or revisit if they have already read "Conflict Management in Practice" with the seven-step approach developed by Deborah weedier-Hatfield and Ellen Raider.
3. Either distribute a handout with the seven steps or have the students number/label their own paper with the seven steps. Lead the group through each of the seven steps as they apply them to their own conflict.
4. Tell the students it is important to write this down, not just think about it. Perhaps give a running example of your own or refer to Jim and Elizabeth's conflict in Chapter 11. Spend two to four minutes on each step.
5. Students will need to guess on step 3. Listen to the other person's needs, or they can write what kind of listening they will engage in.
6. Steps 4–7 are collaborative. Students can do their part and leave a blank space to indicate the person they are in conflict with is brainstorming and evaluating.

Once everyone has completed the seven steps, debrief with the following discussion questions:
1. What was easy about going through these seven steps and what was difficult?
2. How would you feel about actually using this script (or these seven steps in a more casual way) to resolve this conflict with the other person?
3. What are the strengths and weaknesses about resolving a conflict in this manner?

Principles illustrated:
1. Win-win conflict resolution is possible.
2. Conflict resolution requires time and patience.

Recording the Four Horsemen

Approximate Time: class time 10–15 minutes, the activity requires 24 hours to complete

Purpose: To familiarize students with the Four Horsemen

Procedures:

1. Give a mini-lecture or have students read aloud Toxic Conflict: The Four Horsemen. Make sure the students understand what constitutes criticism, defensiveness, contempt and stonewalling.
2. Distribute a colored 8.5 x 11 sheet of paper to everyone in class.
3. Until you meet again as a class the students are going to carry the sheet of paper with them wherever they go (it is best if the class meets every other day, the students will carry the paper with them for about 48 hours.)

4. Instruct the students to rip a small piece off the original paper every time they witness or directly experience on of the four horsemen.
5. When students return to class for the next meeting have them take out their papers and see how much (or little) of the original colored piece of paper is left.

Debrief with the following discussion questions:
1. Why do you think you had this much (or this little) of your paper left?
2. What would have been the difference in this exercise if you had recorded with a pen the person and the words rather than just recording the instance with the small chunk of the paper?
3. After doing this activity can you clarify this sentence from the textbook: "It's easy to see how this kind of communication can be destructive in any relationship…"?

Principles Illustrated:
1. Criticism, Defensiveness, Contempt and Stonewalling exist and are destructive.

Bullies Beware

Approximate Time: 15–20 minutes excluding research and reading time

Purpose: To critically analyze the strategies for coping with bullies available to parents, students and educators

Procedures:

1. There are numerous websites devoted to preventing and managing bullying. They offer strategies and tips for parents, students and educators.
2. Have students in groups of two or three research some of the materials on one of these websites. Students can find their own or you can provide a list. Here are a few samples:

   http://www.pbs.org/teachers/thismonth/conflict/index1.html

   http://www.educationworld.com/a_curr/archives/classroom_management.shtml#bullying

   http://www.stopbullying.gov/

3. After student groups have reviewed the literature have them discuss these questions:

   - Does bullying meet the definition of conflict from your textbook? (Expressed struggle, perceived incompatible goals, etc.)
   - Which of the characteristics of functional/dysfunctional conflicts do you think fits bullying mostly closely? Why?
   - Which of the conflict styles discussed in your book does your research seem to advocate? Avoidance, accommodation, competition, and so on?
   - What are the strengths and the weaknesses of the suggestions/strategies that "the experts" in your research advised?

4. Have groups share their discussion points with the rest of the class.

Principles illustrated:
1. Definition of conflict.
2. Functional and dysfunctional conflicts.

3. Conflict styles

DISCUSSION FORUM PROMPT

Alexandra Levit is a former syndicated columnist for the Wall Street Journal, an author of career guides, such as the best-selling They Don't Teach Corporate in College and Success for Hire. She blogs with up-to-the-minute career advice, and in one post, discusses how to be diplomatic. Read her entry http://blog.alexandralevit.com/wcw/2011/09/how-to-be-diplomatic.html then select a fictional dyad (movies, television) who are dealing with conflict. Briefly describe the problem. Based on Levit's piece, discuss which aspects of diplomacy are being utilized, or could be integrated to smooth over the issue.

JOURNAL PROMPT

Watch John Gottman, Ph.D.'s YouTube video on The Four Horsemen in relationships:

http://www.youtube.com/watch?v=CbJPaQY_1dc

Answer the following questions:

1. Have you had a relationship/friendship which included communication of "the four horsemen" that Gottman notes? (Note: You can select a fictional relationship if you'd prefer not to share one of your own). Describe.
2. Based on the chapter, how could you and your partner use compromise or collaboration to positively affect the communication pattern?
3. What can couples/friends do to prevent reaching the "four horsemen" stage?

PORTFOLIO ENTRY

In class, you were given a Conflict Styles Survey that allowed you to see how you might be inclined to manage conflict. For your Portfolio Entry:
- Report the scores you determined in each of the five categories.
- In essay format (one to three pages) analyze the results for the survey. Do you agree that the scores reflect your style(s) in managing conflict? Use **specific personal examples** to support your conclusions.

FINAL SELF-ASSESSMENT

Now that we are nearly at the end of the semester, reanalyze your own interpersonal communication skills. What are your strengths? Your weaknesses? How does this list compare with the one you made during the first weeks of the semester? How much progress have you mad toward your goals? (one to three pages)

D & A

Complete Invitation to Insight 2 (functional and dysfunctional conflicts) at the end of the chapter (p. 382).

MOVIE ANALYSIS

See the movie analysis of *The Story of Us* at the end of Part III of this manual.

GROUP STUDY

(See the Introductory Essay for further information. Consult the Group Study section in Chapter 1 for additional directions to students.)

TEACHING ACTIVITIES FROM THE *COMMUNICATION TEACHER*

Hanna, M. S. (2000, Spring). Design a role-playing case for study and practice, *14*(3), 12–14.
McGowan, L. (1992, Spring). St. Elmo's Fire as a tool for discussing conflict management, *7*(3), 12–13.
Rancer, A.S. (1994, Spring). Teaching constructive means of handing conflict, *8*(3), 1–2.
Williams, D. (1990, Summer). Interpersonal communication feud, *4*(4), 8–9.

Chapter 12: Communication in Families and at Work

The Boundaries We Build and Tear Down

Approximate Time: 20–30 minutes

Purpose: To identify how boundaries in families are constantly changing

Procedure:
1. Divide students into groups of four to five each.
2. Ask the students to come up with five to six boundaries they remember having when they were growing up. They can by physical, conversational, or systems related (curfew, how many friends could sleep over at a time, etc.).
3. Ask them to review the list and reflect on how these rules changed from age 12, 15, 18, or older. What brought about the change?
4. Discuss as a class.

Discussion Points:
1. List the boundaries on the board, noting similarities and differences.
2. Discuss the age factor and whether these boundaries were openly negotiated at any time.
3. Discuss the impact of culture and gender.
4. Discuss how the students envision boundaries being handled in their future families.
5. How can different expectations of boundaries cause conflict in new family systems?

Principles Illustrated:
1. Boundaries can be very family specific.
2. Boundaries often cause tension within the family system.
3. Boundaries can be difficult to change.

Roles and Expectations

Time: Depends on what setup is selected, from no class time (if done as a report) to one class period

Purpose: To discover the roles and expectations people have of themselves and others in specific categories such as spouse, parent, student, breadwinner, male, and female.

Procedures:
1. Select one of the three setup alternatives:
   a. Ask four to five married students (preferably not from class) to be on a panel. Have the students ask questions regarding the roles and expectations in a marriage.
   b. Divide the class into groups of about six people (three females and three males would be ideal).
   c. Each student interviews six or more individuals from different careers, different socioeconomic income levels, or different ethnic groups.
2. The class may want to create its own questions or ask the following questions and then answer the discussion questions.
   a. What career has each of you chosen for yourself? What type of career is selected by the females, by the males? Are the careers sex-role-oriented? How?
   b. What roles do you expect to play at home? Specify the tasks you are willing or unwilling to play.
   c. What role will/do/did you take as a parent (full-time, half-time, change diapers, single parent, stay-at-home parent)?

d.　What role will/do/did you take as a bread winner?

Discussion Questions:
1. Do you see evidence that today's college students subscribe to traditional sex roles or that they are free of such barriers to independent choice?
2. What messages did you receive as you were growing up regarding specific expectations or behaviors appropriate to your gender?
3. How do you feel your life would be different, if at all, if you were a member of the opposite sex? (Imagine that when you wake up tomorrow and you are the opposite sex) What would you do? How would you act? Would others relate to you differently? What would your expectations of yourself be? How would your expectations change?

The Art of Friendship

Approximate Time: 10 minutes

Purpose: To uncover student's perceptions of friendships

Procedures:

1. Create a PowerPoint with artwork that is somehow connected to friendship. Paintings, photographs and sculptures work well. For example: Degas' "Friends in the Wings" (1879) Picasso's "Friendship" (1908) and Norman Rockwell's "No Swimming" (1921). Because of the subjective nature of art you may choose to include artwork that isn't expressly about friendship.
2. Remind your students that they do not need to be art aficionados to critique artwork.
3. In showing each individual work of art ask your students what they think it says about friendship. (Of course in discussing art, we are discussing ourselves and our perceptions much of the time.) Another way to phrase the question would be to say "What truth about friendship does this work of art seem to convey?"
4. An alternative to this activity is to have students bring in a work of art that they think conveys a truth about friendship.

Principles illustrated:
1. There are different types of friendships.
2. People have expectations about friendships.

Boomerang

Approximate Time: 15–20 minutes (excluding research/reading time)

Purpose: To apply types of family relationships to a modern phenomenon in a family

Procedures:

1. The phrase "boomerang generation" has been used to refer to children who move back in with their parents after finishing college, graduate school or some other form of "adult life." There are numerous articles devoted to this phenomenon. Find one or two articles that offer diverse perspectives on the boomerang generation, a sample is below:

http://www.newyorker.com/humor/2010/05/24/100524sh_shouts_rich

2. Divide the class into as many articles as you have or have pairs read the same article.
3. The groups/pairs use these discussion questions to work their way through the article for a better understanding of family and the boomerang generation:

   o Were there any family narratives mentioned (perhaps not overtly) in the article on the boomerang generation that you read? What were they? Did they come into conflict with the child moving back in with his/her parents?
   o How did the people who wrote or who were mentioned in the articles manage this new wrinkle in the connection-autonomy dialectic?
   o Using the guidelines in "Effective Communication in Families" what advice would you give to a family experiencing this boomerang effect?

4. Students may present their discussion points and findings to the class.

Principles illustrated:
   1. Families are created through communication.
   2. Families have narrative, the connection-autonomy dialectic.
   3. Effective communication in families' guidelines.

Truth, Lies and TV

Approximate Time

Purpose: Your textbook authors note that TV shows often revolve around the friendships of a number of characters. It is difficult not to compare our relationships to the ones we see on TV, but is this wise? Helpful? This activity will allow students to gauge the efficacy of observing/learning about friendship from television.

Procedures:

   1. Have students volunteer to watch a television show that involves friends. The textbook lists some popular ones, but older shows in syndication work well, too.
   2. Give the students a number of things from the textbook to watch for in the show. For example, what types of friendships are present? What gender considerations are present? Do the friends follow any of the guidelines for communication in successful friendships?
   3. Have the students report their findings the next class session.

   Debrief the activity with the following discussion questions:
   1. Do you or your friends find yourself comparing your relationships to the ones you see on television?
   2. Is there anything useful about observing friendships on television?
   3. What are some of the pitfalls of observing friendships on television?
   4. Would you say that you have learned about friendship from television? Why or why not?

Principles illustrated:

1. Types of friendships.
2. Gender has an impact on friendships.
3. Guidelines for communication in successful friendships.

DISCUSSION FORUM PROMPT

Review a movie that focuses on a central family relationship, such as *The Kids are All Right, Easy A, The Blind Side, It's Complicated,* or *My Sister's Keeper.* You can also focus on a television show, such as *Modern Family* or *Raising Hope.* Based on the chapter discussion about families as communication systems, choose one characteristic and describe how the family in your movie or TV show exemplifies those attributes.

JOURNAL PROMPT

Consider two of your friendships and create a cost-benefit chart based on the discussion regarding communication in successful friendships. Analyze your two friendships based on the 10 characteristics noted. Give specific examples of how your friends either meet or do not meet the individual requirements. When you review what you are gaining versus what you are giving in these friendships, does this knowledge change your perspective of their quality? In areas where you feel that your friendship is not reciprocal, what can you do so your friendship needs are met in a more comfortable way?

PORTFOLIO ENTRY

Using an essay format, analyze the communication patterns in your family of origin. Answer the following questions, making sure to include course concepts in your explanation.
1. What couple type do you think your parents are? Explain.
2. If you have siblings, what roles do you and your siblings play in each other's life?
3. Give at least two examples of how your family has interacted as a system.
4. What conflict roles do you and other family members play? Use at least two examples.
5. Do you have any family narratives? How did they develop?
6. What communication rules about conversation and conformity orientation exist? What type of family would you label yours? Provide specific examples.
7. Give at least two examples of family boundaries.
8. Do your family conflicts revolve around any repeating issues?

D & A

1. Understand your own family system better by giving examples of each of the following characteristics:
   - Interdependence of members
   - How the family is more than the sum of its parts
   - Family subsystems and suprasystems
   - How environmental influences affect the family
2. Identify unstated yet important rules that govern communication you have experienced or observed in a family (yours or others'). Discuss rules governing conversation orientation and conformity orientation as well as other areas of communication.

The Story of Us

Discussion Questions Related to Chapters 9, 10, and 11

Approximate Time: Two 1-hour 15-minute class periods
First session: Watch movie
Second session: Watch movie and discuss

Purpose: To give students experience identifying, analyzing, and evaluating course concepts in a "real-life" relationship

Procedures:
1. Distribute the following discussion questions.
2. Have students view *The Story of Us*.
3. Divide the students into groups of three to four members.
4. After the groups have discussed the film, gather for general discussion with the entire class.

The Story of Us Discussion Questions

Chapter 9: Dynamics of Interpersonal Relationships

- What factors caused Ben and Katie to form their relationship at the beginning? How did those factors change over time?
- Map how Ben and Katie's relationship moves through Knapp's stages.
- Which dialectics do you see in Ben and Katie's relationship?
- Explain, based on exchange theory, how the Kirby's helped jumps-tart Ben and Katie's relationship.

Chapter 10: Communication Climate

- What roles do confirming and disconfirming messages play in Ben and Katie's conflict?
- How do Gibb's categories reflect Ben and Katie's communication?
- What will they have to do differently in the future?

Chapter 11: Managing Conflict

- What styles do Ben and Katie use most?
- Is their style of conflict complementary, symmetrical, or parallel?
- Which intimacy/aggression style characterizes their conflict?
- What do you think Ben and Katie will have to do in the future to ensure positive conflict resolution?

Possible Discussion Points

Chapter 9: Dynamics of Interpersonal Relationships

- What factors caused Ben and Katie to form their relationship at the beginning? How did those factors change over time?

  Complementarity—breath of fresh air at the beginning—becomes a source of conflict later in their relationship

  Proximity—met while working for the comedy show

  Rewards—nothing better in the world than "being gotten"

- Map how Ben and Katie's relationship moves through Knapp's stages.

  Initiating: Ben initiated with the paper clips

  Experimenting: Dinner where Katie talks about crossword puzzles and Ben plays checkers with the silverware/utensils; re-experimenting: trying to find common ground and history together—calling about the tree surgeon and caulking in the bathroom, Ben admitting to trying one of her crossword puzzles during dinner after being apart

  Intensifying: spoon story, reintensifying: talking about therapists at dinner after being apart, playing hangman: "I hate Kirby's," "I do too"

  Integrating: Ben's marry me sign; short romantic clips of Ben and Katie and the family; giving Ben the spoon from soup in the park, high points/low points of the day, apartment—"This is where we became an us," feet finding each other under the covers, reintegrating: Katie saying Chow Fun's at the end because "We're an us."

  Bonding: getting married

  Differentiating: when they have kids, their differences in life philosophy surface even more, windshield wiper fluid low, Harold and the purple crayon—differences were attractive to each other at first, now driving them apart: "Where is the girl with the pit helmet?" "I don't know—you beat her out of me"

  Circumscribing: argue about the same thing over and over. Katie: "You're not listening" and Ben: "Everything is always my fault." Katie saying "Fighting becomes the condition, not the exception"

  Stagnating: Katie talking about how after a while when arguing becomes the condition and you retreat in silence to neutral corners (while they are out to eat for their anniversary), calling about the postcards from the kids, but nothing else to say

  Avoiding: Ben moving out, Katie not answering Ben when he asks her why they're doing this when they get back from dropping kids off at bus

  Terminating: Katie saying "It's over," discussing one or two lawyers

- Which dialectics do you see in Ben and Katie's relationship?

  Stability/change

  Ben is too spontaneous and Katie is too rigid.

  Katie wants to write letter to kids before sex—Ben wants to have sex first.

  Katie remembers tooth fairy during sex—needs it taken care of right away.

  Katie not being able to count on Ben to stop the papers for vacation.

  Integration/Separation

  Ben expressing the desire to have one look during the course of the day that would tell him they had a connection, they were on the same page.

  Katie talking about their having less and less eye contact over the years.

  Expression/Privacy

  Katie is hurt over his disclosure to another woman.

  Ben discloses how miserable he's been during dinner, Katie mocks him with kitchenware.

  Katie doesn't tell Rachel right away, Stan tells Rachel after telling Ben he wouldn't.

- Explain, based on exchange theory, how the Kirby's helped jump-start Ben and Katie's relationship—comparison level for alternatives.

Chapter 10: Communication Climate

- What role do confirming and disconfirming messages play in Ben and Katie's conflict?
    Confirming—playing hangman in Italy; Katie's monologue at the end
    Disconfirming—Katie hanging up while Ben's talking about their old apartment (impervious); yelling and name-calling (aggressiveness); Ben ignoring Katie while following the moving truck (impervious, irrelevant); Ben saying "Isn't this when one of us is supposed to say this is stupid, we love each other?"—and Katie getting out of the truck without answering (impervious); Ben forgetting to stop the papers like Katie asked him to (impervious); Katie mentioning that they made less and less eye contact over the years (lack of recognition)
- How do Gibb's categories reflect Ben and Katie's communication?
    Evaluation: Katie saying "You're not listening to me."
    Control: Katie saying "All we've proven is if we're apart weeks at a time we can have a civil dinner for a couple of hours…Ben, it's over."
    Strategy: Ben saying "In Europe, you would have made love first."
    Neutrality: Katie saying "Why don't you ask your girlfriend? I'm sure she can help us get back on track."
    Superiority: Ben saying "It isn't my fault you turned into your goddamn mother."
    Certainty: Ben saying "The kids need some spontaneity in their life."
    What will they have to do differently in the future?

Chapter 11: Managing Conflict

- What styles do Ben and Katie use?
    Passive aggression: Katie sighing when she sees the papers piled up outside their home.
    Direct Aggression: Most of their arguments; Ben saying "… a fucking watermelon." As he pulls the covers off the bed, Katie saying "Fuck you."
- Is their style of conflict complementary, symmetrical, or parallel?
    Symmetrical
- Which intimacy/aggression style characterizes their conflict?
    Intimate- aggressive
- What do you think Ben and Katie will have to do in the future to ensure positive conflict resolution?
    Discuss assertion

Additional Discussion Points If Using as a Semester Review

Chapter 1: Interpersonal Process

- How does Katie's monologue about their relationship at the end of the movie reflect the qualitative definition of interpersonal communication?
    Uniqueness: "I know what mood you wake up in by which eyebrow is higher and you always know I'm a little quiet in the morning and compensate accordingly. That's a dance you perfect over time."
    Irreplaceability: "Building cities on top of cities—I don't want to build another city. I won't be able to say to a stranger Josh has your hands."
    Interdependence: "We made two great kids. There were no people there and now there's people there." "I didn't even know the girl in the pith helmet existed until you brought her out in me."

Disclosure: "I'm no day at the beach."
Intrinsic rewards: "You're a good friend, and good friends are hard to find."

Chapter 2: Culture

- Do Ben and Katie live in a high-context or low-context culture? How would their interaction be different if they lived in the opposite?
  - Low. If lived in high, they would both rely on more on contextual cues to let them know the other is unhappy.
- Do Ben and Katie live in a collective or an individualistic culture? How would their interaction be different if they lived in the opposite?
  - Individualistic. If they lived in collective, they would both work harder at maintaining social harmony; their expectations might be different as well.
- Does power distance affect their relationship?
  - Low power distance

Chapter 3: Communication and the Self

- What role does self-concept play in their relationship?
  - Katie's monologue about "Harold and the Purple Crayon" because he was everything she is not vs. "Harold's wife," and her belief that Ben gave her the role of designated driver of their marriage (reflected appraisal and self-fulfilling prophecy)
  - Katie's moving the dry cleaning and Ben getting a watch with hands (identity management)
  - Katie responding to Ben's high/low at dinner with cookware, "all the while making myself more attractive" (identity management)

Chapter 4: Perceiving Others

- What role does perception play in Katie and Ben's conflict?
  - Ben: "I saw myself through your eyes tonight." (Empathy)
  - Katie: "We were just talking…" (Common tendencies in perception—We judge ourselves more charitably, Empathy)
  - Ben and Katie each focus on the other's character flaws that annoy them the most (Common tendencies in perception—We favor negative impressions)
  - Katie assuming Ben is having an affair because she walks in on him sharing personal information with another woman (Common tendencies in perception—We are influenced by the obvious)
  - Discuss the perceptual shift they both experience from blaming their problems on each other's character flaws to realizing they are both responsible (Punctuation)

Chapter 5: Language

Static Evaluation: She sees Ben as a third child;, he sees Katie as uptight.
Emotive Language: designated driver (implies she's the only one responsible)
Euphemism: watermelon under the bed
Euphemism: Fred and Ethel Mertz
Emotive: Crossword 7 down: "needs" direct attack
They both use a lot of "you" language
Naming and Identity: Dot

Chapter 6: Nonverbal Communication

- How does their nonverbal communication reflect changes in their relationship?

    Paralanguage: Yelling during their arguments, not yelling during their conversation at Ben's apartment

    Proxemics/Intimate Space: Their feet finding each other under the covers, her moving her foot away from his

    Proxemics/Territoriality: Ben moving out of the house

    Chronemics: Ben's watch with no hands, getting a watch with hands; Ben wondering where the furniture guys have been

    Environment: Ben's apartment being organized, having different drinks; Chow Fun's; Stan not replacing the toilet paper roll

    Face and Eyes: Her rolling her eyes when he wakes up the baby; smiling when the kids are watching them row the boat; Katie saying over time there were fewer and fewer times during the day when they made real eye contact

    Touch: Ben's irritation with Katie's checklist before they can make love

    Kinesics/manipulators: Katie taking a towel to answer the door

    Clothing: Katie shutting the bathroom door at the cabin

Chapter 7: Listening

- What poor listening habits do Ben and Katie exhibit?

    Pseudolistening: Katie when Ben calls about their old apartment

    Stage hogging: Ben at dinner with Rachel and Stan

    Insulated listening: Ben not hearing Katie when she talks about not being able to meet everyone of Ben's needs because she's busy with 5,000 things all day

    Defensive listening: Ben responding "I am not a third child" when Katie tries to get him to understand the pressures of raising children; Katie saying "What is that supposed to mean?" when Ben says "In Europe you would have made love first"

    Ambushing: Katie when Ben was trying to explain why he was talking to another woman

Chapter 8: Emotions

Social Conventions: Josh embarrassed by Ben's hug and crying at parents' weekend

Fallacies:

  The fallacy of perfection: Katie

  The fallacy of should: Ben and Katie

  The fallacy of overgeneralization: Ben and Katie

Recognizing feelings:

  Ben and Katie both express anger freely. What other emotions do you think are under the surface? Frustration, loneliness, neglected, defensive, disappointed, resentful, tired, detached, empty?

Chapter 9: Dynamics of Interpersonal Relationships

- What dimensions of intimacy are apparent in Ben and Katie's relationship?

    Physical—sex

    Emotional—"Everything important in the world is in this bed right now"

    Intellectual—talking about their different therapists

    Shared interests—through kids: soccer, baseball

- How does the dialect of intimacy and distance affect their relationship?

They want to be together, they make up reasons to call each other when they're apart, but they argue when together for any length of time.

- How is the game high/low related to intimacy and self-disclosure?

  It's a ritual developed to facilitate self-disclosure.

  Katie breaks the norm of reciprocity when Ben admits missing her as his low and she comments on the garlic press.

- How do Ben and Katie use equivocation and "benevolent lies" to protect their children from their marital problems?

  Katie says their anniversary is their "high."

  Ben and Katie go out to dinner so that the kids see them leaving and coming home together.

  At parents' weekend, Ben tells Erin he made up the couch to do some reading.

  How do Ben and Katie's perception shifts relate to Johari Window?

  Their character flaws (Ben—irresponsible; Katie—rigid) move from their blind area to their open area.

  Gender differences: men's and women's table conversations.

Chapter 10: Communication Climate

- What roles do confirming and disconfirming messages play in Ben and Katie's conflict?

  Confirming: playing hangman in Italy; Katie's monologue at the end

  Disconfirming: Katie hanging up while Ben's talking about their old apartment (impervious)

  Yelling and name-calling (aggressiveness): Ben ignoring Katie while following the moving truck (impervious, irrelevant); Ben saying "Isn't this when one of us is supposed to say this is stupid, we love each other?" and Katie getting out of the truck without answering. (impervious); Ben forgetting to stop the papers like Katie asked him to (impervious); Katie mentioning that they made less and less eye contact over the years (lack of recognition)

- How do Gibb's categories reflect Ben and Katie's communication?

  Evaluation: Katie saying "You're not listening to me"

  Control: Katie saying "All we've proven is if we're apart weeks at a time we can have a civil dinner for a couple of hours. ... Ben it's over!"

  Strategy: Ben saying "In Europe, you would have made love first"

  Neutrality: Katie saying "Why don't you ask your girlfriend. I'm sure she can help us get back on track"

  Superiority: Ben saying "It isn't my fault you turned down your goddamn mother!"

  Certainty: Ben saying "The kids need some spontaneity in their life"

  What will they have to do differently in the future?

Chapter 11: Managing Conflict

- What styles do Ben and Katie use?

  Passive aggression: Katie sighing when she sees the papers piled up outside their home

  Direct Aggression: Most of their arguments; Ben saying, "...a fucking watermelon." As he pulls the covers off the bed, Katie saying "Fuck you!"

- Is their style of conflict complementary, symmetrical, or parallel?

  Symmetrical

- Which intimacy/aggression style characterizes their conflict?

  Intimate/aggressive

- What do you think Ben and Katie will have to do in the future to ensure positive conflict resolution?

  Discuss assertion.

Chapter 12: Communication in Families and at Work

- Which couple type do you think would best describe Ben and Katie's relationship?
    Independent
- How do Ben and Katie's families of origin affect their current view of relationships and their behavior within their relationship?
    Ben—parents more laid back, more pleasure oriented (discuss makeup sex and sing Andrew Sisters song in scene where they're all in bed)
    Katie—Dot has need for perfection, games are "childlike"
- What general principles would Ben and Katie do well to follow?
    Don't sweat the small stuff (Ben's washer fluid)
    Focus on manageable issues (Katie not commenting on directions)
    Share appreciations as well as gripes (Katie complementing Ben at the end)
    Seek win-win solutions (that satisfy Katie's need for order and Ben's need for spontaneity)

PART IV: UNIT WIND-UPS

INSTRUCTION

The following paper was presented at the Speech Communication Association Annual Meeting in November 1995. It explains the concept behind the techniques of group study and use of the Unit Wind-Up. The ideas of the assessment of basic cross-disciplinary proficiencies is also inherent in this approach.

Assessment of Critical Thinking Skills through Collaborative Testing and Case Study Analysis in the Interpersonal Communication Course

Carol Zinner Dolphin
Associate Professor of Communication Arts
University of Wisconsin Center—Waukesha County

Abstract

The basic course in interpersonal communication presents a unique blend of communication theory and application of theory to practical experiences, frequently with the aim of improving daily communication skills. While traditional testing methods—the objective/short answer/essay test—may be adequate in order to judge student understanding of theoretical concepts, these measures fall short in determining the ability of the students to think critically in applying theory to practical situations.

This paper describes an experiment conducted over a period of six semesters in which members of beginning interpersonal communication classes used collaborative learning and group testing experiences in order to link theory and application. The collaborative work was done with the hope that students would be better prepared to demonstrate individually their ability to identify and apply theory on the final exam/case study.

Final results of student grades compare favorably with those in previous semesters where these methods were not used. Notably, however, student satisfaction with this method is very high; in addition, students express a stronger sense of self-confidence about having integrated the theory into their own daily communication behaviors at least to some extent.

Instruction

The introductory interpersonal communication course can be approached in at least three different ways. The instructor may design the course purely as one in beginning theory in which examples are used only as they might illustrate the theory; in this case, the student's grade depends upon his/her mastery of the cognitive elements of theory. On the opposite end of the spectrum, the course might focus predominantly on application and analysis of student expertise in actual and/or role-played interpersonal transactions; in such classes, the student is graded upon the demonstrated ability of skillful interpersonal communication traits. The third—and most common—approach blends the first two methods, presenting a solid body of theory that students must then apply to real and hypothetical situations; with this approach, the student's grade is based upon the ability to master both theory and understanding of application—possibly without regard to the student's actual expertise in interpersonal transactions.

In my own teaching, I have long embraced the third philosophy. It is explicitly stated in the objectives of the course appearing in the syllabus and is emphasized by a number of portfolio or journal assignments that force students to make connections. In all of my lectures, I use personal and hypothetical examples and encourage student additions. I even tell students that, if they understand the theories of the course and learn to *use* what they learn in their daily communication transactions, they can improve the quality of their lives.

Clearly, then, this approach permeates my philosophy teaching the introductory interpersonal communication course. Nevertheless, when I reviewed my teaching materials a few years ago, I noticed one deviance. For many years, I had tested students by using three to four major exams (three "unit" tests and a final cumulative) that assessed primarily the students' understanding of theory. Using traditional objective (true/false and multiple choice) and short response questions, students demonstrated whether or not they had assimilated the information gathered via the textbook and class lectures. I justified this approach by telling myself that the purpose of the tests was, indeed, to test "knowledge" and that I was already evaluating application via the written assignments.

I realized that I had produced for myself a philosophy dilemma. Was I not being untrue to my supposed philosophy by the type of exams that I was administering? Why could not an exam, as well as a written assignment, test for both theory and application?

I had also done a good deal of work in the past years on the use of collaborative learning. In the interpersonal class, I always used carefully focused small-group work, usually with positive results in terms of both student learning and satisfaction. In a course that focused on small-group interaction, I had even introduced the practice of "group testing." I had found it encouraging, during this experiment, to hear students discuss with their peers the theories that I had presented in class and think through the applications out loud. Having a grade attached to the outcome seemed to enhance the seriousness of the work, as well as group productivity. I wondered if this technique could not be successfully transferred to the interpersonal course, frequently taken by first-semester freshmen on our campus.

In addition, I had spent a number of years in investigating the impact of assessment techniques on student learning. From this work, I knew that the best measurement of potential student success is observation of behavior. Study of assessment also increased my awareness of the importance of direct feedback to the student.

This analysis was the seed for the experiment that is described in the following pages. It should be noted that, since this paper began not as a scholarly investigation but as an experiment in a pedagogical approach, it is written in this more casual spirit.

The First Experiment

During the first semester of the experiment (Spring 1993), I worked with a campus colleague, Associate Professor Therese Rozga. Together, we developed chapter quizzes that could be taken by students either individually or in small groups. Usually, these exercises consisted of a number of very brief descriptions of behavior, which students needed to match to the correct communication vocabulary or theory. In addition, students were expected to complete a short objective quiz on the contents of the chapter. (We were both using Adler, Rosenfeld, and Proctor's *Interplay* at the time and relied heavily on suggestions from the instructor's manual.)

Each of us taught two sections of the course. In one of each of our sections, students completed both sections of the quiz individually and then worked together in a small group to come to group consensus on the matching section of the quiz. As each group completed the matching section of the quiz, members received immediate feedback and assessment from the instructor to clarify any errors in thinking. Although all group members participated in the consensus exercise, only those who achieved a certain level on the first quiz were able to earn the group points.

Both of the instructors—as well as the students—liked the second method. It took longer, but it seemed to be time well spent. It was gratifying to hear students discussing the vocabulary and trying to recall text and class examples, thinking aloud and working together to make connections. The scores clearly showed that the students were helping each other to succeed, and many of them expressed satisfaction in a higher level of understanding. Even the better students who tended to contribute the most valuable insights to the group discussions said that they were helped by the interaction to see concepts more clearly. Students also benefited from the "live" feedback and explanations from the instructor, rather than relying solely on a score or other written comments. (Traditional unit tests were also retained at this stage in the experiment.)

But the real test of the process came at the end of the semester. For the final exam, we presented the students with a brief case study (written as a dialogue), which they had to analyze (via directive questions) in the light of the semester's theory. While students who had experienced the collaborative testing throughout the semester performed slightly better on the exam, individuals in all four sections generally did poorly on the final. They appeared overwhelmed with the instrument, and many almost gave up before they completed the entire exam. Only the best students persevered, and, despite the overall quality of the students, there were very few "A's" and many "D's" and "F's." Those who did well expressed satisfaction with the challenge and felt that they had really accomplished something when they had finished. Even some of the "nonperformers" noted that the scenario was probably a good idea but that they felt unprepared for the demands of the exam.

The outcome created a dilemma with, I thought, three possible explanations. Number 1: We were both very poor teachers who didn't know how to teach interpersonal communication. Many years of prior successes (happily) negated this possibility. Number 2: The experiment was a dismal failure. The ideas of collaborative learning, assessment, and an exam that required theory application were all flawed. This second conclusion flew in the face of a great deal of prior research; also, a few students did, indeed, perform well on the exam. Number 3: The method was flawed. Most students were frustrated by the introduction of a new type of instrument along with the stress of a cumulative exam. There must be a better method to prepare students for the final exam.

The Revised Experiment

Despite students' frustration with the final exam, I decided that there was too much promise in this method to accept failure. The second semester, I revised my approach somewhat. Concluding that the problem was not with the instrument itself but with the preparation of the students, I moved forward, applying the revised experimental method to all of my sections of the course. I am still using the following approach at this time.

The collaborative work on individual chapters has been retained; however, it is no longer linked to the quiz grade. Instead, at the request of a number of students, the quiz session begins with the group work, giving the opportunity for further clarification of terms. On these exercises, students earn "group points," which ultimately figure into the final grade, but the quiz is a separate grade.

Next, I have elaborated on the collaborative learning and substituted scenarios for the traditional "unit texts." A series of case studies has been developed, one for each major unit of study (Introductory Theory, Self-Concept, Perception, Listening, Language, Nonverbals, and Relationships and Conflict). Students analyze the case studies, called "Unit Wind-ups," in their small groups. (The groups have sometimes remained the same throughout the semester and have sometimes changed from unit to unit or even from chapter to chapter. This depends upon the particular mix of students in the class, although I prefer to maintain as much group stability as possible.) Just recently, after completing a "Wind-Up" exercise, two students, one who struggles with the concepts and one who assimilates information with ease, were overheard discussing the experience. Both noted how helpful the exercise was to them individually, how it "really showed what we've been learning" and made them "more confident about understanding the material."

A second significant change is that I have also audiotaped the case studies (using on-campus talent). In addition to the written copy, then, students are able to hear the voices of the "participants" and make more accurate judgments about the climate of the transaction by listening to the vocal cues. The tape is an especially helpful modification. I have purposefully chosen audiotape because I believe that it is extremely difficult to produce a quality video, and it is possible that the extra visual stimuli might serve to muddy rather than clarify.

Since the responses are generated by a group, thereby reducing the number of papers that need to be assessed by the instructor, the questions for the "Wind-Ups" have been fairly open-ended and require some degree of explanation. The "Wind-Ups" result in a real grade, and all members receive the same grade for the exercise.

Each analysis takes a full 75-minute class session. The process might be modified for a shorter session by reducing the number and types of questions and/or distributing the case study at the previous meeting so that students could begin to familiarize themselves with the copy. Each of these would speed up the consensus process.

At the final exam session, students receive a similar case study—along with hearing an aural tape—which they must analyze on their own. In consideration of the typical end-of-semester time crunch, the questions on this exam tend to be more directive. For example, on the "Wind-Up," I might ask for them to locate an example of the use of proxemics in the scenario. For the final exam, I'd ask which category of nonverbal communication is illustrated in Speech 17 …

The Model

The model attempts to illustrate the entire learning/assimilation process and to emphasize the key role-played by assessment throughout the process. Initially, theory from a single chapter/topic is presented to students via textbook (or other written) materials, lectures, and discussion. Students' initial individual understanding of the theory is tested by an objective quiz (student behavior); feedback takes the form of individual grade and general clarification on information that was commonly confused. With a foundation in theory understanding, students can begin to use and develop critical thinking skills in the application of theory to practical communication situations.

Concurrent with and following the initial assessment, collaborative work begins using group exercises and testing. Observable behavior may include small-group reports to the general session, written reports to the instructor, and consensus reports on group tests. Instructor feedback, directed to the specific group, is primarily oral. While these activities are occurring in the classroom, students are also individually completing a series of portfolio assignments that require them to identify, explain, and apply the chapter theory to their own personal experiences. Prior to handing in their portfolios, students are required to use a checklist in order to self-assess their own work. Portfolios are collected and graded three times throughout the semester, and students receive relatively detailed feedback from the instructor on their portfolio materials.

Following each unit, students are required to integrate the theories from that unit by analyzing a scenario. These "Unit Wind-Ups" are collaborative efforts that require a written consensus report from the group. Assessment feedback is also written. Finally, for the final exam, students must individually analyze a case study in terms of all of the communication theory studies throughout the semester. The final assessment feedback comes in the form of the semester grade.

Results

The modifications to the initial experiment resulted in a significant improvement on the final exam scores. Whereas during the first semester the scores clustered in the "D" and "F" range, grades now represent the full spectrum and also tend to correlate closely with the grades the students have been receiving throughout the semester. Student surveys confirm that they feel that the group "Wind-Up" exercises have prepared them for the type of exam they can expect for the final.

Somewhat to my disappointment, students are not scoring higher on the case study exam than they did on the more traditional instrument; however, I believe this is offset by the fact that they are being asked to perform at a more sophisticated cognitive level when they need to use critical thinking skills to *apply* theory, rather than simply identify or describe it. The final range of semester grades, then, has remained relatively constant before and during the experiment.

There have been some interesting subordinate findings generated by a questionnaire completed by 128 students immediately following the final exam. It comes as no surprise that students express a high degree of satisfaction with the work done in their small groups and that a full 99 percent either strongly agree (73 percent) or agree (26 percent) with the statement "I enjoyed the group work in COM 101." Clearly, the satisfaction is widespread and is not linked to any particular level of achievement in the course. That is, the "A" students—who might initially express some reservations—find the group work just as positive as the "C" students. In addition, 95 percent agree (agree/strongly agree) that the group exercises and discussions helped them to understand the course concepts; 92 percent agree that the group quizzes were helpful in learning/clarifying course concepts; and 80 percent agree that the group "Wind-Up" exercises helped to prepare them for the final exam. Casual comments and nonverbal indicators also demonstrate that students feel a heightened self-confidence about knowing the material as they enter the final exam situation. Interestingly, 84 percent report that they believe they "probably learned more from the small-group work than they would have from additional lectures," possibly because they are forced to listen, think, and contribute in the small-group situation.

In conclusion, I believe that, although this experiment took a different route than initially expected, it has been largely successful. There is no question that the students are applying theory with greater accuracy and assurance and that they are using critical thinking skills rather than relying strongly on memorization. In addition to test scores, I would point to an increased level of sophistication in their portfolio assignments and more thoughtful questioning during classroom sessions.

As a postscript on the questionnaire, I asked students, "What is the thing that you will remember most about this class?" A sample of responses follow:

"I really enjoyed working in groups. They helped me to remember things that we talked about for tests and quizzes."

"… the group helped me a lot. There are many times when one person doesn't know the answer, but someone else in the group usually does. What is one person's weakness could be another person's strength."

"…the information and how it was *used* in the class. This will be extremely helpful for me in the future. The class was oriented to teach and help the students involved to get good grades."

"…how to look at a situation, evaluate it, and figure out how others feel about it."

"I liked the way the group exercises, quizzes, and wind-up exercises functioned as group study."

"The things that I will remember most are those that I had to write about and make applicable to my own life."

"It has been helpful in my daily life and has improved not only my communication skills but my perception of the world to include a more realistic picture. … I learned more about myself too."

"I will remember to ask myself why I am behaving the way I am. I will remember (hopefully) most of what I've been taught so that I may communicate on a higher level. Finally, I will remember most of the class, but especially my group and the professor."

As educators, what more could we ask?

UNIT WIND-UP 1: "YOU JUST DON'T UNDERSTAND..."

Chapters 1–4: Interpersonal Process, Culture and Communication, Communication and the Self, and Perceiving Others

Procedure:

- Read through the questions at the end of the scenario.
- Read and/or listen to the following scenario carefully. You may mark up this paper in any way you wish.
- Work *as a group* to respond to the questions that follow. Each group will hand in one copy of the responses. The entire group will receive the same letter grade for the exercise; any member who does not participate may, by agreement of the rest of the group, be excluded from signing the group product; however, it is also the joint responsibility of all members to try to involve everyone in the decision-making process. You must work as a group and may not create subgroups to work on different questions simultaneously. You may not use your text or any notes.
- In answering the questions, always explain and illustrate your response by referring to course definitions and the particular case study. When appropriate, you need both to identify the specific Speech Line *and to* describe the situation briefly. Monitor your time so that you are able to complete the exercise within the time limit.

Case Study Participants;

- Richard Karr, Ph.D.—middle-aged college professor in the field of communication; well known and well liked by students; has a reputation for being open and understanding with a no-nonsense attitude
- Cynthia Chambers—freshman in her second semester at he university; average student with about a "C" GPA; outgoing and popular among her peers; school is not necessarily her number-one priority

Situation:

Despite her usual grade of "C" or "D" in the exams in his communication course, Cynthia earned a high "B" on the last exam, leading Professor Karr to look more carefully at her paper. To his dismay, he noticed a number of striking similarities between Cynthia's responses and those of Jayne, an excellent student who sat immediately in front of Cyndi during the exam. Dr. Karr placed the earned grade of "B+" on Cyndi's paper, with a request to see him in his office after class. Because she knows that she has cheated, Cyndi approaches this meeting with a churning stomach and a good deal of trepidation. The following scene takes place in Karr's office.

Case Study:
1. C (*Cyndi knocks timidly at the open door.*) You wanted to see me, Professor Karr?
2. K Yes, Cyndi, come in. (*He gestures for her to sit in the chair next to his desk, and she sits— with some hesitation.*) I wanted to talk with you about your test paper on the last unit.
3. C What about it? I was really happy—I got a "B+"; that's pretty good for me.
4. K You're right. And you know, initially I was really pleased for you because it seemed as if you had studied hard and understood the concepts more clearly.
5. C Right—what do you mean "initially?"
6. K Because shortly after reading your paper, I came to Jayne's—who I recall was sitting right in front of you for the exam. (*Cyndi begins to look down and shift uncomfortably in her chair.*) Do you think that your grade has anything to do with the fact that there was a striking similarity between your answers and those of Jayne?
7. C What are you talking about? What kinds of similarities?
8. K There were a number of times when you listed the characteristics of a theory in exactly the same orders as Jayne, and at least twice you gave the identical examples.

9. C Are you saying that I cheated (*She notices Karr nodding gravely.*)

10. K That's exactly what I am saying. I'm afraid that there were just too many similarities in your two papers for it to be accidental.

11. C Well, you know that Jayne and I are friends. Maybe we just studied together.

12. K Perhaps you did, but I don't think that this would account for answers using exactly the same words—or the same examples.

13. C How do you know that Jayne didn't do the cheating?

14. K Let's be logical, Cyndi. You are the one who had the opportunity to cheat, and, as you yourself mentioned, the "B" grade was pretty good for you. Jayne is someone who has done consistently well this semester, while you have squeaked by with "Cs."

15. C (*She has been thinking things through and has decided to admit her guilt.*) OK—you caught me. I confess! But I don't understand why this is such a big deal. I mean, everyone does it. In my last sociology test, I know of at least six other people who were cheating.

16. K Do you mean that you've also cheated in sociology? (*Cyndi nervously curls her hair around her finger.*)

17. C Well…I'm telling you, those tests are impossible. I mean, she takes sentences from the book and leaves out any old word, and you're supposed to fill it in. Who can study all of that? It's not reasonable—so everyone…takes in a few notes.

18. K Everyone?

19. C No—not everyone—but a lot of people do.

20. K And this makes it all right.

21. C Well, sure. It's only a silly test. It doesn't really mean anything.

22. K Do you think the sociology professor feels that way too?

23. C Of course not—but if she expects people to be able to pass the tests, she has to make them reasonable for us to pass.

24. K (*He leans in toward her slightly.*) Cyndi, I really do understand the pressures that students are under. I can remember feeling pretty stressed out myself when I was in school, but we're getting off the topic. Are you telling me that others also cheated on the communication exam?

25. C No—not that I know of.

26. K Then let's talk about the penalty you'll have to incur for this action.

27. C (*disgruntled*) I suppose I have to give up my "B+" and go back to getting a mediocre "C."

28. K A "C?" You didn't do your own work on the exam.

29. C But I didn't cheat for all the questions, only a few. It's not fair to penalize me for the questions I answered on my own.

30. K Cyndi, I don't think that you understand the seriousness of this situation.

31. C (*Beginning to get worried*) Do you mean that I could get an "F" for the exam? I can't afford that! My grade is bad enough already. I need at least a "C" in order to stay in school.

32. K Perhaps you should have thought of that before you decided to cheat. Do you remember the policy on plagiarism that's printed in the syllabus?

33. C Wait a minute—I didn't plagiarize. It's not like I went to the library and copied some research out of a book and just handed that in for a paper.

34. K What exactly is plagiarism?

35. C It's using someone else's work without giving credit.

36. K And didn't you do exactly that?

37. C No, not exactly. I just looked at someone's paper and wrote that down.

38. K Isn't that using someone else's ideas?

39. C But…

40. K You did use Jayne's ideas, didn't you?

41. C Yes, but…

42. K And I didn't notice that you gave her credit on your paper…

43. C But…

44. K Cyndi, you don't seem to realize that this is really a very serious offense. I have a copy of the syllabus right here. You'll notice that I quoted the policy that explains the severity of the offense.

45. C It says that I could fail the course!

46. K Yes—and it says that you could be expelled from the university with a permanent notation on your transcript.

47. C You wouldn't do that, would you?

48. K I'm not exactly sure what's going to happen. I'm especially disturbed that you've already admitted that this wasn't a one-time event.

49. C It's the only time I've cheated in this class...

50. K But you have admitted to cheating in sociology as well. Ethically, I simply can't hide this—from your professor or from the university. Quite frankly, it makes me wonder how many other times you've used someone else's work and gotten away with it.

51. C This sound like you might even fail me for the semester!

52. K First of all, you chose to fail yourself when you chose to cheat. And secondly, I don't think you are hearing me yet. Your action has ramifications beyond this course. I'm going to have to report your academic misconduct to the administration. I've made a copy of our university's policy on this for you; I suggest you contact your advisor immediately. (*He hands her the policy and rises to gather his materials for class.*)

53. C Wait a minute, Professor Karr. Can't we talk about this? I had no idea that this was so important to you.

54. K It really has nothing to do with me personally. We are talking about ethical responsibility. Right now, I need to get going to my next class. Please see your advisor as soon as possible. I'm sure we'll be talking again in the near future.

Suggested Questions:
1. Of the four chapters in this unit (Communication Process, Culture and Communication, Communication and the Self, and Perceiving Others), which is most involved in the disagreement in this case study?
2. Using a quantitative definition, does this interaction constitute interpersonal communication? Using a qualitative definition? Explain your response.
3. Is this interaction an example of linear, interactive, or transactional communication? Why?
4. What kind(s) of noise are represented during the interaction? Explain.
5. What is punctuation? How might Professor Karr and Cynthia *each* puncture this situation differently?
6. Formulate a perception check that Professor Karr might have used at the beginning of the conversation.
7. Both Professor Karr and Cynthia were influenced by common tendencies of perception. List and define four of the six tendencies, and provide one example of a tendency from this scenario.
8. How does Cynthia use impression management in this transaction? How do you think that her presenting self contrasts with her perceived self?
9. Do you find examples of self-fulfilling prophecy, social comparison, and/or empathy in the case study? If so, indicate the lines of the speech in which they occur.

Brief Sample Answers:
1. Perception—Student and professor differ in their perceptions of the severity of cheating.
2. Quantitative—Yes; there are two individuals involved.
   Qualitative—Depends on the student's explanation
3. Transactional; adequate parenthetical comments indicate that both individuals are sending and receiving messages simultaneously.

4. Psychological noise—Cynthia: unrest about knowing that she has cheated; Karr: concern for how to approach the topic
   Physiological noise—Cynthia's churning stomach and feelings of unrest (External noise—This could be introduced on an audiotape.)
5. Professor Karr—This situation exists because of Cynthia's cheating conduct and her attitude toward it.
   Cynthia—This situation exists because Professor Karr is making such a big deal out of nothing. He doesn't understand that everyone does it.
6. Karr: Cynthia, I've been wondering about the reason for your higher grade on this test. (Description) Did you study harder? (Interpretation 1) Or is it possible that you copied from Jayne's paper? (Interpretation 2) What is your explanation? (Request for clarification)
7. Common tendencies in scenario: Karr is influenced by expectations (Cynthia's past work) and the obvious (Jayne is the better student and Cynthia had the opportunity to cheat); Cynthia assumes others are like her (that everyone thinks cheating is not a big deal).
8. Although she realizes she is guilty of cheating and that this is a punishable act (Perceived Self), Cynthia uses impression management to try to present herself as innocent and naive (Presenting Self).
9. Self-Fulfilling Prophecy—no
   Social Comparison—Speeches 15–17
   Empathy—Speech 24

UNIT WIND-UP 2: "I JUST NEED SOMEONE TO LISTEN"

Chapters 5–8: Language, Nonverbal Communication, Listening, and Emotions

Procedure:
- Read through the questions at the end of the scenario.
- Read and/or listen to the following scenario carefully. Mark up this paper any way you wish.
- Work *as a group* to respond to the questions that follow. Each group will hand in one copy of the responses. The entire group will receive the same letter grade for the exercise. Any member who does not participate may, by agreement of the rest of the group, be excluded from signing the group product; however, it is also the joint responsibility of all members to try to involve everyone in the decision-making process. You must work as a group and may not create subgroups to work on different questions simultaneously. You may not use your text or any notes.
- In answering the questions, always explain and illustrate your response by referring to course definitions and the particular case study. When appropriate, you need both to identify the specific Speech Line *and* to describe the situation briefly. Monitor your time so that you are able to complete the exercise within the time limit.

Case Study Participants:
- Sonja Markios—age 20; bank teller; intelligent, personable, attractive, well groomed
- Mick Grady—age 20; graduate from high school with Sonja; unshaved, small and wiry; dressed in jeans with holes and a soiled flannel shirt
- Andrew Garrett—age 22; graduate student; longtime friend of Sonja; clean-cut and good looking, with a strong physique
- Louanne Briggs—mid-50s; waitress; short and overweight

Situation:
Sonja and Andy have been good friends for over ten years. They both really enjoy each other's company and have found that they are soul mates. They have never been attracted to one another romantically. Sonja has made a midmorning coffee date with Andy at a casual restaurant (such as Denny's, Big Boys, Shoney's) to discuss a personal problem she is having. Sonja arrives at the restaurant first and is seated in a corner booth. While she is waiting, she notices Mick, a high school classmate whom she has not seen since graduation, approaching. She tries to avoid his eyes, playing close attention to the coffee in her cup, but he moves toward her table.

Case Study:
1. M (*His voice is loud enough to make Sonja cringe.*) Hey, Sonja, sweetheart! Long time no see. What's happenin'?
2. S (*She looks up reluctantly, responding unenthusiastically.*) Oh, hi, Mick.
3. M Looks as if you're alone. How about if I join you, and me and you can catch up on old times? (*He sits down without waiting for her response and begins to move in toward her.*)
4. S Well, actually…
5. M Great. Good to see you. Looks like you're doin' pretty good for yourself, Sonja. All dressed up in that snazzy uniform. You must have some fancy job. Let's see what that says on your name tag. (*He moves in close to her to read name tag.*) "First National Bank—Sonja—How may I help you?" Sounds like an invitation to me. Hey, that java smells good. I've gotta get me some before we talk any more. Which girl is our waitress? (*He spots Louanne looking toward the table and waves at her.*) Hey, honey, bring me a cup of this, would ya?

6. S (*She has been quiet during all of this, sometimes almost cringing in embarrassment.*) Mick, if you don't mind, I'd really rather be alone right now.

7. M (*Looking at her with interest, but not moving.*) Yeah, sure.

8. S I'm waiting for someone and my mind is—well, it's just someplace else.

9. M Right. (*He has been keeping his eye on Louanne, who has picked up two plates and is delivering them to an adjacent table.*) Hey, baby, don't forget about that coffee. (*To Sonja*) Huh, what was that you were saying?

10. S Never mind.

11. M It sure is terrific seeing you again after all these years. Time really flies, huh? Seems like just yesterday we were in Krupke's biology class dissecting that old frog. Say—are you busy tomorrow night? How about if you and me hit a few bars together?

12. S Mick—no, really. That's not exactly my style. Now, if you could please leave me alone; I'm kind of engaged...

13. M Kind of engaged? How can anyone be kind of engaged? Either you are or you aren't. Sounds like you and your old man are in trouble. I don't see no ring on that finger neither. What you need is a change, and, baby, I'm here to give it to you.

14. (*Andy arrives—just in time. Sonja jumps up to give him a welcoming hug, which Andy returns warmly, also kissing her on the cheek. He eyes Mick questioningly. Mick is impressed with Andy's physical size.*)

15. S Mick, now if you wouldn't mind...(*She gestures for him to leave.*) Oh, this is Andy Garrett, my...

16. M Hey, I get the picture. You could have just told me, you know. Thanks a lot for embarrassing me. (*Disgruntled, he leaves the restaurant just as Louanne arrives with his coffee. She looks at all of them, confused.*)

17. S (*Sonja speaks to Louanne, smiling.*) He's decided to leave. But I bet Andy would be glad to have that coffee.

18. A Sure, thanks.

19. (*Louanne leave the coffee. Sonja and Andy settle into the booth for their conversation.*)

20. A Who **was** that jerk?

21. S **That** was Mick Grady. (*She rolls her eyes.*) He was my lab partner in high school biology class, and, yes, he was a loser even then. Guess who had to dissect the whole frog? (*She begins to laugh quietly.*)

22. A What are you laughing at? You sounded so serious over the phone.

23. S I just realized...I was trying to get rid of him; so I told him I was kind of engaged—since you were coming. When you showed up...

24. A ...he thought I was your fiancé?

25. S Well, he took one look at you and bolted. It was wonderful.

26. A The look on his face was pretty funny. I wondered what was going on.

27. S I needed that laugh today. And, yes, what I want to talk about to you *is* serious.

28. A (*He moves in to her slightly. Both of their voices become quieter.*) Well...

29. S (*Talking a deep breath*) Well...(*Tears begin to well up in her eyes, and she twists the ring on her right hand.*) This is harder to talk about than I thought it would be. Last week, my mom told me that she and dad are getting a divorce.

30. A I'm sorry.

31. S She asked me not to tell anyone; I just had to talk to someone. I know you went through this a few years ago, so I hoped you could help me to sort this all out. I just don't know what to do.

32. A Did this all really come as a total surprise to you?

33. S Well...more or less. I know that there have been some rough times. A few years ago, we all even went to family counseling, and that seemed to help. But lately, dad seemed to be spending less and less time at home. And mom seemed to be trying to be gone when he was home. I suppose I should have guessed that something was up, but it was easier not to face

the truth. When I think about it, it's been a long time since we've all done much of anything as a family, except for the big holidays.

34. A   So you thought that the counseling worked, but now you realize that maybe things haven't been all that great lately after all, and you're feeling sort of isolated and confused.

35. S   Some…but I think that what I'm mostly feeling is anger. I mean, Andy, they've been married for nearly 25 years. They've gone through dad's business failure and mom's illness, and they've raised three pretty decent kids. And now they're going to throw it all away. It really makes me mad!

36. A   It's OK to be mad. I remember how I felt when I found out about my parents' divorce. I just wanted to punch somebody—mostly them—or myself.

37. S   Yes, that's another thing. I keep thinking how **I** should have done things differently. I should have talked to both of them more. Or maybe I should have been less of a problem to them when I was in high school. At the very least, I should have recognized that this was all happening—and tried to do something.

38. A   (*He touches her arm, and she stops talking.*)

39. S   What?

40. A   You can't blame yourself for what's happening to them. Maybe they've worked really hard to keep things from you. Maybe they also thought that if they ignored the problems they would go away.

41. S   I guess. But it's so hard to see your whole life kind of change before your own eyes. I wish I could figure out what happened—and whose fault this all is. You'd think that someone who's had as many communication courses as I have would be able to handle something this close to home. I just feel like an awful failure.

42. A   I don't think that placing blame is going to help anything or anyone. What you need to do now is to keep the channels of communication open—and try not to take sides.

43. S   That's easier said than done. I've always talked to mom more than dad. After all, she's the one who told me about this whole awful situation. When I see dad staying out later and later and never spending any time with us, it's hard not to take sides.

44. A   Maybe you need to talk to your dad about this—alone.

45. S   Maybe—but I just don't think he's going to have much to say. (*Using a deeper voice*) "This is all between your mother and me. You kids aren't involved." That's what he'll say. But we ARE involved! He's so insensitive!

46. A   Do your brother and sister know about this yet?

47. S   No—and that's pretty awful too. Mom said that she was telling me because I'm the oldest and I deserve to know what's happening. I think that **they** deserve to know too, but mom disagrees. Still, I hate to go behind her back and make her feel even worse.

48. A   It does seem pretty unfair to leave you caught in the middle of things.

49. S   Right—I'm really sorry to dump all of this on you, but I needed to talk to someone.

50. A   That's OK. You know I always have time to listen to you. Of course, I'm no professional. Have you thought about seeing that counselor again?

51. S   You mean the whole family? I don't know.

52. A   No, not the whole family. I mean just you. It sounds as if you could use someone to talk to who can be objective about things.

53. S   You know—that's really a good idea. I hadn't thought of it. Talking to you always helps. Thanks for being such a great friend, Andy. (*She squeezes his hand.*)

54. A   Anytime, Sonja. After all, you've listened to me plenty of times.

55. S   Speaking of that, do you have a little more time? How about another cup of coffee and we can catch up on your life for a while.

56. A   Sorry, Sonja. I really do have to run now. I have a class at noon. Let's get together again soon though.

57. S Soon? (*gently*) The last time we said "soon," it took us six weeks. How about right here next week at the same time?

58. A You're on—and maybe then you can tell me some more about Mick. What a character!

Suggested Questions:

1. Your text discusses the link between languages and credibility and attraction. Based on his use of language, what kinds of judgments might you make about Mick? Why? Be specific.

2. Find an example of each of the following in the scenario:
   Ambiguous language
   Emotional language
   Relative language
   Sexiest language
   Static language
   Powerless language

   In each case, identify the type of language, the specific speech number, and the example itself, and explain *why* your example fits the criteria for this type of language.
   (An alternative approach would be to give the speechnNumber and ask students to identify the type of language illustrated by each example.)

3. Make at least two observations about how this interaction does or does not illustrate the typical differences between genders in the use of language in communication.

4. How do fact and inference operate in this scenario?

5. According to your text, nonverbals serve five functions: to repeat, to substitute, to contradict, to complement, and to regulate. Give examples from the scenario of the following:
   to emphasize
   to regulate
   to substitute

6. Briefly define and give examples of the following types of nonverbal communication:
   kinesics
   proxemics
   paralanguage
   chronemics

7. What does the choice of the environment for this scene communicate?

8. Give one example of a nonlistening behavior (poor listening habit) that appears in the case study.

9. Your text discusses a number of listening response styles. Give an example of four of the following from the case study: *Active Listening Response Styles*: Questioning, Paraphrasing, Empathizing; *Directive Listening Response Styles*: Supporting, Analyzing, Advising, Evaluating.

10. Give an example or two of the emotional fallacies that are discussed in your text (fallacy of approval, causation, catastrophic expectations, helplessness, overgeneralization, perfection, should).

11. In Speech 35, Sonja talks about her anger. In this situation, is her anger a facilitative or a debilitative emotion? Why?

12. Are the emotions exhibited by Sonja first- or second-order emotions? Explain.

Brief Sample Answers:

1. Students should refer to Mick's use of slang, his poor grammar, and, especially, his use of sexist language.

2. Ambiguous Language: Speeches 12–13 "engaged"
   Emotional Language   Speech 20 "jerk"
                         Speech 21 "loser"
                         Speech 58 "character"
   Relative Language   Speeches 56–57 "soon"

Sexiest Language	Speech 1 "sweetheart"
	Speech 5 "honey"
	Speech 9, 13 "baby"
Static Language	Speech 45 "He's so insensitive."
Powerless Language	Speech 15 "if you wouldn't mind"

3. Sonja and Mick's interaction supports generalizations about gender differences: He talks more; he interrupts; he is playing a game; he is using conversation to assert his dominance. Sonja and Andy's interaction is not typical: She speaks more than he does; communication is used as a relational tool, even by Andy; he exposes his feelings at this parents' divorce.

4. *Fact*: Sonja states that she is engaged.
   Inference: Mick infers that Sonja is engaged to be married to Andy.
   Fact: Sonja's parents are getting a divorce.
   Inference: Sonja makes a number of inferences about the causes of the divorce.

5. To Emphasize: Speech 29 "taking a deep breath"
   Speech 21 "She rolls her eyes"
   To Regulate: Speech 38 "He touches her arm, and she stops talking."
   To Substitute: Speech 15 "She gestures for him to leave."

6. Kinesics—use of body   Speech 6 "cringing in embarrassment"
   Speech 15 "gestures for him to leave"
   Proxemics—use of space   Speech 5 "He moves in closer to read her name tag."
   Speech 28 "He moves in to her slightly."
   Paralanguage—use of voice Speech 6 "She has been quiet"
   Speech 28 "Both of their voices become quieter."
   Chronemics—use of time   Speech 50 "You know I always have time to listen."

7. The coffee shop atmosphere is both public and private. This is not an intimate meeting, but it is less casual than meeting in a fast-food environment. Typically, diners are not rushed and are left alone by the wait staff. The midmorning time would also be less crowded, with more opportunity for private conversation.

8. Mick's entire "monologue" is an example of stage hogging. He also pseudo-listens in Speeches 6–10.

9. Questioning: Speech 32
   Paraphrasing: Speech 34
   Empathizing: Speech 36
   Supporting: Speech 30
   Analyzing   Speech 40
   Advising: Speech 44
   Evaluating: Speech 48

10. Fallacy of Should: Speech 37
    Fallacy of Perfection: Speech 40
    Fallacy of Overgeneralization: Speech 45
    Fallacy of Causation: Speech 47

11. It is facilitative because she is expressing it calmly and coherently. There is no evidence that the anger is leaving her out of control or that it is an unreasonable emotion under the circumstance.

12. Second order.

UNIT WIND-UP 3: "CAN'T I PLEASE ANYONE?"

Chapters 9–12: Dynamics of Interpersonal Relationships, Communication Climate, Managing Conflict, Communication in Families and at Work

Procedure:

- Read through the questions at the end of the scenario.
- Read and/or listen to the following scenario carefully. You may mark up this paper in any way you wish.
- Work *as a group* to respond to the questions that follow. Each group will hand in one copy of the responses. The entire group will receive the same letter grade for the exercise. Any member who does not participate may, by agreement of the rest of the group, be excluded from signing the group product; however, it is also the joint responsibility of all members to try to involve everyone in the decision-making process. You must work as a group and may not create subgroups to work on different questions simultaneously. You may not use your text or any notes.
- In answering the questions, always explain and illustrate your response by referring to course definitions and the particular case study. When appropriate, you need both to identify the specific Speech Line *and* to describe the situation briefly. Monitor your time so that you are able to complete the exercise within the time limit.

Case Study Participants:

- Jack Lyons—19-year-old-college student; home for the summer after having been away for the past year; working full time at a local grocery as an assistant manager. Jack has been romantically involved with Rachel since they met at freshman orientation. Rachel lives in the same home town and is also home for the summer.
- Marjorie Lyons—Jack's mother, age 45; attorney. She and Jack had always had a very warm and open relationship, sharing easily with one another.

Situation:

Jack and Marjorie have had a difficult time adjusting to Jack's living at home again after a year away at school. Although Jack has never given her reason to doubt him, Marjorie remains concerned about his welfare. In this light, a curfew has been set for Jack, something he resents, in light of his year of independence. The scene begins at the kitchen table on a Sunday morning. It is about 11:00 am; Jack has just gotten up and is eating breakfast. Marjorie enters. She is annoyed about Jack's late arrival home but is not overtly angry.

Case Study:

1. M So—did you have a good time last night?
2. J (*Distracted*) Oh, yeah. I guess it was fine.
3. M What time did you get in? (*Calmly*)
4. J I don't know. Sometime after midnight, I guess.
5. M (*A little more agitated*) You don't need to lie to me, Jack. Just because I'm in bed doesn't mean that I'm asleep. I heard you come in. It was 2:47!
6. J (*Wearily*) Mom, look, I know that my curfew is 1:30 on weekends. It seems as if I can't please anyone these days. No matter what I...
7. M What I don't need to hear right now is excuses. Jack, I'm just tired of your ignoring the rules of this house. (*Frustrated*)
8. J Mom, could we please not talk about this right now?

9. M Why not? You know the rules. You just can't keep disregarding them time after time. Having you back home for the summer after your year of freedom is hard on both of us, but you need to give a little effort too.

10. J Mom, please, not now, OK?

11. M We can't just keep avoiding the issue, Jack. If you really considered how much I worry when you're out till all hours, doing who knows what, with who knows whom, you'd be considerate enough to come in on time.

12. J (*Serious, almost pleading*) Mom, please, I've got other things on my mind.

13. M (*Changing tones—finally realizing Jack's distraction*) Yes—it sounds as if you really do. (*pause*) Do you want to talk about it?

14. J No—well, yes—I guess I could use a good listener.

15. M So—what's the problem? Does this have anything to do with Rachel?

16. J You've got that one right. She told me last night that she wants to break up. That's why I was so late. We started to talk, and the time just got away on me.

17. M Have you been having any problems to this point?

18. J Not that bad. You know, I'm crazy about Rachel. From the first time I saw her at freshman orientation, I thought she was special. And then the next day, she showed up in the same English class, so we got to see a lot of each other. And we started talking and found out that we had so much in common. And I found out that she's smart too—not brilliant but really smart, especially in things like math that I'm not so good at. We always had such a great time together, and I honestly thought that this was really it for both of us.

19. M And...?

20. J And everything was great until this summer. Now it seems that I just can't please her. She wants to be together all the time. I'm trying to tell her that I really need some breathing space, but she doesn't seem to understand that. She wants me around just about every minute that I'm not working. As a matter of fact, she even thinks I'm working too much.

21. M What exactly does she expect?

22. J That's another problem. She always said that she loved the way I'm so steady and reliable, that she nearly always knows what I'm thinking and what I'll say next. Now she says that she's beginning to think that I'm boring.

23. M Go on...

24. J So last night, I asked her where we stood. I told her that I would do whatever she wants. If she wants me around, I'll be around. If she wants me to do unexpected things, I'll try to do that. If she wants me to listen, I'll listen. If she wants me to talk, I'll talk. And she said that's not the point.

25. M What do you think *is* the point?

26. J It beats me! The next thing I knew she was calling me a wimp—and I was screaming back at her. It was pretty awful.

27. M I guess so. I can understand why you're so upset about all of this.

28. J It just seems as if I don't know Rachel anymore—even in some little ways. Last night, I bought tickets for the baseball game, and she said that she hates baseball. When I brought her a red rose, she said that she likes yellow roses. She didn't even like the music I chose on the radio. I feel as if she's a different person.

29. M Can you just try to talk to her about all of this?

30. J That's another thing. It seems that she wants to know every little last detail about me—what happened in my past and how I'm feeling about everything and who I've dated and—well, you get the picture.

31. M And you don't feel comfortable with this?

32. J I just don't think I always have to share everything I'm feeling all the time. But she tells me everything—and then I feel guilty when I don't do the same.

33. M Have you explained this to her?

34. J I've tried. Believe me, I've tried. Last night she ended up by saying that she really didn't care what I did. I should just please myself and not worry about her. That really made me mad.
35. M Why?
36. J Probably because I know she does care—or at least I sure hope she does. I don't know; we just couldn't stay on the topic last night. I got to the point where I almost made up some stories—just to give her something to think about.
37. M That doesn't sound like such a good idea.
38. J I know…but I was getting desperate.
39. M So—what now?
40. J I thought I'd give her a call and try to see her again tonight—to try to work something out. Maybe we do need some breathing time away from one another.
41. M That sounds like a good idea.
42. J Thanks, Mom. It really did help to talk about this.
43. M Good. Now—what about that curfew issue? (*lightly*) Or did you think I was going to forget all about that?
44. J Mom, you know I hate the curfew. I've just had a whole year on my own. I know that you worry, but I feel as if I'm being treated like a little kid again. Couldn't we work together to find a better solution?
45. M Maybe we can work out a better deal. Could you at least promise—and I really mean promise—that you'll call when you're going to be late?
46. J You mean that you'd be willing to get rid of the time limit as long as I call? That's a deal. Maybe we can both be satisfied with that arrangement. You know I don't stay out all that late very often.
47. M Good—that's at least one problem settled then.
48. J Thanks, Mom. I've got to get going. My shift starts in an hour.
49. M Jack—I really do hope that things work out for you and Rachel. By the way, since you're going to work, we're almost out of milk.
50. J Sure, I'll bring some milk home from the store. I'll drop it off before I go over to talk to Rachel. And yes, I'll call if I'm going to be late.

Questions:
1. Identify the speech in which Jack discusses attraction variables (why we form relationships). Then explain the variables he talks about.
2. Mark Knapp has described five Stages of Coming Together (initiating, experimenting, intensifying, integrating, and bonding). At which stage are Jack and Marjorie? At which stage are Jack and Rachel? Knapp also identifies five Stages of Coming Apart (differentiating, circumscribing, stagnating, avoiding, and terminating). What stage are Jack and Rachel in? Why?
3. How do the dialectical tensions of connection/autonomy, stability/change, and openness/closedness function in this scenario? Give at least two specific examples.
4. Your text discusses a number of compliance-gaining strategies. Identify at least two different strategies in the scenario, and cite the speeches in which they occur.
5. Cite an example of equivocation from the scenario.
6. Identify two concepts about self-disclosure that are illustrated by this scenario.
7. Identify at least one example of a disconfirming response.
8. Recall the categories that Jack Gibb identified as helping to create defensive and supportive communication climates. Note—by speech and by identifying the category name—one example of defensiveness-creating behavior and one example of a supportiveness-creating behavior.
9. According to the definition of conflict given in the text, are Marjorie and Jack involved in a conflict? Are Jack and Rachel? Why?

10. Your text describes five individual conflict styles: nonassertion, indirect communication, passive aggression, direct aggression, and assertion. In addition, four methods of conflict resolution are discussed: win-lose, lose-lose, compromise, and win-win.

    a.   Which individual conflict style is used by Marjorie until Speech 11? Which method of conflict resolution is she using?

    b.   Which individual style does Jack attempt to use?

    c.   Which individual style is illustrated by Jack's response to Rachel as reported in Speech 24?

    d.   Give an example of a way in which Jack might have responded to Rachel using passive aggressive behavior?

    e.   In order to resolve their initial conflict about the curfew, which individual conflict style(s) do Marjorie and Jack use? Which type of conflict resolution method does this resolution illustrate?

    f.   Do Jack and Marjorie live in a collective culture or an individualistic culture? Give at least one reason for your response. Describe at least two ways in which the interaction might be different if they came from another culture.

    g.   Do they live in a high-context culture or a low-context culture? Explain

    h.   Do they live in a culture with low or high power distance? Explain.

Brief Sample Answers:

1. Speech 18. Jack mentions appearance, similarity, complementarity, proximity, and competency in this speech.

2. Jack and Marjorie are probably in the bonding stage since they are "legally" paired as son and mother and because they share a healthy degree of intellectual and emotional intimacy. Jack and Rachel have clearly passed the initiating and experimenting stages and have not yet reached bonding. Students might make a case for either the intensifying or the integrating stage.

3. *Integration/Separation*:

    Jack and Marjorie: Tensions involved in growing up and letting go.

    Jack and Rachel: Rachel wants Jack all the time; Jack needs some freedom.

    Stability/Change:

    Jack and Rachel: Rachel used to like Jack's predictability; suddenly she is finding him boring.

    Expression/Privacy:

    Jack and Rachel: Rachel demands more of Jack in the way of self-disclosure than he is comfortable sharing.

4. Speeches 8, 10, and 12 contain a direct request.

    Speeches 13 and 44 contain a relationship appeal.

    Speech 48 contains an indirect request.

5. Speech 4 illustrates the use of an equivocal response.

6. There are gender differences in self-disclosure.

    Self-disclosure enhances relationships.

    There are numerous reasons for self-disclosure: catharsis, self-clarification, and reciprocity are particularly illustrated in this scenario.

    Self-disclosure has both depth and breadth characteristics.

7. Speech 7 illustrates an interrupting response.

    Speech 6 illustrates a tangential response.

8. Evaluation, Superiority, Control—Marjorie in Speeches 5, 7, and 9

    Neutrality—Rachel (reported by Jack) in Speech 34

    Empathy—Marjorie in Speech 27

    Problem Orientation—Jack and Marjorie in Speeches 43–47

9. Yes to both situations. Both parties are aware of a conflict situation, both see themselves as somewhat interdependent with the other party, both see scarce rewards and the interference of the other in achieving their goals.

10. a Marjorie begins the scene by using direct aggression in a win-lose conflict resolution style.

   b. Jack tries to use avoidance to postpone the potential conflict situation.

   c. Accommodation conflict style

   d. Possible passive aggressive actions: He might have actually made up the stories as he threatened in Speech 36. He might have brought Rachel another red rose. They use assertive behavior leading to a win-win resolution.

   e. They use a collaborative conflict style leading to a Win-Win resolution

   f. Individualistic culture—more concern for personal needs, not social harmony
       Other culture—Son wouldn't question his mother, or in other cultures based on gender differences, a mother wouldn't question her son; more respect for house rules.

   g. Low context—situation was laid out very clearly by the use of language; little was left unsaid.

   h. Low power distance—Jack felt comfortable confronting parental authority.

FINAL WIND-UP: "WHOSE LIFE IS THIS, ANYWAY?"

Cumulative Exam: Chapters 1–12

Note to Instructors:
The case study/scenario that follows was developed for use at the University of Wisconsin Center—Waukesha County. Waukesha is a community located just west of the city of Milwaukee. Chicago's O'Hare Airport is approximately 90 miles south of Milwaukee. Kenosha is located midway between Milwaukee and Chicago; UW-M is the University of Wisconsin—Milwaukee. Instructors are encouraged to alter the locations in this scenario according to the location of their individual campus.

The exam would ordinarily be printed in such a manner as to leave enough room for students to respond to the questions directly on the test form.

Procedure:
- Read through the questions at the end of the scenario.
- Read and/or listen to the following scenario carefully. You may mark up this paper in any way you wish.
- Work *independently* to respond to the questions that follow. You may not use your text or any notes.
- In answering the questions, always explain and illustrate your response by referring to course definitions and this particular case study. When appropriate, you need both to identify the specific Speech Line *and* to briefly describe the situation. Monitor your time so that you are able to complete the exercise within the time limit.

Case Study Participants:
- Sarah Barkley   Age 28; B.A. in communication; employed full time at Mitchell Field in Milwaukee as a ticketing agent for a small airline company. She is the major source of income for the family while husband Brad completes his M.B.A.
- Brad Barkley   Age 31; B.A. in business; employed part time as a shoe salesman while working on his M.B.A. full time at US-M. He expects to finish his degree in a year.
- Tony Barkley   Brad and Sarah's 18-month-old son.

Situation:
Sarah and Brad have been married for four and one-half years. Although the going was pretty tough at first, they are now quite well settled into their current lives. They have just purchased an older home on the east side of Milwaukee—convenient to UW-M and not too long a commute to the airport. Although they need to watch their spending, their current incomes are adequate to manage the house payment, Tony's day care three days a week when Brad is not home to watch him, and even an occasional evening out.

As the scene begins, Brad is just setting the table for their evening meal, which he has prepared. Tony is playing quietly in his playpen in the living room. It is approximately 6:00 pm when Sarah enters, wearing her airline agent's uniform. She is obviously excited as she rushes into the house, sweeps up Tony from his playpen, and moves into the kitchen to involve the three of them in a family hug. During all of this, she is exclaiming...

Case Study:
1. S   I did it! I can't believe it! I did it, I did it! I'm so excited I can hardly stand it. Brad—I actually did it!
2. B   That's terrific, honey. What did you do? (*Immediately the atmosphere changes; he has forgotten.*)

3. S You mean you forget? One of the biggest chances in my life, and you forget?

4. B Aw—geez—I'm sorry. Of course I didn't forget…the big promotion interview. So I guess this means you got the job. (*Suddenly it dawns on him*) You got the job! (*another hug and more squeals*) I told you you could do it.

5. S You told me, and I told me…and it worked. I got it! (*to Tony*) What do you think, kid; your mom's going to be a department manager!

6. B So tell me more. How did it go? What did they ask? When do you start? What do you do?

7. S Well…the interview was at 11:00 this morning…When I walked into the office, I almost died. Six of the company's top execs were there, all staring at me…

8. B Hey—wait a minute! This calls for a toast. (*He moves quickly to the cupboard and takes out two wine glasses, goes to the refrigerator and fills them from the large box of wine in the fridge.*)

9. S (*talks sotto voce to Tony*)…and so your mom had to talk to all of those bigwigs. Pretty tough stuff, huh?

10. B O.K. (*He hands her a glass.*) To my wife, the department manager. (*They clink glasses and drink. There is a brief pause.*) So…go on…

11. S So…there were all these people…

12. (*The sound fades out as Sarah continues her story about the interview. The scene picks up at the end of the description. By this time, Sarah and Brad have moved to the living room couch. Tony has been returned to his playpen and is quietly eating a graham cracker.*)

13. S Its looks as if I'll have charge of the entire local staff for domestic reservations. That's over 100 people! And, of course, there's a nice raise to go along with this. I accepted on the spot!

14. B 100 people? I thought the Milwaukee staff only had about 25.

15. S Oh, oh. I guess I forget a little detail. We have to move to Chicago. The new position is at O'Hare Airport.

16. B That's some little detail.

17. S But, honey, it's such a great opportunity. I couldn't pass it up!

18. B (*He begins to speak more loudly.*) Opportunity or not, this is *our* life, not just yours. Don't you think you should have at least consulted me! I guess this shows what you really think about my going to school.

19. S Brad, that's not fair!

20. B Not fair? What is this? Some kind of game we're playing?

21. S Well, maybe it is! The game of life!

22. B You know, you're making me mad. How about your making a major life-changing decision without any input from me? I'm really getting fed up with the way you're always making *our* decisions for us without even talking to me.

23. S Brad—I can't believe you're reacting like this. This is such a great opportunity. Talk about breaking somebody's bubble.

24. B Sure it's great opportunity—for you. What about me? There's my job and my education to consider too, you know.

25. S Look, let's be realistic. We have a child to take care of. We sure can't do this on your flunky's salary as a part-time shoe clerk! As for school—you can do that anywhere. Heaven knows there are plenty of shoe stores and colleges in Chicago! (*sarcastically*)

26. B (*angry*) I don't want to talk about this anymore. It's pretty clear how much *I* count in this relationship. I'm going to check on the dinner that *I* made for *all of us* while *you* were at your high-class job! (*He storms out of the room.*)

27. T (*Begins to cry*)

28. S Now look what you've done!

29. (*Sarah and Brad eat a very silent dinner, broken only occasionally by Tony's babbles. After dinner, Sarah proceeds to clean up—according to their regular routine—while Brad gets Tony ready for bed. After Tony is tucked in, Brad returns to the living room to try to do some*

homework; Sarah goes to a small office area in their bedroom where she frequently works or reads. After a few minutes, Brad gets up and goes to Sarah in the bedroom. A radio is playing in the background.)

30. B   Honey, I'm sorry. Can you talk about this now?
31. S   Is there anything to talk about?
32. B   Of course there is. It's just that you sprang this on me so fast that I didn't have time to think.
33. S   (*slightly defensive*) Oh—so it's my fault. Why can't anything be your fault?
34. B   (*calmly*) Nothing is anybody's fault. (*He turns off the radio.*) Your news really is terrific. I'm awful proud of you…really. (*He gives her a kiss.*)
35. S   (*She responds coolly, her body still tense.*)
36. B   Honey—are you listening? I mean it. (*He kisses her again.*)
37. S   (*She relaxes a little.*) Does that mean that you've thought this through and you agree with me? That you'll move without kicking and screaming?
38. B   No…I didn't say that.
39. S   Then what's the point of all of this? (*Sarah throws up her hands, rises, and moves away from Brad.*)
40. B   Wait…wait…wait…Can't we talk about this like two adults?
41. S   So—talk.
42. B   I can understand how you were so excited that you just accepted the offer right away. But how about if we try to look at the situation objectively and weigh the alternatives.
43. S   What alternatives? I have a promotion offer, which happens to be in Chicago. Either I take it or I'm stuck here—probably for the rest of my life!
44. B   Please, can't we just *try* this?
45. S   Well, O.K.
46. B   How about if we start by looking at the positives: I'll start. First of all, it's a great opportunity for you in a job and with a company that you like.
47. S   (*She likes his beginning.*) And there's a nice salary increase.
48. B   Chicago isn't too far away. We could still easily visit our parents and Tony could see his grandparents. And it *is* a pretty neat city.
49. S   (*tentatively*) And you *could* find a job at another shoe store, even with the same chain. I guess I have to admit that switching schools isn't such a great idea.
50. B   Now—what about the bad stuff? Want to start this round?
51. S   Well, we've just bought the house; we'd have to go through the hassle of selling and finding a new place…
52. B   One that we could afford—remember, Chicago is more expensive…
53. S   No fair—it's my turn. And even though you could ask for a transfer, you would have to find another job…and we'd have to find a day care place for Tony. And there is the issue of your degree. It doesn't really make much sense for you to change schools at this point. This isn't as much fun as listing the positives.
54. B   And there's one other thing I just thought of. We'd be new residents of Illinois. We'd have to live there a year before I could get in-state tuition.
55. S   And if you commuted to Milwaukee to finish, you'd have to pay out-of-state tuition. Yikes! I never thought of that.
56. B   And remember—Chicago is more expensive in general. We'd have to take a look at how far that extra salary would really go.
57. S   O.K. You're right—anything else?
58. B   Not that I can think of right now. So—how about if we brainstorm for solutions?…
59. S   What do you mean? It seems to me that either I take the job and we move and have to put up with all of those hassles. Or I turn down the promotion and I'm just stuck here with the boredom. It's a no-win situation. One of us is going to be miserable.

60. B You know, it was pretty quiet at dinner. I had a little time to give this some thought, and I think I might just have something that would work. It's not perfect, but…

61. S Go ahead. I'm listening.

62. B Well, how about if we move someplace between here and Chicago?

63. S What do you mean?

64. B Well, we could move somewhere along I-94—like near Kenosha maybe.

65. S Oh—I don't know about that. How does that solve anything? That way we could *both* have enormous commutes!

66. B Listen—it could work. We'd have to sell the house, but we could rent somewhere until I'm finished with school next year. You could take the bus to work—it takes less than an hour and goes right to O'Hare—so we wouldn't need another car, and you could work or sleep on the way.

67. S The rents would be a lot cheaper than Chicago…

68. B I could probably transfer to a store in Kenosha for my job, but I could continue to commute to Milwaukee for school.

69. S And you could also take Tony to day care? That way we wouldn't have to change something we're really happy with.

70. B Sounds good to me…

71. S And by the time you're through with school, we'll have had time to decide if Chicago is the place to relocate to.

72. B And there's always the chance that I'll get a job offer somewhere else in the country…

73. S …and I'll be the one who has to relocate.

74. B What do you think? It could work.

75. S I say we give it a try.

76. B Congratulations, Manager!

77. (*They both laugh and embrace.*)

FINAL EXAM QUESTIONS

Respond to the following questions.

IMPORTANT: When appropriate, you *must* provide BOTH the Speech Line and the example itself. Explain if you wish—or if indicated in the question. Note that the same speech in the scenario may be used to illustrate more than a single interpersonal communication phenomenon. Please write or print legibly; answers that cannot be read easily will be counted as incorrect.

1. The scenario illustrates an example of transactional communication. Explain why or how.

2. Is there an example of self-fulfilling prophecy in this scenario? If so, give the speech where it appears.

3. Illustrate the concept of interpersonal "punctuation" about the conflict in this situation. What might Sarah's interpretation be? What might Brad's view be?

4. Note an example of facilitative emotions in the scenario. Why are they facilitative in this case? Note an example of debilitative emotions. Why are they debilitative?

5. Your text discusses a number of fallacies of thinking: approval, catastrophic, expectations, causation, helpless, overgeneralization, perfection, shoulds, etc.
   a. Which fallacy is illustrated by *Speech 22*, in which Brad says, "You know you're making me mad"?
   b. Which fallacy do you see in *Speech 59*, in which Sarah says, "One of us is going to be miserable"?

6. Identify and give an example of one type of nonlistening you find in the scenario.

7. Which of the listening response styles is illustrated by the following speeches in the scenario? Why? (Explain the style[s] being used.)
   Speech 6:

165

Speech 18:

Speech 42 illustrates two response styles. They are:

8. Design an empathic response that Sarah might have made following *Speech 22*.

9. Briefly define the following types of "troublesome language": emotive words, ambiguous words, static evaluation, euphemisms, relative words

    Speech 25: "your flunky's salary..."

    Speech 65: "enormous commutes..."

    Speeches 19–21: "fair...game"

10. Briefly define each of the following types of nonverbal communication, and give an example of each from the case study: kinesics, proxemics, chronemics, paralanguage

11. What does it mean to say that nonverbals may be used to *regulate*? Give an example from the scenario.

12. Give one example of a dialectical tension that Brad and Sarah are experiencing in this scenario.

13. Mark Knapp discussed five "Stages of Coming Together" (initiating, experimenting, intensifying, integrating, bonding) and five "Stages of Coming Apart" (differentiating, circumscribing, stagnating, avoiding, terminating). Where would you place Sarah and Brad in this taxonomy? Why?

14. Jack Gibb identified six pairs of behaviors that are likely to create defensive or supportive climates (evaluation/description; strategy/spontaneity; control/problem orientation; neutrality/empathy; superiority/equality; certainty/provisionalism). Which one of these behaviors is illustrated by each of the following:

    Speech 42: "I can understand how you were so excited that you just accepted the offer right away."

    Speech 42: "But how about if we try to look at the situation objectively and weigh the alternatives."

    Speech 25: "We sure can't do that on your flunky's salary...!"

15. Your text discusses a number of disconfirming responses. Identify one type of disconfirming response that appears in the scenario.

16. Does Sarah and Brad's situation fit the definition of conflict as given in your text? Why or why not? Is this a functional or a dysfunctional conflict? Why?

17. Briefly explain each of these styles of managing conflict (avoiding, accommodating, compromising, competing, collaborating). Chart the use of conflict in this case study.

    The conflict begins at *Speech #*   .

    From this point until *Speech 26*, the main management style used is:

    Speeches 27–29 illustrate this management style:

    The remainder of the case study primarily uses which management style? *Why?*

18. Culture affects our communication. Is the United States a collectivist or an individualist society? How is this illustrated in the case study? How might the situation (and outcome) have been different if Brad and/or Sarah had come from a different culture or cultures? (Give at least two specific examples.)

19. What conflict roles do Brad and Sarah play?

20. Give an example of family systems present in this scenario.

Brief Sample Answers:

1. Sarah and Brad are sending and receiving messages simultaneously.

2. Yes—Speech 5

3. *Sarah's View*: This conflict started because Brad only thinks about himself—his job and his school. He doesn't care about my opportunity for advancement.

   Brad's View: This conflict started because Sarah went ahead and made a life-changing decision without consulting me.

4. Any number of speeches might be cited for this response.

5. a. Speech 22: fallacy of causation, fallacy of overgeneralization
   b. Speech 59: fallacy of catastrophic expectations
6. Any number of speeches might be cited. Pseudolistening, defensive listening, ambushing, and stage hogging are all present at some point.
7. Speech 6: questioning
   Speech 18: evaluating
   Speech 42: supporting (or empathizing) and advising
8. It sounds as if you are really feeling upset because I went ahead and jumped at this opportunity without consulting you—even though this decision really affects both of us.
9. Definitions are found in the text glossary.
   Speech 25: emotive words
   Speech 65: relative language
   Speeches 19–21: equivocal language
10. Definitions are found in the text glossary. Any number of examples might be cited.
11. There are a number of times when nonverbals are used to regulate in the scenario. Speeches 18, 26, 39, and 43 are all examples.
12. Support might be found for any of the dialectical tensions discussed in the text. The most obvious is that of stability/change.
13. According to Knapp, Sarah and Brad are in the bonding stage, because they are married. The argument is also evidence of differentiating.
14. Speech 42: empathy
    Speech 42: problem orientation
    Speech 25: evaluation
15. There are a number of disconfirming responses through the scenario.
16. Yes, this does fit the definition. The conflict involves a disagreement that is recognized by both parties; they are clearly interdependent; and they believe (initially) that the solution is Win/Lose. Although the conflict might have escalated to be debilitative, it is solved in an equitable manner. It is a facilitative conflict, and their relationship is stronger as a result.
17. The conflict begins at Speeches 15–18.
    Competing—Aggression—Win-Lose
    Avoiding—Nonassertion—Win-Lose
    Collaborating—Assertion—Win-Win
18. The United States is an individualist culture. Sarah might not even be working outside of the home, much less consider making a life-changing decision, without her husband.
19. Sarah plays the blamer, and Brad plays the computer/placater.
20. Tony starts crying when Brad and Sarah are fighting (family members are interdependent); Sarah's need for career development is hindered by the size of the local airport, which affects their relationship (family systems are affected by their environment); they may need to move for Brad next (family members are interdependent).

PART V: TEST QUESTIONS

Code for Test Items

QUESTION TYPES (TYPE):

T = True/False
M = Multiple Choice
K = Matching
E = Essay

Note that multiple choice directions should include the statement "Select the *best* answer."

COGNITIVE TYPES (COG):

R = Recall
C = Conceptual
A = Application

CHAPTER 1: INTERPERSONAL PROCESS

True/False

1. Effective communication can satisfy identity needs.
   ANSWER: T   TYPE: T   COG: R
2. We gain an idea of who we are from the way other react us.
   ANSWER: T   TYPE: T   COG: R
3. In scientific jargon, any interference with communication is termed *noise*.
   ANSWER: T   TYPE: T   COG: R
4. Most people can learn to communicate more effectively.
   ANSWER: T   TYPE: T   COG: R
5. Communication is a process in which messages are generated to create meanings.
   ANSWER: T   TYPE: T   COG: R
6. According to the qualitative definition, all two-person interaction is interpersonal.
   ANSWER: F   TYPE: T   COG: R
7. In interpersonal contexts, the content dimension is more important that the relational dimension of a message.
   ANSWER: F   TYPE: T   COG: R
8. Most people operate at a level of communication effectiveness equal to their potential.
   ANSWER: F   TYPE: T   COG: R
9. Communication competence is defined as using communication that is both effective and appropriate.
   ANSWER: T   TYPE: T   COG: R
10. Communication competence is a trait that a person either possesses or lacks.
    ANSWER: F   TYPE: T   COG: R

11. Verbal communication skills have been identified as most important for career success.
    ANSWER: T   TYPE: T   COG: R
12. *Cognitive complexity* is the term describing the process of paying close attention to one's behavior.
    ANSWER: F   TYPE: T   COG: R
13. Self-monitoring is the ability to construct a variety of different frameworks for viewing an issue.
    ANSWER: F   TYPE: T   COG: R
14. Communication plays a role in satisfying the five human needs that Abraham Maslow calls basic to living a safe and fulfilled life.

ANSWER: T TYPE: T   COG: R

15. At the present time, there is no research to support the hypothesis that a connection exists between social interaction and physical health or longevity.
  ANSWER: F TYPE: T   COG: R

16. According to the transactional model of communication, at any given point in time a person is sending a message *and* receiving a message.
  ANSWER: T TYPE: T   COG: R

17. The qualitative view of communication is more *impersonal* than the quantitative view of communication.
  ANSWER: F TYPE: T   COG: R

18. Communicators who adapt their talk to differing situations possess a characteristic of interpersonal effectiveness.
  ANSWER: T TYPE: T   COG: R

19. From a qualitative perspective when you ask a stranger on the street for directions you are probably not communicating interpersonally with each other.
  ANSWER: T TYPE: T   COG: R

20. Feedback is the listener's verbal and/or nonverbal response to messages received from the speaker.
  ANSWER: T TYPE: T   COG: R

21. Feedback can be verbal and/or nonverbal.
  ANSWER: T TYPE: T   COG: R

22. Communication as defined in the text is always intentional rather than unintentional.
  ANSWER: F TYPE: T   COG: R

23. In some interpersonal contexts the relational dimension of the message may be more important than the content of the message.
  ANSWER: T TYPE: T   COG: R

24. It is a misconception to assume that more communication will always make tense interpersonal situations better.
  ANSWER: T TYPE: T   COG: R

25. The effective communicator is going to make a commitment to the other person but not be concerned with making the relationship clearly useful.
  ANSWER: F TYPE: T   COG: R

26. There is evidence that indicates communication is so important that it's necessary for physical health.
  ANSWER: T TYPE: T   COG: R

27. The ability to ask yourself mentally how you're doing and to change your behavior if necessary is termed *self-monitoring*.
  ANSWER: T TYPE: T   COG: R

28. Qualitatively, interpersonal communication is relatively infrequent, even in many close relationships.
  ANSWER: T TYPE: T   COG: R

29. The concept of communication competence suggests there is no single "ideal" or "effective" way to communicate in every situation.
  ANSWER: T TYPE: T   COG: R

30. Cognitive complexity and self-monitoring are both identified as factors that impede (reduce) communication competence.
  ANSWER: F TYPE: T   COG: R

31. From a quantitative perspective, the terms *dyadic communication* and *interpersonal communication* are interchangeable.
  ANSWER: T TYPE: T   COG: R

32. A group of senior executives cite lack of interpersonal communication skills as a deficit in today's workforce.
  ANSWER: T TYPE: T   COG: R

33. Research suggests that communication competence is an inborn rather than a learned characteristic.
  ANSWER: F TYPE: T   COG: R

34. In the last 20 years for Americans, the average number of friendships has increased.
    ANSWER: F   TYPE: T   COG: R
35. Early models of communication were complex and were better at explaining public speaking.
    ANSWER: F   TYPE: T   COG: R
36. One of the features that distinguishes qualitatively interpersonal communication from less personal exchanges is interdependence."
    ANSWER: T   TYPE: T   COG: R
37. According to research everyday talk is insignificant in maintaining relationships.
    ANSWER: F   TYPE: T   COG: R
38. In communication, meanings exist in the messages themselves.
    ANSWER: F   TYPE: T   COG: R
39. Fields like engineering, accounting and computer science have little need for interpersonal communication on a daily basis."
    ANSWER: F   TYPE: T   COG: R
40. Even positive qualities such as self-monitoring and cognitive complexity can be ineffective when carried to excess.
    ANSWER: T   TYPE: T   COG: C

Multiple Choice

41. Which of the following allows us to use the terms *dyadic communication* and *interpersonal communication* interchangeably?
    a. quantitative
    b. qualitative
    c. situational
    d. functional
    e. interactional
       ANSWER: a   TYPE: M   COG: R
42. An example of psychological noise is
    a. cigarette smoke in a crowded room
    b. fatigue
    c. insecurity
    d. poor sound
    e. illness
       ANSWER: c   TYPE: M   COG: A
43. Which of the following is *not* a valid reason for studying communication?
    a. wanting to learn new ways of viewing a familiar topic
    b. wanting to manipulate weakness in others
    c. wanting to understand that we spend a significant amount of time communicating
    d. wanting to use more effective communication in relationships
    e. decreasing errors in the workplace based on communication
       ANSWER: b   TYPE: M   COG: R
44. A discernible response to a message is
    a. encoding
    b. channel
    c. feedback
    d. noise
    e. none of the above
       ANSWER: c   TYPE: M   COG: R
45. Your first encounter at a job interview is affected by the interviewer's scowling facial expression. Which characteristic of communication best describes the situation?
    a. Communication is dyadic.
    b. Communication is a transactional process.

c. Communication is static.

d. Communication is dependent on personalized rules.

e. None of the above describes it.

ANSWER: b   TYPE: M   COG: A

46. Because it's often impossible to distinguish sending and receiving, your text's communication model replaces these roles with the more accurate term:

a. speaker

b. listener

c. communicator

d. empathizer

e. none of the above

ANSWER: c   TYPE: M   COG: R

47. Which of the following characterizes transactional communication?

a. Communication must be sent through a channel.

b. Communication involves communicators' occupying different but overlapping environments.

c. We may be receiving and responding to messages from another person at the same time that she or he is receiving and responding to us.

d. Noise may be both physical and psychological.

e. All of the above characterize it.

ANSWER: e   TYPE: M   COG: R

48. The first communication models characterized communication as:

a. a Ping-Pong game

b. a one-way event

c. a transactional event

d. an ongoing process

e. none of the above

ANSWER: b   TYPE: M   COG: R

49. The idea that it is often necessary to negotiate a shared meaning in order for satisfying communication to occur relates to which characteristic of the communication model?

a. Sending and receiving are usually simultaneous.

b. Meanings exist in and among people.

c. Environment and noise affect communication.

d. Channels make a difference.

e. none of the above

ANSWER: b   TYPE: M   COG: R

50. That fact that college students who have been enrolled in debate classes tend to become more verbally aggressive than those who have not is related to which communication concept?

a. external noise

b. channel

c. transactional

d. environment

e. none of the above

ANSWER: d   TYPE: M   COG: C

51. Environments are also referred to as:

a. contexts

b. homes

c. relationships

d. cognitive complexity

e. self-monitoring

ANSWER: a   TYPE: M   COG: R

52. Which of the following are outlined in your text as important characteristics of communication?
    a. sending and receiving are usually simultaneous
    b. meanings exist in and among people
    c. environment and noise affect communication
    d. channels make a difference
    e. all of the above
        ANSWER: e   TYPE: M   COG: R
53. The text suggests a "qualitative" definition of an interpersonal relationship. Which of the following is *not* one of the criteria for that definition?
    a. context
    b. irreplaceability
    c. disclosure
    d. interdependence
    e. All are criteria.
        ANSWER: a   TYPE: M   COG: R
54. The term created by Julia Wood to describe the unique ways that people interact with each other in close relationships is:
    a. impersonal interactions
    b. relational culture
    c. self-disclosure
    d. metacognition
    e. none of the above
        ANSWER: b   TYPE: M   COG: R
57. The idea that "nothing" never happens refers to which communication principle?
    a. Communication is transactional.
    b. Communication can be intentional or unintentional.
    c. Communication has a content and relational dimension.
    d. Communication is irreversible.
    e. none of the above
        ANSWER: b   TYPE: M   COG: A
58. Sandra interprets her coworker's comment "Thanks a lot" as negative. This is an example of which communication principle?
    a. content dimension
    b. relational dimension
    c. noise
    d. communication is unintentional
    e. communication is irreversible
        ANSWER: b   TYPE: M   COG: A
59. The explicit, dictionary definition of a message is referred to as:
    a. content dimension
    b. relational dimension
    c. context dimension
    d. relative dimension
    e. none of the above
        ANSWER: a   TYPE: M   COG: R

60. Mike and Sue are happily married and always say, "I love you" before ending their telephone conversations. The fact that the words do not have the same emotional impact as the first time they were spoken is indicative of:
    a.   Communication is transactional.
    b.   Communication is unrepeatable.
    c.   Communication is unintentional.
    d.   Communication is irreversible.
    e.   none of the above
        ANSWER: b   TYPE: M   COG: A

61. When a religious person listens to a speaker who uses profanity, he or she would probably experience
    a.   external noise
    b.   cognitive complexity
    c.   relational noise
    d.   physiological noise
    e.   psychological noise
        ANSWER: e   TYPE: M   COG: A

62. Being unable to hear a speaker's remarks because you are sitting in the rear of an auditorium is an example of:
    a.   external noise
    b.   psychological noise
    c.   physiological noise
    d.   static
    e.   none of the above
        ANSWER: a   TYPE: M   COG: A

63. An example of physiological noise is:
    a.   anger
    b.   poor sound
    c.   insecurity
    d.   fatigue
    e.   none of the above
        ANSWER: d   TYPE: M   COG: R

64. An emailed love letter not having the same impact as a handwritten one is related to the _____ of the message.
    a.   channel
    b.   context
    c.   noise
    d.   environment
    e.   none of the above
        ANSWER: a   TYPE: M   COG: A

65. The dynamic process that participants create through their interaction with one another is termed:
    a.   environment
    b.   noise
    c.   transactional
    d.   context
    e.   none of the above
        ANSWER: c   TYPE: M   COG: R

66. Which of the following is not true about communication competence?
    a.   There is no single "ideal" or "effective" way to communicate.
    b.   Competence is situational.
    c.   Competence can be learned.
    d.   Competence involves a large repertoire of skills.
    e.   none of the above
        ANSWER: e   TYPE: M   COG: C

67. Which of the following means the same things as "Communication is irreversible"?
    a. Erasing or replacing spoken words or acts is not possible.
    b. You can't erase an impression you've created.
    c. It's impossible to "unreceive" a message.
    d. Words said are irretrievable.
    e. All mean the same as the statement.
        ANSWER: e   TYPE: M   COG: C
68. Effective communication includes the dimension(s) of
    a. commitment to the other person
    b. commitment to the relationship
    c. concern about the message being received
    d. a desire to make the relationship useful
    e. all of the above
        ANSWER: e   TYPE: M   COG: R
69. According to researcher Mark Redmond, which kind of message is communicatively competent by definition?
    a. an assertive message
    b. an empathic message
    c. a feedback message
    d. a linear message
    e. all of the above
        ANSWER: b   TYPE: M   COG: R
70. Which characteristic applies to interpersonal communication?
    a. intentional or unintentional
    b. impossible not to communicate
    c. irreversible
    d. unrepeatable
    e. all of the above
        ANSWER: e   TYPE: M   COG: R
71. Which is true of communication?
    a. Everyone does it.
    b. More is always better.
    c. It can solve all problems.
    d. It is a natural ability.
    e. All of the above are true.
        ANSWER: a   TYPE: M   COG: R
72. Which of the following is a reason to study communication?
    a. It gives you a new look at a familiar topic.
    b. We spend a staggering amount of time communicating/
    c. None of us communicates as effectively as we could.
    d. All of the above are reasons.
    e. Only a and b are reasons.
        ANSWER: d   TYPE: M   COG: R
73. Which of the following are social needs met by communication?
    a. helping others and being helped
    b. having fun
    c. giving and receiving affection
    d. all of the above
    e. a and c only
        ANSWER: d   TYPE: M   COG: R

77. Communication is defined as
    a. continuous and transactional
    b. having overlapped environments
    c. simultaneously sending and receiving messages
    d. distorted by physical and psychological noise
    e. all of the above
        ANSWER: e   TYPE: M   COG: R

78. Interpersonal communication can be distinguished from impersonal communication based on qualities of:
    a. uniqueness
    b. interdependence
    c. intrinsic rewards
    d. all of the above
    e. a and b only
        ANSWER: d   TYPE: M   COG: R

79. A study conducted by Patrick O'Sullivan revealed that undergraduates would prefer to use e-mail to send which type of message?
    a. complicated
    b. positive
    c. negative
    d. valuable
    e. none of the above
        ANSWER: c   TYPE: M   COG: R

80. The definition of what kind of communication is appropriate
    a. is very similar in all cultures
    b. varies slightly between cultures
    c. varies considerably between cultures
    d. is irrelevant in different cultures
    e. none of the above
        ANSWER: b   TYPE: M   COG: R

81. Which of the following is true about overly casual e-mails from students to professors?
    a. Professors are less likely to fulfill the requests in overly casual e-mails
    b. Professors were especially bothered by e-mails that were not signed
    c. Professors were especially bothered by short cuts like "BTW" instead of "by the way"
    d. Students received a lower assessment by their professors when they wrote highly casual e-mails
    e. All of the above
        ANSWER: e   TYPE: M   COG: R

82. Communication is more effective when communicators
    a. are different
    b. vary
    c. are identical
    d. adapt
    e. none of the above
        ANSWER: d   TYPE: M   COG: R

83. Which of the following human needs that Maslow identified is connected to communication?
    a. safety
    b. social
    c. self-esteem
    d. self-actualization
    e. all of the above
        ANSWER: e   TYPE: M   COG: R

84. One study showed that high self-monitors often experience
    a. less intimacy in their romantic relationships
    b. less satisfaction in their romantic relationships
    c. less commitment in their romantic relationships
    d. all of the above
    e. none of the above
        ANSWER: d   TYPE: M   COG: R
85. Sarah and Jim are driving to a friend's house. She is about to suggest a different route when she stops herself because she knows Jim hates it when she "takes over" while he's driving. This is an example of which communication concept?
    a. self-monitoring
    b. cognitive complexity
    c. communication is unrepeatable
    d. messages
    e. none of the above
        ANSWER: a   TYPE: M   COG: A

Essay

86. Your text claims that "We all need to communicate." Explain that claim, and give two examples of what needs communication can fulfill.
        ANSWER: TYPE: E   COG: A
87. You book claims that the nature of transactional communication is rather like dancing with partners. Explain what this statement means. Explain why this is true.
        ANSWER: TYPE: E   COG: A
88. Discuss the content and relational dimensions of the statement "I'm glad you're here." How might your interpretation differ if the two individuals were siblings? Lovers? Working partners? Enemies?
        ANSWER: TYPE: E   COG: A
89. Discuss how the quality of parent–child interaction is a transactional process.
        ANSWER: TYPE: E   COG: A
90. Using specific examples that one might find in a teacher/student/classroom setting discuss the idea that communication can be intentional or unintentional.
        ANSWER: TYPE: E   COG: A
91. Explain how social rituals we engage in reflect the idea that not all communication seeks understanding.
        ANSWER: TYPE: E   COG: C
92. Consider a recent exchange you experienced or observed (coworkers, teacher-student, family members or friends) and provide examples for each of the following elements of a communication model:
    a. one person in the dyad's personal environment and the other person's environment
    b. channels
    c. physical noise
    d. psychological noise
        ANSWER: TYPE: E   COG: A
93. According to the qualitative definition of communication, it is neither possible nor desirable to communicate interpersonally all the time. Consider the following relationships:
    a. a newly married couple
    b. a couple celebrating 25 years of marriage
    c. siblings
    d. friends
    e. student/teacher
    How do you think their communication is reflected on the interpersonal/impersonal continuum?
        ANSWER: TYPE: E   COG: A

94. Using specific examples show how your communication throughout a typical day fulfills each of the needs discussed in your text.

      ANSWER: TYPE: E   COG: A

95. Using the characteristics of competent communication and specific examples evaluate your own communication. In what areas do you demonstrate competence? What areas do you need to work on?

      ANSWER: TYPE: E   COG: A

96. Choose a current relationship and explain how it is qualitative by using the features that distinguish qualitatively interpersonal communication from less personal exchanges.

      ANSWER: TYPE: E   COG: A

97. Discuss the difference between effective communication and appropriate communication as they relate to communication competence.

      ANSWER: TYPE: E   COG: A

Matching

98. Match the five human needs that Abraham Maslow identifies, below, with the statements illustrating them:

      1. "to develop happy relationships with partners"
      2. "to become the most complete person I can be"
      3. "to have sufficient air, water, and food to survive"
      4. "to protect myself from real or perceived threats"
      5. "to believe that I have value as a person"

      a. physical
      b. safety
      c. social
      d. self-esteem
      e. self-actualization

      ANSWER: c, e, a, b, d TYPE: K   COG: A

99. March the letter of the term that best identifies each of the numbered situations. Be sure to clarify the terms before you begin, and pay particular attention to underlined words and phrases. Identify which principle influences the self-concept in each example.

a. cognitive conservatism
b. reflected appraisal
c. distorted feedback
d. significant other

e. social comparison
f. "facework"
g. self-fulfilling prophecy

_____ 1. *Your father has always told you* that you *have* mechanical abilities. The first time you try to fix your bike, *you fail* miserably.

_____ 2. You always scored more points than anyone else on your team *in high school*. You *still* think you're the best, even though your college teammates *outscore you* in every game.

_____ 3. Even though Jim is six feet tall, he describes himself as "a shrimp" when he is with his friends who are members of the Milwaukee Bucks.

_____ 4. Kerby knows that his usual use of grammar is often incorrect and sloppy. At his boss's party, he carefully monitors himself so that he *appears educated and intelligent.*

_____ 5. Because Peggy's parents and teachers have always encouraged her in her undertakings, *Peggy sees herself* as a worthwhile human being.

_____ 6. Sheila is doing average work in college, but she likes to hang around with her friends who are working in a factory because it makes her feel smart.

_____ 7. *Your parents tell you*, their friends, and all your relatives about all your wonderful accomplishments, *even though you have only average achievements.*

_____ 8. You anticipate that the party on Saturday night will be boring; when you go, you have a terrible time.

_____ 9. Although Jerry is late for his job interview because he took a wrong turn on the way, he tries to preserve his image by commenting on the long train he also encountered.

_____ 10. High school senior Kim really admires *her English teacher, Ms Rudolph.* When *Ms. Rudolph* suggests that Kim consider a career in education, Kim pays special attention to her.

_____ 11. Even though he doesn't know *his fiancée Amy's* parents well, jasper listens carefully to their advice.

_____ 12. Your father has always *told you that you have above-average mechanical abilities.* The first time you try to fix your bike, *you succeed easily.*

_____ 13. Ever since the third grade, when Erin's teacher told her that she war poor at art, Erin *has believed* that she is not artistic.

_____ 14. Because of your preparation and positive attitude, you feel assured of success at your job interview; you get the job.

_____ 15. You still think of yourself as a shy fifth grader despite being at the hub of social activity in at least three clubs on your college campus.

ANSWER KEY:
1. c	6. e	11. d
2. a	7. c	12. g
3. e	8. g	13. b
4. f	9. f	14. g
5. b	10. d	15. a

CHAPTER 2: CULTURE AND COMMUNICATION

True/False

1. Marshall McLuhan's "global village" metaphor suggests that the world's cultures are becoming increasingly disconnected and independent.
    ANSWER: F   TYPE: T   COG: R
2. Culture is, to a great extent, a matter of perception and definition.
    ANSWER: T   TYPE: T   COG: C
3. Jews, soccer mom, homosexuals, and Baby Boomers would all be examples of co-cultures.
    ANSWER: T   TYPE: T   COG: C
4. "Out-groups" are groups we perceive to be different from ourselves.
    ANSWER: T   TYPE: T   COG: R
5. High-context cultures rely more on nonverbal cues than do low-context cultures.
    ANSWER: T   TYPE: T   COG: R
6. Mainstream North American culture tends to be more low context than high context.
    ANSWER: T   TYPE: T   COG: R
7. Interculturalness means that a student moving to a different state would have the same "culture shock" as an international traveler visiting the United States.
    ANSWER: F   TYPE: T   COG: C
8. Social scientists use the term "salience" to describe how much weight we attach to a particular person or phenomenon.
    ANSWER: T   TYPE: T   COG: R
9. Leets's research on racist messages found that the kinds of messages that are most harmful are relatively the same from culture to culture.
    ANSWER: F   TYPE: T   COG: R
10. Autonomy, change, and initiative are associated with individualistic cultures.
    ANSWER: T   TYPE: T   COG: R
11. Gudykunst and Kim's research suggests that intercultural factors weigh more heavily than interpersonal factors in business and personal interactions.
    ANSWER: F   TYPE: T   COG: C
12. Care for extended family before self is typical of collectivist cultures.
    ANSWER: T   TYPE: T   COG: R
13. "Power distance" describes the degree to which members of a society accept the unequal distribution of power among members.
    ANSWER: T   TYPE: T   COG: R
14. Cultures with high power difference believe in minimizing the difference between various social classes.
    ANSWER: F   TYPE: T   COG: R
15. Challenging authority is acceptable in cultures that endorse low power distance.
    ANSWER: T   TYPE: T   COG: R
16. People in India tend to use more emoticons in their e-mails because of their low-context tendencies.
    ANSWER: T   TYPE: T   COG: C
17. In countries that avoid uncertainty, deviant people and ideas are considered dangerous and intolerance is high.
    ANSWER: T   TYPE: T   COG: C
18. Nurturing societies emphasize cooperation and show little difference between the expected behaviors for men and for women.
    ANSWER: T   TYPE: T   COG: R
19. When offering identification information, one's personal name will be given before one's family name in every culture.
    ANSWER: F   TYPE: T   COG: C

20. Hyperpersonal communication means that we typically withhold information from others online.
    ANSWER: F   TYPE: T   COG: C
21. Edward Hall found that people in the Middle East stand much closer when conducting business than Americans do.
    ANSWER: T   TYPE: T   COG: R
22. Online communicators can create idealized and unrealistic views of others.
    ANSWER: T   TYPE: T   COG: R
23. The way members of a culture are taught to think and reason shapes the way they interpret others' messages.
    ANSWER: T   TYPE: T   COG: R
24. When you text with a friend, you cannot see their facial expressions, or hear their nonverbal tones. Social scientists call this "richness."
    ANSWER: T   TYPE: T   COG: R
25. Tolerance for ambiguity is a characteristic of intercultural competence.
    ANSWER: T   TYPE: T   COG: R
26. Ethnocentrism is the attitude that one's culture is superior to others.
    ANSWER: T   TYPE: T   COG: R
27. The way members of a culture are taught to think and reason has little to do with how messages are interpreted.
    ANSWER: F   TYPE: T   COG: C
28. Samovar and Porter suggest that attitude and motivation are more "culture general," whereas knowledge and skill are more "culture specific."
    ANSWER: T   TYPE: T   COG: R
29. A chat conducted via e-mail or on the Internet exercises a high level of control over the receiver's attention.
    ANSWER: F   TYPE: T   COG: R
30. Posting to a discussion forum in an online environment is considered asynchronous communication.
    ANSWER: T   TYPE: T   COG: C
31. The permanence of digital messages has only negative consequences.
    ANSWER: F   TYPE: T   COG: C
32. Research regarding the impact of online relationships on face-to-face interactions is mixed with both "cyberpessimists" and studies that support positive effects on relationships.
    ANSWER: T   TYPE: T   COG: C
33. Instant messaging has high effectiveness for detailed messages.
    ANSWER: F   TYPE: T   COG: C
34. Voicemail has high effectiveness for detailed messages.
    ANSWER: F   TYPE: T   COG: C
35. An impulsive message or post on social media can haunt you for a lifetime, also known as "disinhibition."
    ANSWER: T   TYPE: T   COG: C
36. When you are at a restaurant with a friend and continuously check your phone for messages, some people are insulted when you divide your attention between technology and your face-to-face interactions.
    ANSWER: T   TYPE: T   COG: C
37. Derogatory texts, e-mail messages, or blog posts are known as "firing."
    ANSWER: F   TYPE: T   COG: C
38. If a person finds that their time on social media is subtracting from their interpersonal relationships, they may want to re-evaluate their time spent on mediated communication.
    ANSWER: T   TYPE: T   COG: C
39. The fastest growth in social networking has come from users 74 and older.
    ANSWER: T   TYPE: T   COG: R

Multiple Choice

40. Marshall McLuhan's "global village" metaphor suggests:
    a.   members of every nation are connected by communication technology
    b.   members of certain villages are connected by communication technology
    c.   members of countries with reliable Internet access share information to create a village
    d.   none of the above
          ANSWER: a   TYPE: M   COG: C

41. Teenagers may see the elderly as a(n):
    a.   co-culture
    b.   in-group
    c.   low context
    d.   out-group
    e.   none of the above
          ANSWER: d   TYPE: M   COG: A

42. Gangs fit the definition of a co-culture because they:
    a.   have a well defined identity
    b.   achieve a sense of belonging
    c.   use distinctive language
    d.   use distinctive nonverbal markers
    e.   all of the above
          ANSWER: e   TYPE: M   COG: C

43. In North American culture categories such as age, ethnicity, race, gender, sexual orientation, physical disabilities and religion are all considered
    a.   anticultures
    b.   focus groups
    c.   co-cultures
    d.   inner groups
    e.   none of the above
          ANSWER: c   TYPE: M   COG: A

44. Rather than classifying some exchanges as intercultural and others as free from cultural influences, it's more accurate to talk about
    a.   degrees of cultural significance
    b.   high and low context
    c.   power distance
    d.   co-cultures
    e.   none of the above
          ANSWER: a   TYPE: M   COG: C

45. Low-context cultures tend to value and emphasize
    a.   straight talk and assertiveness
    b.   face-saving and social harmony
    c.   nonverbal cues
    d.   all of the above
    e.   none of the above
          ANSWER: a   TYPE: M   COG: R

46. High-context cultures tend to:
    a.   value and emphasize subtle, often nonverbal cues to maintain social harmony
    b.   value straight talk and assertiveness
    c.   value verbal cues
    d.   all of the above
    e.   none of the above
          ANSWER: a   TYPE: M   COG: R

47. When an Israeli views an Arab as being evasive while the Arab views the Israeli as overly blunt, they are encountering value differences primarily associated with
    a. high vs. low context
    b. individualism vs. collectivism
    c. power distance
    d. uncertainty avoidance
    e. achievement vs. nurturing
    ANSWER: a   TYPE: M   COG: A
48. When a North American answers the question "Who am I?" by citing individual factors while an Asian person answers the same question by identifying groups in which she/he is a member, they are expressing value differences associated with
    a. high vs. low context
    b. individualism vs. collectivism
    c. power distance
    d. uncertainty avoidance
    e. achievement vs. nurturing
    ANSWER: b   TYPE: M   COG: R
49. When Austrian students are praised for asking their teachers questions while Filipino students see questioning their teachers as inappropriate, they are exhibiting values associated with which concept?
    a. high vs. low context
    b. individualism vs. collectivism
    c. power distance
    d. uncertainty avoidance
    e. achievement vs. nurturing
    ANSWER: c   TYPE: M   COG: A
50. The degree to which members of a culture feel threatened by ambiguous situations and try to stay away from them is known as
    a. power distance
    b. uncertainty avoidance
    c. cultural perception
    d. all of the above
    e. none of the above
    ANSWER: b   TYPE: M   COG: R
51. A "hard" culture is a culture that values
    a. achievement
    b. collectivism
    c. low power distance
    d. nurturing
    e. high power distance
    ANSWER: a   TYPE: M   COG: R
52. When a German believes men should be "hard" and women should be "soft" while a Spaniard believes there is little difference between expected behaviors for men and women, they are experiencing value differences associated with
    a. high vs. low context
    b. individualism vs. collectivism
    c. power distance
    d. uncertainty avoidance
    e. achievement vs. nurturing
    ANSWER: e   TYPE: M   COG: A

53. The Korean language has separate terms for older brother, oldest brother, younger sister, youngest sister, and so on. This is a reflection of:
   a. cultural perspective
   b. power distance
   c. uncertainty avoidance
   d. individualism vs. collectivism
   e. none of the above
      ANSWER: b   TYPE: M   COG: C

54. Which of the following contrasting pairs is associated with features of verbal communication styles?
   a. directness/indirectness
   b. elaborate/succinct
   c. formal/informal
   d. all of the above
   e. none of the above
      ANSWER: d   TYPE: M   COG: R

55. Cultural differences in decoding messages occur because of differences in
   a. translation
   b. attributional variations
   c. patterns of thought
   d. all of the above
   e. none of the above
      ANSWER: d   TYPE: M   COG: R

56. Collectivist cultures, in comparison to individualist cultures, tend to
   a. see the world in terms of either/or dichotomies
   b. define themselves as part of a group
   c. define themselves in terms of what they do
   d. tolerate conflict easily
   e. none of the above
      ANSWER: b   TYPE: M   COG: R

57. Most scholars believe intercultural competence requires
   a. motivation and attitude
   b. knowledge
   c. skill
   d. all of the above
   e. none of the above
      ANSWER: d   TYPE: M   COG: R

58. Patiently dealing with the uncertainty that surrounds most intercultural encounters is a sign of
   a. tolerance for ambiguity
   b. intercultural competence
   c. ethnocentrism
   d. a and b
   e. all of the above
      ANSWER: d   TYPE: M   COG: R

59. Which of the following is *not* associated with intercultural competence?
   a. tolerance for ambiguity
   b. open-mindedness
   c. interaction management
   d. display of respect
   e. stereotyping
      ANSWER: e   TYPE: M   COG: R

60. The ideas that all women are emotional and that all older people are out of touch with reality are examples of
   a. patterns of thought
   b. open-mindedness
   c. stereotypes
   d. power distance
   e. none of the above
      ANSWER: c TYPE: M COG: A

61. Technological changes have given us new options for communicating personally. What is the term used in your textbook to identify technologically enhanced communication?
   a. communication competence
   b. metacommunication
   c. computer-mediated communication (CMC)
   d. e-mail
   e. none of the above
      ANSWER: c TYPE: M COG: R

62. Research conducted by Patrick O'Sullivan to learn about preferences for face-to-face versus mediated channels for sending messages concluded that
   a. face-to-face is always better than mediated channels
   b. negative messages should be sent face-to-face
   c. positive messages should be sent using mediated channels
   d. mediated channels are appealing for sending negative messages
   e. channels people choose for sending messages don't contribute to communication competence
      ANSWER: d TYPE: M COG: R

63. If a group of preschool children play in a park and do not notice that their parents come from different countries or that they speak different languages, they are experiencing:
   a. intercultural communication
   b. minimal salience on culture
   c. interpersonal communication
   d. cultural identity
   e. high salience on culture
      ANSWER: b TYPE: M COG: A

64. Residents of countries with continuous wartime activity experience a high degree of:
   a. intercultural communication
   b. power distance
   c. low-context exchanges
   d. nurturing cultures
   e. uncertainty avoidance
      ANSWER: e TYPE: M COG: A

65. Your new friend Nguyen feels uncomfortable responding to a professor's question in class. He says that in his culture, this is not appropriate. Nguyen is describing:
   a. uncertainty avoidance
   b. high power distance
   c. low power distance
   d. high context
   e. low context
      ANSWER: b TYPE: M COG: A

66. You want to learn more about your new friend Shira's clothing, particularly her hijab (head covering). According to Berger, what strategy would be the most risky?
    a. passive observation
    b. asking an expert
    c. watching a film about Muslim women
    d. confessing cultural ignorance
    e. reading about the clothing of Muslim people
        ANSWER: d   TYPE: M   COG: A

67. Workers in factories of _____ cultures do not expect to be consulted over managerial decisions.
    a. high-context
    b. low-context
    c. achieving
    d. nurturing
    e. none of the above
        ANSWER: a   TYPE: M   COG: C

68. When asked to identify themselves, what cultures are most likely to give their first name, surname, street, town and country?
    a. American
    b. Canadian
    c. Australian
    d. European
    e. All of the above
        ANSWER: e   TYPE: M   COG: C

69. An important element of _____ is stereotyping.
    a. high-context culture
    b. prejudice
    c. intercultural incompetence
    d. power distance
    e. uncertainty avoidance
        ANSWER: e   TYPE: M   COG: R

70. In a _____ culture, elders remain in the family home and are highly valued and respected for their position, wisdom, and age.
    a. high power distance
    b. individualistic
    c. achieving
    d. collective
    e. social
        ANSWER: d   TYPE: M   COG: A

71. _____ makes all channels of remote personal communication possible.
    a. The Internet
    b. Texting
    c. Social media
    d. E-mail
    e. None of the above
        ANSWER: c   TYPE: M   COG: A

72. Your friend sent you an instant message on Facebook and said, "No, I'm not going to the party." You couldn't tell if she was angry. Social scientists would say this is due to the message lacking
_____.
    a.   richness
    b.   clarification
    c.   an exclamation mark
    d.   an emoticon
    e.   more sentences
       ANSWER: a   TYPE: M   COG: A

73. Contributing to a Wiki or blog occurs as _____ communication.
    a.   synchronous
    b.   asynchronous
    c.   mediated
    d.   technological
    e.   all of the above
       ANSWER: a   TYPE: M   COG: A

74. Research that supports online communication as being positive for relationships cites:
    a.   Couples who talk frequently via cell phone feel more loving and committed.
    b.   Sixty percent of American teenagers believe the Internet helps them make new friends.
    c.   People who have both in-person and online contact with friends are less lonely.
    d.   Partners in long-distance relationships who communicate via social media feel greater intimacy and higher levels of trust.
    e.   All of the above
       ANSWER: e   TYPE: M   COG: C

75. You need to talk to your boss about a change in schedule. You want to gauge your boss's response to your request as she is listening to your words. What modes of communication would likely work best?
    a.   voice mail
    b.   face-to-face conversation
    c.   e-mail
    d.   text messaging
    e.   a and b only
       ANSWER: e   TYPE: M   COG: A

76. You need a quick answer from your father about a type of beef he asked you to pick up from the store. A quick exchange of this type could benefit from:
    a.   Twitter
    b.   text messaging
    c.   face-to-face conversation
    d.   voice mail
    e.   e-mail
       ANSWER: b   TYPE: M   COG: A

77. "Netiquette" components include:
    a.   respecting others' need for undivided attention
    b.   keeping your tone civil
    c.   being mindful of bystanders
    d.   balancing mediated and face time with others
    e.   all of the above
       ANSWER: e   TYPE: M   COG: R

78. Japanese insurance companies warn their policyholders who are visiting the United States to avoid their cultural tendency to say "Excuse me" or "I'm sorry" if they are involved in a traffic accident, because of cultural differences in

a. translation
b. attributional variations
c. patterns of thought
d. reflections of power distance
e. none of the above
ANSWER: a   TYPE: M   COG: A

Essay

79. Describe, using terms from the text, some difficulties that might occur in a business meeting with participants from the United States, Japan, and Saudi Arabia.
    ANSWER: TYPE: E   COG: A

80. Explain how Gudykunst and Kim's two-by-two matrix reflects the relationship between interpersonal communication and cultural significance.
    ANSWER: TYPE: E   COG: C

81. Explain the primary cultural influences that affect interpersonal communication. Include in your discussion the following:
a. high versus low contexts
b. individualism versus collectivism
c. power distance
d. uncertainty avoidance
e. achievement versus nurturing
    ANSWER: TYPE: E   COG: A

82. Explain how a person's cultural tendency toward uncertainty avoidance could impact their tolerance for ambiguity.
    ANSWER: TYPE: E   COG: C

83. Identify three specific challenges faced by communicators when using different verbal and nonverbal communication systems.
    ANSWER: TYPE: E   COG: C

84. How might interpersonal conflict be viewed differently by high-context vs. low-context cultures?
    ANSWER: TYPE: E   COG: A

85. Explain how the concepts *shy* and *assertive* may be seen differently in individualistic cultures and collectivistic cultures.
    ANSWER: TYPE: E   COG: A

86. Explain why multinational companies need to consider fundamental differences in power distance when they set up shop in a new country.
    ANSWER: TYPE: E   COG: C

87. Explain how a country's need for uncertainty avoidance might affect innovation vs. imitation of products and ideas.
    ANSWER: TYPE: E   COG: C

88. What is the role of perception in intercultural communication?
    ANSWER: TYPE: E   COG: A

89. How does someone develop intercultural communication competence?
    ANSWER: TYPE: E   COG: A

90. Explain how translation, attributional variations, and patterns of thought make the decoding of messages especially difficult for communicators from different cultures.
    ANSWER: TYPE: E   COG: A

91. What are some of the challenges facing communicators who belong to co-cultures within a dominant culture?
    ANSWER: TYPE: E   COG: A

92. Explain how the classroom atmosphere might be different given the following cultural influences:
a. high vs. low context

    b. power distance

    c. individualism vs. collectivism

        ANSWER: TYPE: E   COG: C

93. Compare and contrast a message that could be stated face-to-face and one sent via social media channels that could be distorted due to lack of richness.

        ANSWER: TYPE: E   COG: C

94. Explain a time that someone text messaged you when a communication mode with more richness would have created a more seamless interaction.

        ANSWER: TYPE: E   COG: A

95. Describe three potential ramifications of failing to scrutinize the content that you post on social media outlets.

        ANSWER: TYPE: E   COG: R

96. Your professor includes a "netiquette" statement in his/her syllabus. Discuss how "disinhibition" and "flaming" would relate to this policy.

        ANSWER: TYPE: E   COG: C

97. Your friend Selwynn is planning a trip to Germany. Selwynn has mastered textbook German but is concerned about intercultural communication competence. What *specific strategies* would you provide Selwynn to improve the three dimensions of intercultural communicative competence before the trip to Germany?

        ANSWER: TYPE: E   COG: A

Matching

98. Match the cultural values and norms with their definition.

    _____ a.   High vs. Low Context

    _____ b.   Individualism vs. Collectivism

    _____ c.   Power Distance

    _____ d.   Uncertainty Avoidance

    _____ e.   Achievement vs. Nurturing

1. The degree to which a culture views their primary responsibility as themselves or their group.
2. The degree to which societies place value on material success vs. support of relationships.
3. The degree to which people feel threatened by ambiguous situations.
4. The degree to which a culture values direct verbal communication or subtle, often nonverbal communication.
5. The degree to which members of a society accept an unequal distribution of power.

        ANSWER: a. 4; b. 1; c. 5; d. 3; e. 2   TYPE: K   COG: R

99. Match the letter of the term that best identifies each of the numbered situations. Begin by clarifying the terms as they have been defined in your text

a. collectivism
b. co-culture
c. ethnocentrism
d. high-context culture
e. high-power structure
f. individualism
g. intercultural communication

h. in-group
i. out-group
j. low-context culture
k. low-power structure
l. stereotyping
m. uncertainty avoidance

_____ 1. James, a British citizen, believes it is important for him to achieve on his own—and to be recognized for his accomplishments.

_____ 2. All the boys in the neighborhood formed a club for "boys only."

_____ 3. Leonard, a gay male, recognized that he and other gays have certain unique problems.

_____ 4. Jason is proud of being a U.S. citizen because he considers his own culture superior to others in the world.

_____ 5. When Young Sun, a Japanese executive, continually proposes to take care of an issue "later," his subordinates understand that he is really denying their request.

_____ 6. Young Sun is especially proud of an award that names his unit of the company "Outstanding Division of the Year."

_____ 7. Sylvia feels left out because all the other interns go out after work and she is never invited.

_____ 8. Pamela Sils is especially proud of an award that names her "Executive of the Year."

_____ 9. Father Brady and Rabbi Silbert enjoy their friendly discussions about their different religious perspectives.

_____ 10. Jennie, a high school senior, feels comfortable challenging her teachers in class.

_____ 11. The sales representatives for the biotech company felt their company was much better than others, and hence they didn't want to associate with other sales representatives at the conference.

_____ 12. Lana chooses not to travel to foreign countries because she is wary of new environments and customs.

_____ 13. Kim is given special respect in his family because he is the oldest brother.

_____ 14. Max, Frances, Louie, Enid, and Muriel, all octogenarians, enjoy their weekly card sessions at the Senior Center.

_____ 15. Because Amy is Chinese, the music teacher expected her to choose to play the violin.

ANSWER KEY:

1. f	6. a	11. h
2. h	7. j	12. m
3. b	8. f	13. e
4. c	9. g	14. b
5. d	10. k	15. l

CHAPTER 3: COMMUNICATION AND THE SELF

True/False

1. Positive self-esteem guarantees interpersonal success.
     ANSWER: F   TYPE: T   COG: R
2. Self-concept is a largely changeable set of perceptions you hold of yourself.
     ANSWER: F   TYPE: T   COG: R
3. At about six or seven months of age, a child begins to recognize "self" as distinct from surroundings.
     ANSWER: T   TYPE: T   COG: C
4. Very early in life, self-concept is almost exclusively physical.
     ANSWER: T   TYPE: T   COG: C
5. In reflected appraisal, messages received from significant others are particularly powerful.
     ANSWER: T   TYPE: T   COG: C
6. Self-esteem has a powerful effect on communication behavior.
     ANSWER: T   TYPE: T   COG: C
7. Men who compare themselves to media-idealized male physiques evaluate their bodies negatively.
     ANSWER: T   TYPE: T   COG: R
8. The significance we attach to the features of the self is unrelated to the opinions of others.
     ANSWER: F   TYPE: T   COG: C
9. People seldom look at others as a way of judging themselves.
     ANSWER: F   TYPE: T   COG: C
10. Social comparison offers a way of reshaping unsatisfying self-concepts, in that we control who is available for comparison.
     ANSWER: T   TYPE: T   COG: R
11. The way we view ourselves is usually identical with others' perception of us.
     ANSWER: F   TYPE: T   COG: C
12. The tendency to resist revision of our self-perception is strong.
     ANSWER: T   TYPE: T   COG: R
13. Research shows that people are more critical of themselves when they are in a positive mood than when they are in a negative mood.
     ANSWER: F   TYPE: T   COG: C
14. The tendency to seek information that conforms to an existing self-concept has been labeled *cognitive conservatism*.
     ANSWER: T   TYPE: T   COG: R
15. Unfortunately, self-concepts are fixed and not subject to change.
     ANSWER: F   TYPE: T   COG: C
16. The self-concept can actually affect the future behavior of others.
     ANSWER: T   TYPE: T   COG: C
17. The reference groups against which we compare ourselves play an important role in shaping our view of ourselves.
     ANSWER: T   TYPE: T   COG: R
18. Research shows that people with low self-esteem are inclined to seek out people who view them favorably.
     ANSWER: F   TYPE: T   COG: C
19. Communicators who believe they are incompetent are more likely than others to pursue rewarding relationships.
     ANSWER: F   TYPE: T   COG: C
20. Specific influential individuals are the single source of self-concept information.
     ANSWER: F   TYPE: T   COG: C
21. While children may be born with some social characteristics, self-concept is almost totally determined by social interaction.
     ANSWER: T   TYPE: T   COG: R

22. Growing up in an overly critical family is one of the most common causes of a negative self-image.
    ANSWER: T   TYPE: T   COG: C
23. One reason for negative evaluation of self is that our culture subscribes to the myth of perfection.
    ANSWER: T   TYPE: T   COG: C
24. People often cling to outmoded and unrealistic self-concepts, even when the new image would be more favorable than the old one.
    ANSWER: T   TYPE: T   COG: C
25. Self-fulfilling prophecies occur when strong expectations make the expected outcome more likely than it otherwise would have been.
    ANSWER: T   TYPE: T   COG: R
26. Research has shown that there are situations where people misrepresent themselves to gain the trust of others.
    ANSWER: T   TYPE: T   COG: R
27. To connect the concept of self-fulfilling prophecy with "the power of positive thinking" is an oversimplification.
    ANSWER: T   TYPE: T   COG: R
28. Once the self is firmly rooted, only a powerful force can change it.
    ANSWER: T   TYPE: T   COG: R
29. Self-concept must change in order to stay realistic.
    ANSWER: T   TYPE: T   COG: R
30. A significant other is someone who has given us primarily positive reinforcement.
    ANSWER: F   TYPE: T   COG: R
31. The term *face* is used by social scientists to describe the presenting self.
    ANSWER: T   TYPE: T   COG: R
32. Each of us possesses several selves, not merely one self.
    ANSWER: T   TYPE: T   COG: R
33. People are likely to reveal all of their perceived self to others.
    ANSWER: F   TYPE: T   COG: R
34. People rarely manage impressions to accomplish personal goals.
    ANSWER: F   TYPE: T   COG: C
35. The decision to be spontaneous can be a form of impression management.
    ANSWER: T   TYPE: T   COG: R
36. Face management is something that is necessary only in actual face-to-face encounters.
    ANSWER: F   TYPE: T   COG: R
37. Identity management is not as pervasive in computer-mediated communication as it is in face-to-face interaction.
    ANSWER: F   TYPE: T   COG: C
38. True self-disclosure has to be honest.
    ANSWER: T   TYPE: T   COG: R
39. The self-disclosure nature of a statement can come from the context in which it is shared.
    ANSWER: T   TYPE: T   COG: R
40. John Suler's research indicates that changing age, history, personality, and even gender are all ways people manage their identities in cyberspace.
    ANSWER: T   TYPE: T   COG: R

Multiple choice

41. The view that self-concept can be seen as a product of the messages you've received throughout your life is known as
    a. reflected appraisal
    b. social comparison
    c. multidimensional self
    d. subjective self-concept
    e. self-fulfilling prophecy
    ANSWER: a   TYPE: M   COG: R

42. Which of the following is supported by research related to how the self-concept develops?
    a. Self-concept does not exist at birth.
    b. Self-concept is almost totally a product of social interaction.
    c. Children recognize "self" as distinct from surroundings at about age 6 or 7 months.
    d. All of the above are supported.
    e. None of the above are supported.
    ANSWER: d   TYPE: M   COG: R

43. For a reflected appraisal to be regarded as important it must be
    a. from a competent source
    b. perceived as highly personal
    c. reasonable in light of what we believe about ourselves
    d. consistent and repeated
    e. all of the above
    ANSWER: e   TYPE: M   COG: C

44. Which of the following is *not* a characteristic of self-concept?
    a. denotative
    b. multidimensional
    c. subjective
    d. flexible
    e. resists change
    ANSWER: a   TYPE: M   COG: R

45. The communication strategies people use to influence how others view them is called
    a. cognitive conservatism
    b. impression management
    c. reflected appraisal
    d. self-concept
    e. social comparison
    ANSWER: b   TYPE: M   COG: R

46. Compared to low self-monitors, people who are high self-monitors
    a. have a more simple, focused idea of who they are
    b. can easily identify their true feelings
    c. are typified by the phrase "What you see is what you get"
    d. are good "people readers"
    e. have a narrow repertoire of behaviors
    ANSWER: d   TYPE: M   COG: C

47. When some professional athletes doggedly insist they can be of value to the team when past their prime, they are displaying which characteristic of self-concept?
    a. multidimensional
    b. subjective
    c. flexible
    d. resists change
    e. none of the above
    ANSWER: d   TYPE: M   COG: A

48. Rosenthal and Jacobson's report that a change in teachers' expectations of randomly selected "special" children led to an actual change in their intellectual performance most nearly illustrates
   a. changing self-concept
   b. characteristics of self-concept
   c. self-fulfilling prophecy
   d. social comparison
   e. psychological vultures
      ANSWER: c   TYPE: M   COG: A
49. If you ever gave a speech and forgot your remarks, not because you were unprepared but because you were afraid, saying "I know I'll blow it," you experienced
   a. changing self-concept
   b. characteristics of self-concept
   c. self-fulfilling prophecy
   d. social comparison
   e. feedback
      ANSWER: c   TYPE: M   COG: A
50. You can change your self-concept by having
   a. realistic expectations
   b. a realistic perception of yourself
   c. the will to change
   d. the skill to change
   e. all of the above
      ANSWER: e   TYPE: M   COG: R
51. The communication strategies people use to influence how others view them is called
   a. public self strategies
   b. social comparison strategies
   c. reflected appraisal strategies
   d. identity management strategies
   e. perceived self strategies
      ANSWER: d   TYPE: M   COG: R
52. Children with cruel "friends" suffer from
   a. bragging
   b. inaccurate feedback of others
   c. perfection
   d. multidimensional self-concept
   e. subjective self-concept
      ANSWER: b   TYPE: M   COG: C
53. Even though others disagree, Diandra thinks of herself as a tremendously effective communicator. She reinforces this image by surrounding herself with people who are very shy and socially naive. Diandra's unrealistic handling of this situation provides an example of
   a. the theory of significant others
   b. social comparison theory
   c. self-discipline theory
   d. similarity theory
   e. consistency appraisal theory
      ANSWER: b   TYPE: M   COG: A
54. Which of the following is (are) *not* characteristics of identity management?
   a. We strive to construct multiple identities.
   b. Identity management is collaborative.
   c. Identity management can be unconscious.
   d. People are equally aware of their identity management behaviors.
   e. Both c and d
      ANSWER: d   TYPE: M   COG: A

55. People manage impressions to
    a. follow social rules
    b. achieve relational goals
    c. accomplish personal goals
    d. All of the above are correct.
    e. Only a and c are correct.
        ANSWER: d   TYPE: M   COG: C
56. Which of the following has the power to be a self-fulfilling prophecy?
    a. astrological horoscopes
    b. placebos
    c. sex-linked stereotypes
    d. labels of shyness
    e. all of the above
        ANSWER: e   TYPE: M   COG: A
57. Which of the following is used in face-to-face interactions to manage impressions?
    a. words
    b. nonverbal actions
    c. personal items
    d. physical setting
    e. all of the above
        ANSWER: e   TYPE: M   COG: R
58. Two concepts that describe how interaction shapes the way individuals view themselves are
    a. comparison appraisal and social reflection
    b. reflected appraisal and social comparison
    c. social reflection and intrapersonal comparison
    d. self-esteem and self-concept
    e. reflected comparison and social appraisal
        ANSWER: b   TYPE: M   COG: R
59. Significant others are those people
    a. whose evaluations are especially influential to us
    b. who were a negative force in our lives
    c. whom we view as highly competent
    d. with whom we spend a great deal of time
    e. c and d
        ANSWER: a   TYPE: M   COG: R
60. Social comparison allows us to decide
    a. if we are superior or inferior to others
    b. if we are the same or different from others
    c. if we like or dislike others
    d. all of the above
    e. a and b only
        ANSWER: e   TYPE: M   COG: R
61. Seeking information that conforms to an existing self-concept is called
    a. presenting self
    b. reflected appraisal
    c. cognitive conservation
    d. self-fulfilling prophecy
    e. social comparison
        ANSWER: c   TYPE: M   COG: R

62. Which of the following is *not* true about identity management in computer-mediated communication (CMC)?
    a. Identity management is just as pervasive in CMC interactions.
    b. CMC allows a sender to say difficult things without forcing the receiver to respond immediately.
    c. CMC is not as effective for identity management as face-to-face communication.
    d. CMC can actually be an advantage for communicators who want to manage the impressions they make.
    e. CMC allows communicators to choose the desired level of clarity.
       ANSWER: c   TYPE: M   COG: R

63. The *Michelangelo phenomenon* describes
    a. how individuals resist negative feedback about themselves
    b. how we strive to construct multiple identities
    c. how we manage impressions
    d. how significant others sculpt one another's self-concept
    e. how the self-concept fulfills its own prophecy
       ANSWER: d   TYPE: M   COG: R

64. Even though he has a nice singing voice, Kevin still believes he is a terrible singer because his first grade teacher told him he couldn't sing well. This is an example of how _____ shapes our self-concept.
    a. reference groups
    b. reflected appraisal
    c. self-esteem
    d. social comparison
    e. none of the above
       ANSWER: b   TYPE: M   COG: A

65. Joe thinks he is smart compared to everyone else in his algebra class. This is an example of how _____ can define our self-concept.
    a. self-monitoring
    b. facework
    c. identity management
    d. cognitive conservatism
    e. reference groups
       ANSWER: e   TYPE:M   COG: A

66. Still thinking you are a good student even after failing classes for two years is an example of which reason for having a self-concept others would regard as unrealistically favorable?
    a. low self-esteem
    b. distorted feedback
    c. obsolete information
    d. a and c
    e. none of the above
       ANSWER: c   TYPE: M   COG: A

67. The fact that being ignored by an acquaintance hurts more than being ignored by someone familiar to us tells us that
    a. people are poor judges of their own communication skills
    b. the self-concept is objective
    c. family plays a strong role in shaping our identity
    d. who counts as a significant other isn't always obvious to us
    e. none of the above
       ANSWER: d   TYPE: M   COG: C

68. When studying the relationship between individuals' self-evaluation as communicators and their ability to perform those communication skills, researchers found that
   a. subjects accurately evaluated their performance
   b. subjects inaccurately judged their own abilities
   c. subjects predictions were inaccurately negative when they were in a good mood
   d. subjects succumbed to a self-fulfilling prophecy
   e. none of the above
      ANSWER: b   TYPE: M   COG: R

69. The Myth of Perfection describes
   a. how self-esteem is affected by societal models that are unrealistically perfect
   b. how our self-concept is formed based on distorted feedback
   c. how social comparison theory isn't perfect in nature
   d. how we used identity management to appear more perfect than we are
   e. how no one comes from a perfect family
      ANSWER: a   TYPE: M   COG: R

70. Seeing yourself as being "patient at work but not patient at home" demonstrates how
   a. cognitive conservatism works
   b. the self-concept does not resist change
   c. the self-concept is flexible
   d. the self-concept is objective
   e. all of the above
      ANSWER: c   TYPE: M   COG: A

71. The person you believe yourself to be in moments of honest examination is your
   a. intuitive self
   b. perceived self
   c. public self
   d. presenting self
   e. both c and d
      ANSWER: b   TYPE: M   COG: R

72. The term used to describe the verbal and nonverbal ways we act to maintain our own and others' presenting images is
   a. facework
   b. multiple identity construction
   c. self presentation
   d. identity performance
   e. self-esteem maintenance
      ANSWER: a   TYPE: M   COG: R

73. When we use items such as cars to influence how others see us, we are managing impressions by using
   a. setting
   b. manner
   c. appearance
   d. attitude
   e. b and c
      ANSWER: a   TYPE:M   COG: C

74. What is a reason(s) for excessively negative self-evaluation?
   a. obsolete information
   b. distorted feedback
   c. myth of perfection
   d. social expectations
   e. all of the above
      ANSWER: e   TYPE: M   COG: R

75. If one parent has a good self-concept and the other a poor self-concept the child is most likely to
   a. choose a parent with the good self-concept as the model
   b. choose the parent with the poor self-concept as the model
   c. have a self-concept somewhere between good and poor
   d. The parent's self-concept has no impact on the child
   e. none of the above
      ANSWER: a   TYPE: M   COG: R

76. A spouse who asks their partner if they did the right thing in disciplining their child by giving the child a time-out, in the hopes of getting their partner's approval, is demonstrating what benefit of self-disclosure?
   a. catharsis
   b. self-clarification
   c. self-validation
   d. reciprocity
   e. impression formation
      ANSWER: c   TYPE: M   COG: A

77. Which of the following is an equivocal reaction to this question: "How do you like this dress I just bought?"
   a. I don't like it at all.
   b. It's an interesting design.
   c. I love it!
   d. It doesn't fit you.
   e. None of the above.
      ANSWER: b   TYPE: M   COG: A

78. Which of the following is NOT an alternative to self-disclosure?
   a. silence
   b. lying
   c. equivocation
   d. hinting
   e. All of the above are alternative to self-disclosure.
      ANSWER: e   TYPE: M   COG: A

79. Since studies show that Chinese, Germans, Japanese, and Americans all manage identities differently in conflicts, we can deduce that facework is influenced by
   a. conflict
   b. self-esteem
   c. culture
   d. social comparison
   e. impression management
      ANSWER: c   TYPE: M   COG: C

Essay

80. Using terminology from the chapter, discuss the meaning and significance of the following line from Dorothy Nolte's *Children Learn What They Live:* "If a child lives with encouragement he learns confidence."
      ANSWER: TYPE: E   COG: A

81. How is it possible to change one's self-concept? In answering the question address the subjective, resistant nature of the self-concept.
      ANSWER: TYPE: E   COG: C

82. List three aspects of your self-concept. Then, for each of the three, list a reference group you would use.
      ANSWER: TYPE: E   COG: C

83. Discuss the relationship between these terms: *perceived self, presenting self, impression management, honesty,* and *communication competence.* Offer an example that illustrates the relationship in action.
        ANSWER: TYPE: E   COG: C

84. Explain how messages shape the self-concept by comparing and contrasting reflected appraisal and social comparison.
        ANSWER: TYPE: E   COG: A

85. Describe two specific strategies that can be used to improve your self-image.
        ANSWER: TYPE: E   COG: A

86. Explain the phenomenon called the *self-fulfilling prophecy.* Describe the two types of self-fulfilling prophecies (not positive and negative), and give an example of each.
        ANSWER: TYPE: E   COG: A

87. List and explain with examples the four requirements that must be met for an appraisal to be regarded as important.
        ANSWER: TYPE: E   COG: A

88. What are the primary influences that shape development of the self-concept?
        ANSWER: TYPE: E   COG: R

89. Compare and contrast identity management in face-to-face interaction with identity management in computer-mediated communication. Under which circumstances would you use one over the other?
        ANSWER: TYPE: E   COG: A

Matching

90. Match the following examples of responses to risky self-disclosure to their appropriate categories.

      _____1. Loss of Influence
      _____2. Loss of Control
      _____3. Hurt the Other Person
      _____4. Negative Impression
      _____5. Rejection

  a.   "Have you told Sylvia that? I think I should."
  b.   "You don't have a degree? Why was I listening to you?"
  c.   "I think we need to break up."
  d.   "You haven't saved a dime towards retirement? That's not good."
  e.   "It's sort of dumb that you ever thought that."

    Answer
  1. b
  2. a
  3. e
  4. d
  5. c
                             TYPE: K   COG: A

CHAPTER 4: PERCEIVING OTHERS

True/False

1. Research suggests that typical dyads can only interpret and explain 25 to 50 percent of each other's behavior accurately.
   ANSWER: T   TYPE: T   COG: R
2. If your mother gives you a kiss goodbye, this is considered a second-order reality.
   ANSWER: F   TYPE: T   COG: C
3. *Interpretation* is a term used by communication theorists to describe the determination of causes and effects in a series of interactions.
   ANSWER: F   TYPE: T   COG: R
4. The way a communication sequence is punctuated affects its perceived meaning.
   ANSWER: T   TYPE: T   COG: R
5. Age, health, fatigue, and hunger are all psychological factors that influence perceptual judgments.
   ANSWER: F   TYPE: T   COG: R
6. A person you have a crush on calls you "sweetheart" and you believe that they must have a crush on you, too. This is known as second-order reality.
   ANSWER: T   TYPE: T   COG: C
7. Sandra Bem's sex type research suggests that stereotypical masculine and feminine behaviors are opposite poles of a single continuum.
   ANSWER: F   TYPE: T   COG: C
8. People commonly imagine that others possess the same attitudes and motives that they do.
   ANSWER: T   TYPE: T   COG: C
9. A friend is talking to you, but another friend is standing nearby yelling on the phone. You pay attention to the friend on the pone due to "selection."
   ANSWER: T   TYPE: T   COG: C
10. *Attribution* is the term social scientists use to describe the process of attaching meaning to behavior.
    ANSWER: T   TYPE: T   COG: R
11. When others suffer, we often blame the problem on their personal qualities; when we're the victims, we find explanations outside ourselves.
    ANSWER: T   TYPE: T   COG: R
12. People who are "fixtures" in our lives become more noticeable to us due to attention.
    ANSWER: F   TYPE: T   COG: C
13. *Self-serving bias* is the term used by social scientists to label our tendency to judge ourselves in the most generous terms possible.
    ANSWER: T   TYPE: T   COG: R
14. Role constructs in the organization stage include social position.
    ANSWER: T   TYPE: T   COG: R
15. You are at a restaurant and the server seems to throw your food down. You figure she is lazy or doesn't like her job very much. this is an example of punctuation.
    ANSWER: T   TYPE: T   COG: A
16. Androgynous behaviors are solely the product of biological sexual differences.
    ANSWER: F   TYPE: T   COG: R
17. The perception process must occur in the same sequence of selection, organization, and interpretation.
    ANSWER: F   TYPE: T   COG: R
18. We cannot avoid making initial judgments, and we usually cling to these first impressions even if they are wrong.
    ANSWER: T   TYPE: T   COG: R
19. Gundykunst and Kim's research suggests that intercultural factors weigh more heavily than interpersonal factors in business and personal interactions.
    ANSWER: F   TYPE: T   COG: C

20. Research shows us that it's hardest to empathize with people who are radically different from us.
    ANSWER: T   TYPE: T   COG: R
21. When couples' narratives share similar narratives about how their relationship began, they have a better chance for smooth communication.
    ANSWER: T   TYPE: T   COG: R
22. Problems arise with first impressions when the labels we attach are inaccurate and we tend to hang on to them.
    ANSWER: T   TYPE: T   COG: R
23. People who are sleep deprived perceive time intervals realistically.
    ANSWER: F   TYPE: T   COG: C
24. When analyzing the connection between mood and happiness, research is mixed on whether perceptual outlook or the amount of relational satisfaction comes first.
    ANSWER: T   TYPE: T   COG: C
25. If a person feels like they are a "loser" in society, compared to other people who are more successful, this is an example of standpoint theory.
    ANSWER: T   TYPE: T   COG: C
26. In Zimbardo's prison experiment, the participants knew it was a fictitious situation, so they did not react intensely or perceive themselves differently.
    ANSWER: F   TYPE: T   COG: C
27. Perceptual schema are tendencies to misinterpret data.
    ANSWER: F   TYPE: T   COG: R
28. The Taoist saying of "one who speaks does not know; one who knows does not speak" is consistent with Asian perception that less talking is ideal.
    ANSWER: T   TYPE: T   COG: C
29. Collective cultures may have less success in perspective taking than individualistic cultures.
    ANSWER: F   TYPE: T   COG: C
30. Empathy requires open-mindedness, imagination, and commitment.
    ANSWER: T   TYPE: T   COG: R
31. Gender is one of the most fundamental schema people use to organize their perceptions.
    ANSWER: T   TYPE: T   COG: R
32. When an instructor sees a group of students on the first day of class as motivated and interested in learning, (s)he is generalizing.
    ANSWER: T   TYPE: T   COG: A
33. Research has shown that there is no correlation between the degree of empathy an individual exhibits and his/her tendency to commit violent crimes.
    ANSWER: F   TYPE: T   COG: R
34. Beliefs about the value of talk do not differ from one culture to another.
    ANSWER: F   TYPE: T   COG: R

Multiple Choice

35. We attach meaning to our experiences using which of the following?
    a. physiology, culture, and society
    b. selection, organization, interpretation, and negotiation
    c. social roles, self-concept, and perception
    d. empathy, sympathy, and interpretation
    e. all of the above
       ANSWER: b   TYPE: M   COG: R

36. Which step of perception is based on the fact that we notice some messages and ignore others?
   a. selection
   b. organization
   c. interpretation
   d. negotiation
   e. none of the above
   ANSWER: a   TYPE: M   COG: R

37. You and your friend have an entirely different interpretation of a comment that a third friend made. This is due to:
   a. different first-order realities
   b. different second-order realities
   c. different backgrounds
   d. different perceptions
   e. different levels of sensitivity
   ANSWER: b   TYPE: M   COG: A

38. A server believes that all teenagers do not tip well. This is an example of:
   a. Using an organizing scheme to make generalizations about members of groups.
   b. Using a perception check ot determine if assumptions are accurate.
   c. Using empathy to understand that teenagers don't always have a lot of money.
   d. All of the above.
   e. None of the above.
   ANSWER: a   TYPE: M   COG: A

39. A person you just went out with doesn't call you back after a first date. You figure that they just didn't like you. Your analysis of the situation is known as:
   a. interpretation
   b. empathy
   c. perceptual schemata
   d. punctuation
   e. attention
   ANSWER: d   TYPE: M   COG: A

40. A hungry person sees restaurants everywhere because of which factor of attention?
   a. motives
   b. contrast or change
   c. repetition
   d. intensity
   e. organization
   ANSWER: a   TYPE: M   COG: R

41. Perceptual schema include which constructs?
   a. physical and role
   b. interaction
   c. psychological
   d. all of the above
   e. none of the above
   ANSWER: d   TYPE: M   COG: R

42. A form of organization used to identify causes and effects in interaction is called
   a. grammar
   b. syntax
   c. punctuation
   d. spelling
   e. capitalization
   ANSWER: c   TYPE: M   COG: R

43. Which step of perception is involved when you wonder if the person who smiles at you across the room is interested in romance or is just being polite?
    a. selection
    b. organization
    c. interpretation
    d. negotiation
    e. none of the above
         ANSWER: c   TYPE: M   COG: A
44. Exaggerated beliefs associated with a categorizing system are known as
    a. empathy
    b. perspective taking
    c. stereotyping
    d. salience
    e. punctuation
         ANSWER: c   TYPE: M   COG: R
45. The process by which individuals influence each others perceptions through communication is known as
    a. selection
    b. organization
    c. interpretation
    d. punctuation
    e. negotiation
         ANSWER: e   TYPE: M   COG: R
46. Kim thinks her roommate Julie's constant cleaning is obsessive, and Julie thinks that Kim is a slob. Kim and Julie are experiencing a clash of
    a. role constructs
    b. narratives
    c. punctuation
    d. all of the above
    e. none of the above
         ANSWER: b   TYPE: M   COG: A
47. We interpret situations based on:
    a. perception
    b. assumptions about human behavior
    c. how much talking someone does when we meet them
    d. friendliness of others
    e. empathy
         ANSWER: b   TYPE: M   COG: C
48. Which sex type is probably characterized by competitive interaction, seeing relationships as opportunities to win something?
    a. masculine males
    b. masculine females
    c. feminine females
    d. androgynous males
    e. undifferentiated females
         ANSWER: a   TYPE: M   COG: R
49. Which sex type differs little in perceptions of interpersonal relationships?
    a. masculine
    b. male–female dichotomy
    c. feminine
    d. androgynous
    e. undifferentiated
         ANSWER: d   TYPE: M   COG: C

50. Stanford psychologist Philip Zimbardo's experiment with young men, assigning some as prisoners and some as guards, was a dramatic example of the significance of which role in perception?
    a. sexual
    b. occupational
    c. mood
    d. self-concept
    e. cultural
        ANSWER: b   TYPE: M   COG: C

51. When our _____ clash with others, we can either hang on to our own point of view, or try to negotiate common ground.
    a. opinions
    b. personalities
    c. ideas
    d. facts
    e. narratives
        ANSWER: e   TYPE: M   COG: C

52. Long-married, happy couples may distort facts about their relationship, but they share similar stories. This reveals that:
    a. Shared narratives don't have to be accurate to be powerful.
    b. Shared narratives should be discussed by people who remember them accurately.
    c. Shared narratives can't be trusted.
    d. Shared narratives should be agreed upon before telling others.
    e. Shared narratives confuse others when the message is inconsistent.
        ANSWER: a   TYPE: M   COG: C

53. The term social scientists use to describe the process of attaching meaning to behavior is
    a. selection
    b. attribution
    c. punctuation
    d. perception checking
    e. none of the above
        ANSWER: b   TYPE: M   COG: R

54. When we engage in self-serving bias,
    a. we tend to judge ourselves in the most generous terms possible
    b. we tend to blame others' problems on their personal qualities
    c. we find explanations outside ourselves when we have problems
    d. all of the above
    e. none of the above
        ANSWER: d   TYPE: M   COG: A

55. In Western cultures, such as the United States, silence is most often viewed as
    a. a sign of social grace
    b. an embarrassment
    c. an indication of communication competence
    d. a sign of physical strength
    e. all of the above
        ANSWER: b   TYPE: M   COG: R

56. If you have the flu and become angry with a friend for not calling you, whereas ordinarily you would have thought, "Oh, he's just busy" is an example of:
    a. physiological influence
    b. psychological influence
    c. emotional influence
    d. role influence
    e. perceptual influence
        ANSWER: a   TYPE: M   COG: A

57. Physiological influences that can impact us include:
    a. age
    b. our senses
    c. biological cycles
    d. neurobehavioral challenges
    e. all of the above
        ANSWER: e   TYPE: M   COG: R

58. You feel good about your relationship and charitable about your partner. This leads to increased happiness and more satisfaction in other parts of your life. You're experiencing:
    a. physiological state influencing your perception
    b. psychological state influencing your perception
    c. cognitive state influencing your perception
    d. functional state influencing your perception
    e. sexual state influencing your perception
        ANSWER: b   TYPE: M   COG: A

59. Which of the following is *not* a type of perceptual schema that allows us to organize the raw data we have selected?
    a. physical constructs
    b. role constructs
    c. interaction constructs
    d. psychological constructs
    e. selective constructs
        ANSWER: e   TYPE: M   COG: R

60. All of the following influence what we think of ourselves and others *except*
    a. self-concept
    b. socialization
    c. social norms
    d. mood
    e. none of the above
        ANSWER: c   TYPE: M   COG: R

61. Your friend sees your mother give you a kiss goodbye. This would be considered a:
    a. second-order reality
    b. first-order reality
    c. meaningful reality
    d. perceptual reality
    e. all of the above
        ANSWER: b   TYPE: M   COG: C

62. You see your sweetheart as great looking and you overlook the fact that she is not as neat as you'd like. This is an example of:
    a. true love
    b. empathy that your sweetheart is too busy to clean up
    c. relational roles affecting perception
    d. psychological state influencing your perception
    e. maturity
        ANSWER: c   TYPE: M   COG: A

63. You have a fight with your brother. Your mother thinks that you're "just acting like normal siblings." Your brother thinks you are jealous of him. This is an example of _____ reality.
    a. distorted
    b. first-order
    c. empathetic
    d. perceptual
    e. second-order
        ANSWER: e   TYPE: M   COG: A
64. Second-order realities involve
    a. observable qualities of a thing
    b. our attaching meaning to first-order things or situations
    c. objective facts
    d. visible situations
    e. none of the above
        ANSWER: b   TYPE: M   COG: R
65. Andersen's research regarding perceptual differences within a single national culture revealed:
    a. Climate and geographic latitude accurately predicted communication predispositions.
    b. Climate and geographic latitude inaccurately predicted communication predispositions.
    c. Climate and geographic latitude were not connected.
    d. Climate and geographic latitude were not studied.
    e. None of the above.
        ANSWER: a   TYPE: M   COG: R
66. _____ narratives provide the best chance for smooth communication.
    a. Organized
    b. Psychological
    c. Intense
    d. Shared
    e. Social
        ANSWER: d   TYPE: M   COG: C
67. Scientists developed _____ to describe how a person's position in a society shapes his or her view of society and of specific individuals.
    a. Social theory
    b. Interaction theory
    c. Standpoint theory
    d. Social role theory
    e. Self-concept theory
        ANSWER: c   TYPE: M   COG: R
68. If after several months you begin to lose patience from empathetically listening to a friend's constant family problems, you may be experiencing
    a. compassion fatigue
    b. empathetic termination
    c. sympathetic termination
    d. reflection fatigue
    e. perception fatigue
        ANSWER: a   TYPE: M   COG: A
69. Treating people as individuals instead of assuming they possess the same characteristics as every other member of the group to which you assign them is called
    a. punctuating
    b. decategorizing
    c. empathizing
    d. sympathizing
    e. stereotyping
        ANSWER: b   TYPE: M   COG: C

70. Jake is embarrassed to find that the "dumb blond" jokes he told in class were offensive to several of his classmates. John made the common perception mistake of
    a. being influenced by the obvious
    b. clinging to first impressions
    c. assuming others are like us
    d. incorporating the halo effect
    e. none of the above
         ANSWER: c   TYPE: M   COG: A

71. Which component is missing from the following perception-checking statement?
    "When you hung up on me, I got mad. What were you feeling?"
    a. a request for clarification for how to interpret the behavior
    b. an empathizing statement
    c. providing two possible interpretations of the behavior
    d. emotional contagion
    e. No components are missing.
         ANSWER: c   TYPE: M   COG: A

72. Immediately disliking a blind date after hearing negative evaluations about him from others is an example of how perception is
    a. influenced by the obvious
    b. influenced by our expectations.
    c. influenced by negative impressions.
    d. influenced by self-serving bias.
    e. none of the above
         ANSWER: b   TYPE: M   COG: A

73. Empathy requires
    a. open-mindedness
    b. imagination
    c. commitment
    d. all of the above
    e. a and c only
         ANSWER: d   TYPE: M   COG: R

Essay

74. Provide an example from your own experience of how each of the following factors affects perception and, hence, your interpersonal communication:
    a. psychological sex types
    b. occupational roles
    c. cultural differences
    d. physiological factors
         ANSWER: TYPE: E   COG: A

75. Briefly explain the concept of selection in the perception process and give one example of it in action.
         ANSWER: TYPE: E   COG: A

76. Select and explain two constructs you would use to classify the students in this class. How would your relationship to the students be affected differently by the two constructs?
         ANSWER: TYPE: E   COG: C

77. The text divides the act of perception into a four-part process. Name each of these parts. Then, using an event from your own experience, describe how each part functions.
         ANSWER: TYPE: E   COG: A

78. What skills and attitudes does an empathic person possess? Use examples to distinguish an empathetic person from a nonempathetic person.
         ANSWER: TYPE: E   COG: A

79. Here is a situation: Your best friend has just arrived to pick you up for a movie date. For the fifth time in a row, he is more than 15 minutes late. Write a perception-checking statement you might use in this situation. Indicate the parts of the statement.
    ANSWER: TYPE: E   COG: A
80. There are several factors that cause us to interpret a person's behavior in one way or another. Identify three of these factors, and explain how they affect interpretation.
    ANSWER: TYPE: E   COG: R
81. What do the authors mean by the statement, "Shared narratives don't have to be accurate to be powerful"?
    ANSWER: TYPE: E   COG: C
82. Select a privileged and underprivileged group and discuss how standpoint theory relates to each group.
    ANSWER: TYPE: E   COG: C
83. Why is relational satisfaction so powerful in interpretation? Explain.
    ANSWER: TYPE: E   COG: A
84. Give an example of a situation that represents confirmation bias.
    ANSWER: TYPE: E   COG: A
85. Give an example of a situation that represents self-serving bias.
    ANSWER: TYPE: E   COG: A
86. Explain whether or not you believe that empathy and ethics are related.
    ANSWER: TYPE: E   COG: A
87. Explain how perception-checking varies in low-context and high-context cultures.
    ANSWER: TYPE: E   COG: A
88. Explain how a person could "decategorize" others in order to avoid stereotyping.
    ANSWER: TYPE: E   COG: A
89. How we select, organize, and interpret data about others is influenced by a variety of factors. Explain how your perceptual judgments are affected by physiology, culture, social, and psychological factors.
    ANSWER: TYPE: E   COG: A

Matching

90. Match each definition with its corresponding term.

_____ 1. Stories we use to describe our personal worlds.
_____ 2. Determination of causes and effects in a series of interactions.
_____ 3. How a person's position in a society shapes their view of society in general.
_____ 4. Tendency to form an overall positive impression of a person on the basis of one positive characteristic.
_____ 5. Seeking out and organizing impressions to support an opinion.
_____ 6. Judging ourselves in the most generous terms possible.
_____ 7. The ability to recreate another person's perspective.

a. self-serving bias
b. standpoint theory
c. empathy
d. halo effect
e. narratives
f. punctuation
g. confirmation bias
h. store owner
i. investor
j. geologist

ANSWER: e, f, b, g, d, a, c   TYPE: K   COG: R

91. Mark the letter of the term that best identifies each of the numbered situations. Be sure to clarify the terms before you begin, and pay particular attention to underlined words and phrases.

a. punctuation
b. interpretation
c. empathy
d. first-order reality
e. second-order reality
f. androgynous behavior
g. halo effect
h. selection

_____ 1. Holly communicated *her understanding* of her friend's housing problem to that friend.
_____ 2. Susan assumes that her friend's silence in class mean that she has nothing to say; Ye Sun believes that this same silence indicated respect for authority.
_____ 3. Now that he is shopping for a car, Ken seems to notice more car advertisements.
_____ 4. You figure your friend's smile means she's happy.
_____ 5. Janice *noticed* that her boss walked right into the conference room without greeting anyone.
_____ 6. Janice *figured her boss was pretty mad* when he didn't say hello to anyone.
_____ 7. You say you're late because your partner's never ready on time; your partner says she takes her time getting ready because you're always late.
_____ 8. Tracy exhibits both sensitivity and strength when faced with a difficult decision.
_____ 9. Even though Peter isn't especially interested in the life cycle of a worm, he listens carefully in class because he knows the material will be on the test.
_____ 10. Donna is so pretty that everyone assumes she is a nice person, too.

For each of the following, identify which element of the perception-checking statement is missing.

a. This statement doesn't describe behavior.
b. This statement doesn't give two distinctly different interpretations.
c. This statement neglects to request clarification of the perception.
d. There is nothing missing from this perception-checking statement.

_____ 11. "When you told everyone my parents own the company, you must have been indicating I was hired here only because of them. Is that what you think?"
_____ 12. "Dad, when you told my friend Art what a great athlete you think I am, I thought either you were really proud of me and wanted to brag a little or maybe you wanted to see what Art and I had in common by the way he responded. What were you up to?"
_____ 13. "I'm really wondering—are you angry with me or just sulking?"
_____ 14. "When your told me you expected to get an outline with my report, I thought you were trying to trick me into doing more work, or maybe you didn't realize that wasn't part of my job."
_____ 15. "Why is it you're smiling all the time today? Did you win the lottery or get a new job? What's up?"

ANSWER KEY:

1. c	6. e	11. b
2. b	7. a	12. d
3. h	8. f	13. a
4. b	9. h	14. c
5. d	10. g	15. d

CHAPTER 5: LANGUAGE

True/False

1. The "study of symbols" would be an accurate description for the "study of language."
   ANSWER: T   TYPE: T   COG: C
2. Words are arbitrary symbols that have no meaning in themselves.
   ANSWER: T   TYPE: T   COG: R
3. An important task facing communicators is to establish a common understanding of the words they use to exchange messages.
   ANSWER: T   TYPE: T   COG: C
4. Research suggests that bilingual speakers think differently when they change languages.
   ANSWER: T   TYPE: T   COG: C
5. Some languages contain words that have no English equivalents.
   ANSWER: T   TYPE: T   COG: R
6. To the extent that our language is both sexist and racist, our view of the world is affected.
   ANSWER: T   TYPE: T   COG: C
7. While language may shape thoughts and behavior, it doesn't dominate them absolutely.
   ANSWER: T   TYPE: T   COG: R
8. Syntax deals with structure; semantics govern meaning.
   ANSWER: T   TYPE: T   COG: R
9. Coordinated management of meaning (CMM) theory describes some types of pragmatic rules that operate in everyday conversation.
   ANSWER: T   TYPE: T   COG: R
10. Ogden and Richards' *triangle of meaning* shows a direct relationship between a word and the thing or idea it represents.
    ANSWER: F   TYPE: T   COG: R
11. Research indicates that names shape the way others think of us, the way we view ourselves, and the way we act.
    ANSWER: T   TYPE: T   COG: R
12. The preconceptions we hold about people because of their names have little influence on our behavior toward them.
    ANSWER: F   TYPE: T   COG: C
13. The labels we choose for ourselves and encourage others to use say a great deal about who we think we are and how we want others to view us.
    ANSWER: T   TYPE: T   COG: C
14. Research shows that linguistic differences are often more a function of gender roles than of the speaker's biological sex.
    ANSWER: T   TYPE: T   COG: C
15. Linguistic relativism asserts that culture is shaped and reflected by the language its members speak.
    ANSWER: T   TYPE: T   COG: R
16. Communication researchers call the process of adapting one's speech style to match that of others with whom the communicator wants to identify *divergence*.
    ANSWER: F   TYPE: T   COG: C
17. Powerful speech is most likely to get desired results regardless of the country in which it is used.
    ANSWER: F   TYPE: T   COG: C
18. Language can shape the way we perceive and understand the world.
    ANSWER: T   TYPE: T   COG: C
19. Competent communicators understand that ambiguity and vagueness can sometimes serve useful purposes.
    ANSWER: T   TYPE: T   COG: R

20. Behavioral descriptions are less specific than abstract ones.
    ANSWER: F   TYPE: T   COG: R
21. Coordinated management of meaning (CMM) theory describes pragmatic rules operating in everyday conversations.
    ANSWER: T   TYPE: T   COG: R
22. The language we use describes our perceptions but does not affect our perceptions.
    ANSWER: F   TYPE: T   COG: C
23. Research suggests that common names are generally viewed as being more active and likeable than unusual ones.
    ANSWER: T   TYPE: T   COG: R
24. Like ambiguity, high-level abstractions also can help communicators find face-saving ways to avoid confrontations and embarrassment by being deliberately unclear.
    ANSWER: T   TYPE: T   COG: R
25. Name choice can be a powerful way to make a statement about cultural identity.
    ANSWER: T   TYPE: T   COG: R
26. Research suggests that a mixture of powerful and polite speech is usually more effective than a powerful-only or polite-only style.
    ANSWER: T   TYPE: T   COG: C
27. The goal of language is always to be perfectly clear to another person.
    ANSWER: F   TYPE: T   COG: C
28. Language that is open to several interpretations should not be used by a competent communicator.
    ANSWER: F   TYPE: T   COG: C
29. High-level abstractions can help communicators avoid confrontations and embarrassment.
    ANSWER: T   TYPE: T   COG: R
30. "I" language reflects the speaker's willingness to take responsibility for her or his beliefs and feelings.
    ANSWER: T   TYPE: T   COG: R
31. Research suggests that "I" language in large doses can sound egotistical.
    ANSWER: T   TYPE: T   COG: C
32. "We" language implies that the issue is the concern and responsibility of both the speaker and the receiver of a message.
    ANSWER: T   TYPE: T   COG: R
33. "The climate in Portland is better than in that in Seattle" is an example of a factual statement.
    ANSWER: F   TYPE: T   COG: A
34. Gender research indicates that there is no significant difference between male and female speech in areas such as the use of profanity, qualifiers, and vocal fluency.
    ANSWER: T   TYPE: T   COG: R
35. Euphemisms are typically used to strengthen the impact of information that might be weak.
    ANSWER:F   TYPE: T   COG: R
36. To say, "It bothers me when you sleep in late" is a way to deny responsibility for a feeling.
    ANSWER: T   TYPE: T   COG: A
37. A complete "I" statement has two parts: the other person's behavior and the consequences.
    ANSWER: F   TYPE: T   COG: R
38. Emotive words are really stating a point of view.
    ANSWER: T   TYPE: T   COG: R
39. One analysis of over 1,200 research studies found that only 1 percent of variance in communication behavior resulted from sex differences.
    ANSWER: T   TYPE: T   COG: R
40. Differences between the way men and women speak are determined by a wide variety of factors that may have little or nothing to do with biological sex.
    ANSWER: T   TYPE: T   COG: C

Multiple Choice

41. The features that characterize all languages are:
    a. symbolic.
    b. rule-governed.
    c. subjective.
    d. all of the above
    e. a and b only
    ANSWER: d   TYPE: M   COG: R

42. The notion that words are arbitrary and have no meaning in themselves refers to which characteristic of language?
    a. symbolic
    b. rule-governed
    c. powerful
    d. equivocal
    e. static
    ANSWER: a   TYPE: M   COG: R

43. Rules that tell us what uses and interpretations of a message are appropriate in a given context are:
    a. phonological rules.
    b. syntactic rules.
    c. pragmatic rules.
    d. semantic rules.
    e. none of the above
    ANSWER: c   TYPE: M   COG: R

44. The fact that the words "whiskey makes you sick when you're well," when arranged differently, "Whiskey, when you're sick, makes you well," create a totally different meaning is related to which rule of language?
    a. pragmatic
    b. syntactic
    c. phonological
    d. semantic
    e. none of the above
    ANSWER: b   TYPE: M   COG: R

45. Brandon's stomach begins to churn when his boss pokes his head in his office and says, "I want to see you." This is because of which kind of language rules?
    a. pragmatic rules
    b. syntactic rules
    c. phonological rules
    d. semantic rules
    e. none of the above
    ANSWER: a   TYPE: M   COG: A

46. The fact that *love* means many things, ranging from "Eros" (romantic love) to agape (selfless love), suggests which quality of troublesome language?
    a. ambiguity
    b. static nature
    c. inferential
    d. emotive
    e. relativeness
    ANSWER: a   TYPE: M   COG: A

47. Alfred Korzybski suggested the linguistic device of "dating" to cope with which form of troublesome language?
    a. ambiguity
    b. static nature
    c. inferential
    d. emotive
    e. relativeness
    ANSWER: b   TYPE: M   COG: A

48. Terms like *angry* and *exciting* that announce the speaker's attitude point to which quality of troublesome language?
    a. ambiguity
    b. static nature
    c. inferential
    d. emotive
    e. relativeness
    ANSWER: d   TYPE: M   COG: A

49. The notion that the worldview of a culture is shaped and reflected by the language its members speak is known as:
    a. prejudice.
    b. ethnocentrism.
    c. egocentrism.
    d. co-culture.
    e. linguistic relativism.
    ANSWER: e   TYPE: M   COG: R

50. Research demonstrates that names are more than just a simple means of identification. Name choices can:
    a. be distinctive.
    b. make a powerful statement about cultural identity.
    c. be an indicator of status.
    d. be unusual.
    e. all of the above
    ANSWER: e   TYPE: M   COG: R

51. The Sapir–Whorf hypothesis is associated with:
    a. linguistic relativism.
    b. demographics.
    c. technology.
    d. in-groups.
    e. out-groups.
    ANSWER: a   TYPE: M   COG: R

52. Overly abstract language can cause which of the following problems?
    a. stereotyping
    b. confusion
    c. serious misunderstandings
    d. leaves you less clear about your own thoughts
    e. all of the above
    ANSWER: e   TYPE: M   COG: C

53. Language shapes our impression of:
    a. credibility.
    b. status.
    c. power.
    d. racism and sexism.
    e. all of the above
    ANSWER: e   TYPE: M   COG: R

54. Statements that have the effect of canceling the thought that precedes them are:
    a. questions.
    b. "but" statements.
    c. "if" statements.
    d. "you" statements.
    e. "we" statements.
    ANSWER: b   TYPE: M   COG: R

55. Language can express an unwillingness to take responsibility through the use of:
    a. "it" statements.
    b. "you" language.
    c. "but" statements.
    d. all of the above
    e. none of the above
    ANSWER: d   TYPE: M   COG: R

56. The statement "Claudia is a beautiful person" is an example of which troublesome characteristic of language?
    a. evasion
    b. sexism
    c. euphemism
    d. static evaluation
    e. none of the above
    ANSWER: d   TYPE: M   COG: R

57. Language can have a strong effect on our perceptions and how we regard one another based on:
    a. power.
    b. credibility and status.
    c. naming.
    d. affiliation and attraction.
    e. all of the above
    ANSWER: e   TYPE: M   COG: R

58. Euphemisms are:
    a. pleasant words substituted for blunt ones.
    b. terms such as *freedom, truth*, and *democracy.*
    c. words that appear to describe but actually announce a speaker's attitude.
    d. words that gain their meaning by making comparisons.
    e. not defined by any of the above.
    ANSWER: a   TYPE: M   COG: R

59. Which of the following statements is the lowest-level abstraction of the word *considerate*?
    a. She helps me around the house.
    b. She calls me on Fridays before she goes shopping to see if I need anything.
    c. She thinks of others.
    d. She always follows the rules of politeness.
    e. She follows the Golden Rule.
    ANSWER: b   TYPE: M   COG: A

60. The statement "Americans are materialistic" is an example of which problem caused by overly abstract language?
    a. a euphemistic statement
    b. syntactic confusion
    c. the Sapir–Whorf hypothesis
    d. stereotyping
    e. none of the above
    ANSWER: d   TYPE: M   COG: A

61. Teaching kids to "go potty" instead of "urinating in the toilet bowl" is an example of:
    a. ambiguous language.
    b. euphemisms.
    c. emotive language.
    d. static evaluation.
    e. relative language.
    ANSWER: b   TYPE: M   COG: A

62. Being surprised at paying $20 a plate at your friend's suggested "inexpensive" restaurant reflects which type of language?
    a. ambiguous language
    b. euphemism
    c. emotive language
    d. static evaluation
    e. relative language
    ANSWER: e   TYPE: M   COG: A

63. The statement "For me, a good dinner is fresh seafood, white wine, and French pastry" is an example of:
    a. emotive language.
    b. behavioral description.
    c. intentional orientations.
    d. semantic ambiguity.
    e. a euphemistic statement.
    ANSWER: b   TYPE: M   COG: A

64. Language usage that has a high frequency of terms implying superior male traits and inferior female traits or a high frequency of terms of superior female traits and inferior male traits is known as:
    a. metacommunication.
    b. androgynous language.
    c. paralanguage.
    d. sexist language.
    e. none of the above
    ANSWER: d   TYPE: M   COG: R

65. The implication of the statement "Sign language is symbolic, not literal" is:
    a. that there are many different sign languages because there are many possible symbols for each concept.
    b. that there is only one correct sign language because the signs are universally recognized.
    c. the connection between a concept and its visual representation is obvious and direct.
    d. experts should work more to unify the major sign languages.
    e. sign language is more impersonal than verbal language.
    ANSWER: a   TYPE: M   COG: C

66. The rules that tell us which interpretation of a message is appropriate in a given context are:
    a. syntactic.
    b. semantic.
    c. pragmatic.
    d. all of the above
    e. a and b
    ANSWER: c   TYPE: M   COG: R

67. Ambiguous language refers to the fact that words have:
    a. unique sounds.
    b. unique spellings.
    c. one commonly accepted definition.
    d. more than one commonly accepted definition.
    e. different levels of abstraction.
    ANSWER: d   TYPE: M   COG: R

215

68. In the statement "Mekelle is a good student," the word that is troublesome due to static evaluation is:
    a. Mekelle.
    b. is.
    c. a.
    d. good.
    e. student.
          ANSWER: b   TYPE: M   COG: A
69. Arguments often result when we label our inferences as:
    a. facts.
    b. opinions.
    c. ambiguous language.
    d. personal.
    e. descriptive.
          ANSWER: a   TYPE: M   COG: R
70. Saying "You look nice" instead of "That color of dress looks good on you" is an example of:
    a. a euphemism.
    b. abstraction.
    c. emotive language.
    d. a behavioral description.
    e. a hedge.
          ANSWER: b   TYPE: M   COG: A
71. In a study that compared men's and women's use of words that show a stance (words that express attitude, emotion, certainty, doubt, commitment, etc.), what was the only type of stance word that showed a significant difference between men and women?
    a. opinion words (like "happy")
    b. hedges (like "almost")
    c. expletives (like "damn")
    d. empathic words (like "absolutely")
    e. factuality words (like "sure")
          ANSWER: c   TYPE: M   COG: R
72. Which of the following is a fact, not an inference?
    a. You're so moody.
    b. Why are you so down?
    c. You are so silly.
    d. It's obvious you are bored.
    e. You are yawning.
          ANSWER: e   TYPE: M   COG: A
73. Which of the following is NOT part of a complete "I" statement?
    a. the other person's behavior
    b. your feelings
    c. consequences the other person's behavior has for you
    d. what you intend to do about the other person's behavior
    e. all of the above are part of a complete "I" statement
          ANSWER: d   TYPE: M   COG: R
74. Your textbook authors warn about using "but" statements because:
    a. people usually don't listen to them.
    b. "but" can cancel the thought that precedes it.
    c. people don't like two part sentences.
    d. "but" can dehumanize the receiver.
    e. people find the word "but" patronizing.
          ANSWER: b   TYPE: M   COG: R

75. The use of a numeric pain scale in health care is to avoid what type of troublesome language?
    a. racist
    b. sexist
    c. euphemism
    d. relative
    e. static evaluation
        ANSWER: d   TYPE: M   COG: R
76. Why does sociolinguist Deborah Tannen like giving orders using polite speech?
    a. She finds the request gets done more quickly.
    b. She likes that it protects the dignity of her assistants.
    c. She likes that as a woman a man will do as she asks.
    d. She likes that her assistants are surprised by it.
    e. None of the above.
        ANSWER: b   TYPE: M   COG: R
77. When members of an ethnic group use their own dialect, even though they are fluent in the dominant language, it could be an example of:
    a. powerful speech.
    b. abstraction.
    c. affiliation.
    d. convergence.
    e. divergence.
        ANSWER: e   TYPE: M   COG: R
78. Your textbook authors report that people with names that are spelled unusually often get:
    a. higher-paying jobs.
    b. lower-paying jobs.
    c. negative assessments.
    d. positive assessments.
    e. their names misspelled.
        ANSWER: c   TYPE: M   COG: R
79. The fact that some people have come out against the use of the term "vegetable" in reference to someone who may be brain dead illustrates what linguistic principle?
    a. linguistic relativism
    b. language is subjective
    c. affiliation
    d. abstraction ladder
    e. language of responsibility
        ANSWER: b   TYPE: M   COG: A
80. Which statement does not contain powerless language?
    a. I really hope you can understand.
    b. This assignment is not too difficult.
    c. Call me later, won't you?
    d. This may not be fair, but I don't like Charlyce.
    e. Let's meet for lunch tomorrow.
        ANSWER: e   TYPE: M   COG: A

Essay

81. "Climb down" the abstraction ladder by suggesting three successively more concrete meanings for the following words: *independent, selfish,* and *nosy.* Explain how these meanings are more concrete.
        ANSWER: TYPE: E   COG: A
82. Identify and explain the language problem(s) illustrated in the following statement: "Camille is insensitive." Rewrite the statement to be less troublesome, adding any necessary information.
        ANSWER: TYPE: E   COG: A

83. Discuss two ways of eliminating sexist language.
          ANSWER: TYPE: E   COG: C

84. Emotive language seems to describe something but really describes the speaker's attitude toward it. The following is a statement of a personality trait: "My child is high-spirited." Give two versions to show how the trait can be viewed either favorably or unfavorably, according to the label people give it.
          ANSWER: TYPE: E   COG: A

85. Rewrite the following statements so that the speaker takes responsibility for the feelings expressed:
    a. "It's really annoying to have to wait for people."
    b. "You never know what's going to happen with Marlon."
    c. "We really should get going."
    d. "Are you doing anything later?"
          ANSWER: TYPE: E   COG: A

86. Explain and give an example of the disruptive language concept "Fact–opinion confusion."
          ANSWER: TYPE: E   COG: A

87. Using the word *but* in a statement has the effect of canceling everything that came before it. Rewrite the following two statements so that they more clearly express the speaker's thoughts and feelings:
    a. "I really enjoy the time we spend together, but I think we should see other people more."
    b. "You're a good worker, but your habitual lateness makes it hard for your coworkers to do their jobs."
          ANSWER: TYPE: E   COG: A

88. Your close friend has a habit of interrupting you whenever you try to share a personal story. Offer an example of how you might describe this problem to your friend, using "I," "You," and "We" language as recommended in the text.
          ANSWER: TYPE: E   COG: A

89. Distinguish between phonological, syntactic, semantic, and pragmatic rules. Provide an example of each.
          ANSWER: TYPE: E   COG: A

90. The general public seems to be captivated by the topic of gender differences in language. Your textbook offers two approaches to gender and language. Describe the two different views offered, and discuss the significance of each.
          ANSWER: TYPE: E   COG: C

Matching

91. Label each of the following as fact (F) or inference (I).

       _____ Bernie's face is turning red.
       _____ Shameeka's happy she won the prize.
       _____ You're ten minutes late.
       _____ You didn't call me last night.
       _____ You only like me because I'm a football star.
          ANSWER: F, I, F, F, I   TYPE: K   COG: C

CHAPTER 6: NONVERBAL COMMUNICATION

True/False

1. Nonverbal communication is best defined as "messages expressed by nonlinguistic means."
   ANSWER: T   TYPE: T   COG: R

2. In real life, spontaneous nonverbal expressions are frequently unclear and difficult to interpret.
   ANSWER: T   TYPE: T   COG: C

3. Emblems are usually delivered intentionally.
   ANSWER: T   TYPE: T   COG: C

4. Researchers have found that people who hear content-free speech can consistently recognize the emotion being expressed as well as identify its strength.
   ANSWER: T   TYPE: T   COG: C

5. Persuasiveness increases when one person mirror's another's movements.
   ANSWER: T   TYPE: T   COG: R

6. Social scientists use the term *paralanguage* to describe nonverbal vocal messages.
   ANSWER: T   TYPE: T   COG: R

7. Listeners pay more attention to the content of words than to paralanguage when asked to determine a speaker's attitudes.
   ANSWER: F   TYPE: T   COG: R

8. Cognitively complex people are better at decoding nonverbal behavior than are those who are less cognitively complex.
   ANSWER: T   TYPE: T   COG: C

9. Sarcasm is one instance in which we use both emphasis and tone of voice to change a statement's meaning to the opposite.
   ANSWER: T   TYPE: T   COG: C

10. Low self-monitors are usually better at hiding their deception than communicators who are more aware.
    ANSWER: F   TYPE: T   COG: R

11. We generally rate highly expressive liars as more honest than those who are more subdued.
    ANSWER: T   TYPE: T   COG: R

12. *Proxemics* is the term social scientists use to describe the study of how people communicate through bodily movements.
    ANSWER: F   TYPE: T   COG: R

13. Research shows that we tend to comply with requests when they are delivered at a rate that is not similar to our own speaking rate.
    ANSWER: F   TYPE: T   COG: R

14. The physical exterior of a home does not give viewers any accurate perceptions of the home owner.
    ANSWER: F   TYPE: T   COG: R

15. While it's possible to avoid verbal communication, it's impossible to stop sending nonverbal messages.
    ANSWER: T   TYPE: T   COG: R

16. The term *haptics* is used to label the study of space.
    ANSWER: F   TYPE: T   COG: R

17. Appropriate touch increases liking and boosts compliance.
    ANSWER: T   TYPE: T   COG: C

18. *Paralanguage* is a scientific term given to speech that includes slang peculiar to a specific group.
    ANSWER: F   TYPE: T   COG: R

19. *Territory* and *personal space* are used interchangeably to describe the invisible bubble that serves as an extension of our physical being.
    ANSWER: F   TYPE: T   COG: R

20. Proxemics is the study of how people use the space around them.
      ANSWER: T   TYPE: T   COG: R

21. Emblems are culturally understood substitutes for verbal expressions.
      ANSWER: T   TYPE: T   COG: R

22. You stand up at the end of a meeting with your boss. This is known as a nonverbal regulator.
      ANSWER: T   TYPE: T   COG: C

23. Rita wears a business suit to an interview because she wants to look professional and educated. This is an example of managing identity through manner.
      ANSWER: F   TYPE: T   COG: A

24. Someone studying oculesics would watch people's facial expressions as they look at others.
      ANSWER: F   TYPE: T   COG: C

25. All fidgeting indicates uneasiness.
      ANSWER: F   TYPE: T   COG: R

26. "Um," "er," and "uh" are known as disfluencies.
      ANSWER: T   TYPE: T   COG: R

27. Ingrid stands too close to Marci when talking with her. Marci looks away, leans backwards, and folds her arms. This is known as barrier behavior.
      ANSWER: T   TYPE: T   COG: A

28. Research shows that clothing can send a message of trustworthiness, level of sophistication, and moral character.
      ANSWER: T   TYPE: T   COG: R

29. Students see professors who have well decorated office as more credible than those who have less attractive work areas.
      ANSWER: T   TYPE: T   COG: R

30. Chronemics is the study of how people use color.
      ANSWER: F   TYPE: T   COG: R

Multiple Choice

31. All of the following are characteristics of nonverbal communication *except:*
    a.   all behavior has communicative value.
    b.   nonverbal communication is primarily relational.
    c.   nonverbal communication is ambiguous.
    d.   nonverbal communication is specific.
    e.   All of the above are characteristics of nonverbal communication.
      ANSWER: d   TYPE: M   COG: R

32. When a speaker seeks a response, he or she "signals" by looking at the listener, creating a brief period of mutual gaze called:
    a.   gaze window.
    b.   stare.
    c.   eye contact.
    d.   bliss factor.
    e.   cues
      ANSWER: a.   TYPE: M   COG: R

33. The fact that it is impossible to think about and control all nonverbal behavior suggests which characteristic of nonverbal communication?
    a.   multiple channels
    b.   continuous
    c.   unconscious
    d.   ambiguous
    e.   nonverbal impact
      ANSWER: c   TYPE: M   COG: C

34. The fact that most nonverbal cues are vague implies which characteristic of nonverbal communication?
    a. multiple channels
    b. continuous
    c. ambiguous
    d. unconscious
    e. nonverbal impact
    ANSWER: c   TYPE: M   COG: C

35. Observers rely more on women's nonverbal behavioral cues to their social position, whereas men are rated more on their:
    a. attire.
    b. attitude.
    c. posture.
    d. facial expressions.
    e. none of the above
    ANSWER: a   TYPE: M   COG: R

36. Metts and Grohskopf's review of professional journal articles on constructing good impressions found that there are several ways of managing identity nonverbally. These include:
    a. the way we act, or our manner.
    b. the way we dress, or our appearance.
    c. the physical items we surround ourselves with, or setting.
    d. all of the above
    e. both a and b
    ANSWER: d   TYPE: M   COG: R

37. Which of the following are nonverbal signals that indicate a speaker has finished talking and is ready to yield to a listener?
    a. lack of change in vocal intonation
    b. a drawl on the first syllable
    c. a drop in vocal pitch or loudness
    d. all of the above
    e. a and b only
    ANSWER: c   TYPE: M   COG: C

38. Which type of nonverbal communication is considered the most noticeable?
    a. face
    b. posture and gesture
    c. touch
    d. voice
    e. proxemics and territoriality
    ANSWER: a   TYPE: M   COG: R

39. Research by Berger and diBattista showed that when communicators gave directions that weren't followed, in their second attempt they would:
    a. change their wording.
    b. talk faster.
    c. talk louder.
    d. use more gestures.
    e. talk softer.
    ANSWER: c   TYPE: M   COG: R

40. The ability to consider more than one possible interpretation for nonverbal behavior is a characteristic of:
    a. cognitive complexity.
    b. ambiguity.
    c. paralanguage.
    d. proxemics.
    e. kinesics.
        ANSWER: a   TYPE: M   COG: R

41. The voice communicates through:
    a. tone and pitch.
    b. speed and volume.
    c. pauses and disfluencies.
    d. all of the above
    e. a and b only
        ANSWER: d   TYPE: M   COG: R

42. Edward T. Hall considers intimate distances to be:
    a. 0 to 18 inches.
    b. 18 inches to 4 feet.
    c. 4 feet to 12 feet.
    d. 12 feet to 25 feet.
    e. 25 feet and beyond.
        ANSWER: a   TYPE: M   COG: R

43. At which distance can you keep someone "at arm's length"?
    a. intimate
    b. personal
    c. social
    d. public
    e. none of the above
        ANSWER: b   TYPE: M   COG: C

44. Edward T. Hall considers social distance to be:
    a. 0 to 18 inches.
    b. 18 inches to 4 feet.
    c. 4 feet to 12 feet.
    d. 12 feet to 25 feet.
    e. 25 feet and beyond.
        ANSWER: c   TYPE: M   COG: R

45. Which is *not* barrier behavior?
    a. touch
    b. sneeze
    c. decrease eye contact
    d. scratch
    e. backing away
        ANSWER: a   TYPE: M   COG: R

46. The effect of an attractive room on the people working in it is an example of which type of nonverbal communication?
    a. environment
    b. territoriality
    c. proxemics
    d. touch
    e. paralanguage
        ANSWER: a   TYPE: M   COG: R

47. Culturally understood substitutes for verbal expressions are known as:
    a. emblems.
    b. illustrators.
    c. regulators.
    d. paralinguistic cues.
    e. none of the above
    ANSWER: a   TYPE: M   COG: R

48. In an experiment done by Aldert Vrij and colleagues, trained observers were able to spot liars 78 percent of the time. What kinds of things did the observers notice?
    a. Liars make fewer hand and finger movements.
    b. Liars have more speech disturbances.
    c. Liars pause longer before offering answers than do truth-tellers.
    d. all of the above
    e. none of the above
    ANSWER: d   TYPE: M   COG: C

49. Which distance is being used when a child sits on your lap?
    a. intimate
    b. personal
    c. social
    d. public
    e. territorial
    ANSWER: a   TYPE: M   COG: A

50. Which distance is typically used when a teacher lectures in front of a large lecture class?
    a. intimate
    b. personal
    c. social
    d. public
    e. territorial
    ANSWER: d   TYPE: M   COG: A

51. At what distance are a couple of friends likely to stand when in public?
    a. intimate
    b. personal
    c. social
    d. public
    e. territorial
    ANSWER: b   TYPE: M   COG: A

52. Which distance is being used when an employer talks with an employee as they are seated across from each other at an office desk?
    a. intimate
    b. personal
    c. social
    d. public
    e. territorial
    ANSWER: c   TYPE: M   COG: A

53. Nonverbal messages are best at communicating:
    a. thoughts.
    b. ideas.
    c. feelings.
    d. concepts.
    e. negative emotions.
    ANSWER: c   TYPE: M   COG: R

54. Morton and Trehub's study of children's interpretation of mixed messages concluded that:
    a. children rely on nonverbal cues more than words for understanding.
    b. children rely on words more than nonverbal cues for understanding.
    c. children become confused when words and nonverbal cues contradicted each other.
    d. children are more accurate than adults at interpreting mixed messages.
    e. none of the above
       ANSWER: b   TYPE: M   COG: C

55. Proxemics is the study of how communication is:
    a. divided down into distances.
    b. affected by the use, organization, and perception of space and distance.
    c. the social relationship between two or more individuals.
    d. equal to the level of the relationship.
    e. none of the above
       ANSWER: b   TYPE: M   COG: R

56. Everyday Carlos sits in the third seat in the third row. One day Bonita sits in this seat, and Carlos is very angry. What type of nonverbal communication is Carlos displaying?
    a. touch
    b. proxemics
    c. territoriality
    d. time
    e. body movement
       ANSWER: c   TYPE: M   COG: A

57. Punctual mainlanders often report the laid-back Hawaiian approach to time as welcoming. This is an example of:
    a. kinesics.
    b. proxemics.
    c. chronemics.
    d. territoriality.
    e. touch.
       ANSWER: c   TYPE: M   COG: A

84. Which of the following is not a social function of nonverbal communication?
    a. It defines the type of relationship we want with others.
    b. It conveys emotions we may be unwilling or unable to express.
    c. It involves identity management.
    d. all of the above
    e. both b and c
       ANSWER: d   TYPE: M   COG: C

85. Which of the following conclusions can be reached from the study showing those touched lightly on the arm were 70 percent more likely to complete a rating scale?
    a. Touching someone lightly is more persuasive than a heavier touch.
    b. Touching someone on the arm is the most persuasive location for compliance.
    c. Touch increases compliance.
    d. Touch increases understanding.
    e. If you touch someone, she or he will do what you want.
       ANSWER: c   TYPE: M   COG: C

86. Paralanguage includes the vocal qualities of:
    a. rate and pitch.
    b. disfluencies and pauses.
    c. tone and volume.
    d. all of the above
    e. a and c only
       ANSWER: d   TYPE: M   COG: R

87. Evidence suggests that:
    a. as we get to know more about people and like them, we start to regard them as better looking.
    b. we view others as beautiful or ugly not just on the basis of their appearance.
    c. posture, gestures, facial expressions, and other behaviors can increase the attractiveness of an otherwise-unremarkable person.
    d. all of the above
    e. none of the above
    ANSWER: d   TYPE: M   COG: A

88. A positive impression is associated with _____ between our verbal and nonverbal behavior.
    a. differences
    b. consistency
    c. management
    d. a and c only
    e. none of the above
    ANSWER: b   TYPE: M   COG: R

89. Research shows that clothing can convey the following nonverbal elements:
    a. level of sophistication.
    b. trustworthiness.
    c. moral character.
    d. educational background.
    e. all of the above
    ANSWER: e   TYPE: M   COG: R

90. Jessie twirls her hair while she watches television. This is an example that demonstrates:
    a. fidgeting signals uneasiness.
    b. manipulators often happen while relaxing.
    c. fidgeting always has meaning.
    d. manipulators should happen in private.
    e. gestures produce a wide range of meaning.
    ANSWER: b   TYPE: M   COG: C

91. Liars tend to have more _____ than truth-tellers.
    a. paralanguage
    b. proxemics
    c. unintentional pauses
    d. eye contact
    e. none of the above
    ANSWER: c   TYPE: M   COG: R

92. Surgeons whose voices were regarded as dominating and indifferent were more likely to be sued for malpractice than those with a less threatening style. This is an example of:
    a. vocal factors influencing the way a speaker is perceived by others.
    b. disfluencies influencing the way a speaker is perceived by others.
    c. manipulators influencing the way a speaker is perceived by others.
    d. inflection influencing the way a speaker is perceived by others.
    e. accents influencing the way a speaker is perceived by others.
    ANSWER: a   TYPE: M   COG: R

93. Burgoon and Levine's research on deception detection indicates that we are accurate in detecting deception:
    a. just over half the time.
    b. just under half the time.
    c. about 80% of the time.
    d. less than 70% of the time.
    e. about 20% of the time.
    ANSWER: a   TYPE: M   COG: R

94. The display of involvement signaled by physical closeness, eye contact, movement, and touch is known as:
    a. nonverbal manipulators.
    b. disfluencies.
    c. paralanguage.
    d. nonverbal immediacy.
    e. chronemics.

    ANSWER: d   TYPE: M   COG: R

95. When working at a call center as a telephone salesperson, Mischa was trained to speak at an even pace, not talk too loudly or softly, and use friendly inflection. This is an example that demonstrates:
    a. voice qualities change the meaning of a statement.
    b. voice qualities make us sound confident.
    c. voice qualities influence listeners.
    d. voice qualities are used intentionally to manipulate listeners.
    e. voice qualities can be used to shift emphasis from one word to another.

    ANSWER: c   TYPE: M   COG: R

96. Social rules may discourage us from performing some manipulators in public, but people still do so without noticing. Which of the following is not a manipulator?
    a. yelling at a friend
    b. pinching a body part
    c. fidgeting
    d. twirling a strand of hair
    e. rubbing a sore leg

    ANSWER: a   TYPE: M   COG: A

Essay

97. Assume you are at a restaurant with a friend. He or she flirts with the server. Write a one-sentence statement you could use to check out your interpretation of this nonverbal communication. Assume you will say the sentence to your friend.

    ANSWER: TYPE: E   COG: A

98. Discuss how nonverbal communication is influenced by culture. Provide an example of how understanding can be impacted as a result of cultures having different nonverbal behaviors.

    ANSWER: TYPE: E   COG: C

99. In many situations, the right kinds of gestures can increase persuasiveness. List and explain a few types of gestures that are effective for persuasion.

    ANSWER: TYPE: E   COG: A

100. Anthropologist Edward T. hall defined four distances we use in our everyday lives. Name and briefly describe each of the four distances. Provide an example of the kind of communication that goes on at each range.

    ANSWER: TYPE: E   COG: A

101. For each of the following settings, describe how the environment is likely to be designed to suit the needs of the person who inhabits it.
    a. fast-food restaurant
    b. airport waiting areas
    c. a professor's office
    d. a gambling casino
    e. a movie theater

    ANSWER: TYPE: E   COG: A

102. Explain and provide an example for three of the five functions that nonverbal communication can serve.

    ANSWER: TYPE: E   COG: C

103.	Explain the meaning of the statement, "Nonverbal messages convey emotions that we may be unwilling or unable to express, or ones we may not even be aware of."
	ANSWER:		TYPE: E		COG: R
104.	Describe a time when you jumped to conclusions over the ambiguity of someone's nonverbal behavior. Discuss how you could perception-check that same situation.
	ANSWER:		TYPE: E		COG: A
105.	Do you agree or disagree with Burgoon and Levine's research that "we overestimate our abilities to detect others' lies"? Explain.
	ANSWER:		TYPE: E		COG: C
106.	Pick a celebrity and describe how that person uses manner, appearance, and setting for identity management.
	ANSWER:		TYPE: E		COG: C
107.	Describe how vocal factors can influence the way a person is perceived by others.
	ANSWER:		TYPE: E		COG: C
108.	Discuss cultural barriers that can occur based on chronemics.
	ANSWER:		TYPE: E		COG: C
109.	Explain how clothing conveys trustworthiness and moral character.
	ANSWER:		TYPE: E		COG: C
110.	Do you agree with research that states "as we get to know more about people and like them, we start to regard them as better looking"? Why or why not?
	ANSWER:		TYPE: E		COG: A
111.	Which specific nonverbal behaviors suggest a communicator is attempting an act of deception?
		ANSWER:		TYPE: E		COG: A

Matching

112.	Match the letter of the term that best identifies each of the given examples.
	A.	kinesics
	B.	proxemics
	C.	territoriality
	D.	physical environment
	E.	chronemics

	_____ Juan was annoyed that someone else was sitting in "his seat" in class.

	_____ The lovers were sitting only inches apart.

	_____ The executive folded her arms and stood ramrod straight while she made her report to the Board.

	_____ Karen waited three days before answering Raul's e-mail message.

	_____ Antonio and Clyde decorated their apartment with posters and lights.

	ANSWER: C, B, A, E, D		TYPE: K		COG: C

113. Match the letter of the term that best identifies each of the numbered examples given. Begin by clarifying the terms as they have been defined in your text.

a. kinesics
b. paralanguage
c. proxemics
d. territoriality
e. haptics
f. chronemics

_____ 1. The executive *folded her arms and stood ramrod straight* while she made her report to the Board.
_____ 2. Jeremy put a *"NO ENTRANCE" sign* on *the door to his room*.
_____ 3. Mohammed went every day to the hospital just *to hold* his premature infant son.
_____ 4. Anne *stepped back three feet* from her friend.
_____ 5. Martin *turned his body away* from his brother.
_____ 6. Rob's *voice softened* when he spoke to her.
_____ 7. Chrissie *waited three days* before answering Erin's e-mail message.
_____ 8. Even though she was really busy, Susan *found time* to spend with Todd.
_____ 9. Mitchell *sighed* audibly.
_____ 10. Kevin was annoyed that someone else was *sitting in "his seat"* in class.
_____ 11. Nick always *put his arm around* his son when he wanted to give him advice.
_____ 12. The officer *pointed* in the correct direction.
_____ 13. When Jennifer got into the elevator, she chose to *stand in the corner farthest from the other passengers*.
_____ 14. The lovers were sitting *only inches* apart.
_____ 15. No one dared to sit in *Archie Bunker's chair*.

ANSWER KEY:

1. a	6. b	11. e
2. d	7. f	12. a
3. e	8. f	13. c
4. c	9. b	14. c
5. a	10. d	15. d

CHAPTER 7: LISTENING

True/False

1. Listening is defined as the process of receiving and responding to others.
    ANSWER: T   TYPE: T   COG: R
2. Research indicates that executives spend approximately 60 percent of their communication time listening.
    ANSWER: T   TYPE: T   COG: C
3. Listening involves much more than the passive act of hearing.
    ANSWER: T   TYPE: T   COG: R
4. Despite the frequency with which we use listening, listening skills tend to be recognized as of little importance by business leaders.
    ANSWER: F   TYPE: T   COG: C
5. In committed relationships, listening to personal information in everyday conversation is considered an important ingredient of satisfaction.
    ANSWER: T   TYPE: T   COG: C
6. Listening is a communication skill that can be developed and improved through instruction and training.
    ANSWER: T   TYPE: T   COG: R
7. "Failing to take the other's perspective when listening" is one of the most frequent marital communication problems.
    ANSWER: T   TYPE: T   COG: R
8. Listening is a natural activity that people do without conscious effort.
    ANSWER: F   TYPE: T   COG: R
9. Because every person interprets data uniquely, we have to accept the fact that we can never completely understand another person.
    ANSWER: T   TYPE: T   COG: R
10. Research indicates that the average person spends much more time speaking than listening in a normal day.
    ANSWER: F   TYPE: T   COG: R
11. The ability to make sense of messages is closely related to the listener's intelligence.
    ANSWER: T   TYPE: T   COG: R
12. Personality traits of listeners do not affect their ability to understand messages.
    ANSWER: F   TYPE: T   COG: R
13. Evaluative responses have the best chance of being received when the person with the problem hasn't requested an evaluation.
    ANSWER: F   TYPE: T   COG: C
14. A major difference between effective and ineffective listening is the kind of feedback offered.
    ANSWER: T   TYPE: T   COG: R
15. Mindless listening occurs when we react to others' messages automatically and routinely, without much mental investment.
    ANSWER: T   TYPE: T   COG: R
16. The ability to repeat a statement you just heard doesn't guarantee that you understood it.
    ANSWER: T   TYPE: T   COG: R
17. There are times when the best response is no response.
    ANSWER: T   TYPE: T   COG: R
18. Mindful listening involves giving careful and thoughtful attention and responses to the messages we receive.
    ANSWER: T   TYPE: T   COG: R
19. Sincere questions are attempts to send a message rather than receive one.
    ANSWER: F   TYPE: T   COG: R

20. The meaning and intent of any statement is shaped by its context.
                ANSWER: T   TYPE: T   COG: R

21. To have an "invitational" attitude is to learn more about perspectives other than your own.
                ANSWER: T   TYPE: T   COG: R

22. Questioning is an example of a listening response from the "more reflective/less evaluative" end of the listening response continuum.
                ANSWER: T   TYPE: T   COG: R

23. Listening is only a marginal skill when it comes to building good relationships.
                ANSWER: F   TYPE: T   COG: C

24. Listening automatic; hearing is not.
                ANSWER: F   TYPE: T   COG: R

25. Most communicators accurately evaluate their ability to listen and understand others.
                ANSWER: F   TYPE: T   COG: C

26. Paraphrasing is feedback that restates, in your own words, the message you thought the speaker sent.
                ANSWER: T   TYPE: T   COG: R

27. Sometimes, because of information overload, we choose to listen mindlessly rather than mindfully.
                ANSWER: T   TYPE: T   COG: R

28. Physiological factors do not contribute to listening since listening is a psychological process.
                ANSWER: F   TYPE: T   COG: C

29. Empathizing requires both understanding of and agreement with another person's message.
                ANSWER: F   TYPE: T   COG: C

30. Women are more prone than men to give supportive responses when presented with another person's problem.
                ANSWER: T   TYPE: T   COG: A

31. In analyzing a situation, the listener offers an interpretation of a speaker's message.
                ANSWER: T   TYPE: T   COG: R

32. Research on listening reveals that people only remember about half of what they hear immediately after hearing it.
                ANSWER: T   TYPE: T   COG: C

33. Communicators should use the one or two response styles at which they are the most skilled.
                ANSWER: F   TYPE: T   COG: R

34. Pseudolisteners give the appearance of being attentive, but their minds are in another world.
                ANSWER: T   TYPE: T   COG: R

35. When approached with another's problem, the most common reaction is advising.
                ANSWER: T   TYPE: T   COG: R

Multiple Choice

36. Recall is related to which component of hearing?
    a. hearing
    b. attending
    c. understanding
    d. remembering
    e. all of the above
            ANSWER: d   TYPE: M   COG: R

37. The ability to recall is a function of:
    a. the number of times information is repeated.
    b. how much information there is.
    c. whether the information may be "rehearsed."
    d. all of the above
    e. a and b only
            ANSWER: d   TYPE: M   COG: R

38. Reasons for improving listening skills include:
    a. to understand and retain information.
    b. to build and maintain relationships.
    c. to help others.
    d. to evaluate messages.
    e. all of the above
         ANSWER: e   TYPE: M   COG: R

39. Researcher Ellen Langer uses the terms _____ and _____ to describe the way that we listen.
    a. mindful, mindless
    b. attentive, nonattentive
    c. cognitive, mindless
    d. fruitful, fruitless
    e. none of the above
         ANSWER: a   TYPE: M   COG: R

40. Silent listening is the best response to use when:
    a. your interjections wouldn't be appropriate.
    b. you don't want to encourage a speaker to keep talking.
    c. you are open to the speaker's ideas.
    d. you want the speaker to talk through their own solution.
    e. all of the above
         ANSWER: d   TYPE: M   COG: R

41. Barriers to listening include:
    a. information overload.
    b. rapid thought and noise.
    c. other-affirmation.
    d. all of the above
    e. a and b only
         ANSWER: e   TYPE: M   COG: R

42. Which of the following is not a contributing factor for understanding messages?
    a. knowledge about the source of the message
    b. the listener's mental abilities
    c. the context of the message
    d. the volume of the message
    e. all of the above are contributing factors
         ANSWER: d   TYPE: M   COG: R

43. The fact that we spend five or more hours a day listening contributes to:
    a. hearing problems.
    b. information overload.
    c. personal concerns.
    d. rapid thought.
    e. noise
         ANSWER: b   TYPE: M   COG: R

44. Distractions presented by our physical and mental worlds contribute to:
    a. hearing problems.
    b. noise.
    c. personal concerns.
    d. rapid thought.
    e. information overload.
         ANSWER: b   TYPE: M   COG: R

45. After hearing about the car accident that Dan was in, Jenny responded with "What did you do then?" This type of questioning response is used to
   a. clarify meanings
   b. learn about others' thoughts and feelings
   c. learn about others' wants
   d. encourage discovery
   e. gather more facts and details
      ANSWER: e   TYPE: M   COG: A

46. Fatigue is which barrier to listening?
   a. hearing problem
   b. information overload
   c. personal concerns
   d. rapid thought
   e. noise
      ANSWER: e   TYPE: M   COG: R

47. Susan's professors think she is always listening to their lectures because of her eye contact, nods, and note-taking. In reality, Susan is using the class time to catch up on her personal diary. Susan is guilty of:
   a. pseudolistening.
   b. filling in the gaps.
   c. insulated listening.
   d. defensive listening.
   e. none of the above
      ANSWER: a   TYPE: M   COG: A

48. Barry is more concerned about how much and how long he can talk, rather than listening to others. Barry is guilty of:
   a. pseudolistening.
   b. insensitive listening.
   c. stage hogging.
   d. ambushing.
   e. selective listening.
      ANSWER: c   TYPE: M   COG: A

49. At least four of his friends have told Spencer that his girlfriend is dating others, but Spencer never seems to hear what they are saying. Spencer is probably a(n):
   a. pseudolistener.
   b. insulated listener.
   c. stage hogger.
   d. defensive listener.
   e. ambusher.
      ANSWER: b   TYPE: M   COG: A

50. Which of the following is an example of a question that carries a hidden agenda?
   a. "Are you busy Sunday evening?"
   b. "You called her back already?"
   c. "Why don't you ever listen?"
   d. "Do you think my new haircut is nice?"
   e. "Are you going to let him get away with that?"
      ANSWER: a   TYPE: M   COG: A

51. It's hard to talk to Edie because she always seems to take things the wrong way and to try to support herself and her side of the story. Edie is a(n):
    a. pseudolistener.
    b. insulated listener.
    c. stage hogger.
    d. defensive listener.
    e. ambusher.
        ANSWER: d   TYPE: M   COG: A
52. It's hard to talk to Kit because she never really seems to listen; she is just waiting for you to make a mistake and then she pounces. Kit is a(n):
    a. pseudolistener.
    b. insulated listener.
    c. stage hogger.
    d. defensive listener.
    e. ambusher.
        ANSWER: e   TYPE: M   COG: A
53. Restating in your own words what you thought a speaker has told you is known as:
    a. emphatic communication.
    b. paraphrasing.
    c. pseudolistening.
    d. stage hogging.
    e. empathizing.
        ANSWER: b   TYPE: M   COG: R
54. The listening response that involves staying attentive while being nonverbally responsive is known as:
    a. silent listening.
    b. questioning.
    c. paraphrasing.
    d. interjecting.
    e. advising.
        ANSWER: a   TYPE: M   COG: R
55. Which response style is associated with the "less reflective/more evaluative" end of the listening response continuum?
    a. questioning
    b. empathizing
    c. paraphrasing
    d. analyzing
    e. none of the above
        ANSWER: d   TYPE: M   COG: R
56. Reflecting a speaker's thoughts, feelings, and wants is associated with which type of listening response?
    a. paraphrasing
    b. analyzing
    c. advising
    d. evaluating
    e. supporting
        ANSWER: a   TYPE: M   COG: R
57. All of the following are misconceptions about listening except:
    a. listening is a skill that can be taught.
    b. listening and hearing are the same thing.
    c. listening is easy.
    d. All listeners receive the same message.
    e. None of the above is applicable.
        ANSWER: a   TYPE: M   COG: R

233

58. Which of the following is not an example of a counterfeit question?
    a. "Are you finally off the phone?"
    b. "Are you busy Friday night?"
    c. "Honey, do you think I'm overweight?"
    d. "Why aren't you listening to me?"
    e. "You said we were going too fast. Could you be more specific?"
    ANSWER: e   TYPE: M   COG: R
59. Paraphrasing means:
    a. using gestures, nods, and facial expressions to respond to the speaker.
    b. restating, in your own words, the message you think the speaker just sent.
    c. repeated use of questions.
    d. mentally questioning the speaker's intentions and arguments.
    e. all of the above
    ANSWER: b   TYPE: M   COG: R
60. All of the following represent the "more reflective/less evaluative" end of the listening continuum
    except:
    a. questioning.
    b. paraphrasing.
    c. empathizing.
    d. analyzing.
    e. none of the above
    ANSWER: d   TYPE: M   COG: R
61. Which of the following is *not* one of the five components of listening mentioned in your text?
    a. hearing
    b. attending
    c. understanding
    d. advising
    e. responding
    ANSWER: d   TYPE: M   COG: R
62. When listeners attempt to show solidarity with the people to whom they are listening, they are using
    which listening response style?
    a. silent listening
    b. paraphrasing
    c. supporting
    d. analyzing
    e. evaluating
    ANSWER: c   TYPE: M   COG: R
63. The residual message is the
    a. most important component
    b. least important component
    c. message "lost" through lack of recall
    d. part of the message we remember
    e. connections listeners make with their own culture
    ANSWER: d   TYPE: M   COG: R
64. A listening model that includes responding is a _____ model.
    a. transactional
    b. transmission
    c. residual
    d. proactive
    e. nonverbal
    ANSWER: a   TYPE: M   COG: R

65. Which of the following is the most accurate example of an empathizing response?
   a. "Don't worry about it."
   b. "Hey, it's only a game."
   c. "You'll feel better tomorrow."
   d. all of the above
   e. none of the above
      ANSWER: e   TYPE: M   COG: R

66. Which of the following is a more reflective/less evaluative listening response?
   a. supporting
   b. questioning
   c. analyzing
   d. advising
   e. evaluating
      ANSWER: b   TYPE: M   COG: R

67. Which statement about the following conversation is accurate?
   Speaker: Trent is such a jerk; he always takes me for granted.
   Listener: You're disgusted with the way Trent has been treating you.
   a. The listener used pseudolistening.
   b. The listener gave a poor paraphrase because it doesn't use the speaker's words.
   c. The listener should have used a question before trying to paraphrase.
   d. The listener used a paraphrase to try and understand the speaker's message.
   e. Both a and b are accurate.
      ANSWER: d   TYPE: M   COG: A

68. The difference between an empathizing response and a supporting response is:
   a. a supporting response is less effective.
   b. an empathizing response is less effective.
   c. an empathizing response is more evaluative and directive.
   d. a supporting response is more evaluative and directive.
   e. none of the above
      ANSWER: d   TYPE: M   COG: C

69. Which is *not* an example of a counterfeit question?
   a. questions that make statements
   b. questions that carry hidden agendas
   c. questions based on unchecked assumptions
   d. questions that gather more facts and details
   e. all of the above
      ANSWER: d   TYPE: M   COG: R

70. When offering a supporting response it is important to:
   a. use touch as well as verbal support.
   b. be sure your support is sincere.
   c. be sure the speaker can accept your support.
   d. focus on the future.
   e. b and c only
      ANSWER: e   TYPE: M   COG: R

71. When offering an analyzing response it is important to:
   a. use tentative phrasing.
   b. be reasonably sure you are correct.
   c. be sure the other person will be receptive.
   d. be sure your motive for offering an analysis is truly to help.
   e. all of the above
      ANSWER: e   TYPE: M   COG: R

72. Which of the following is an analyzing response phrased in a tentative way?
    a. Your teacher doesn't understand you.
    b. Perhaps your teacher wants you to work harder.
    c. You need to talk to the teacher.
    d. Most teachers are like that.
    e. What did your teacher say?
        ANSWER: b   TYPE: M   COG: A
73. Silent listening is defined as:
    a. listening without words.
    b. listening without giving the speaker feedback.
    c. listening without eye contact or head movement.
    d. listening attentively with nonverbal responses.
    e. None of the above is silent listening.
        ANSWER: d   TYPE: M   COG: R
74. Why is "parrot-phrasing" not a good idea?
    a. you sound foolish
    b. you sound hard of hearing
    c. you still might misunderstand
    d. none of the above
    e. all of the above
        ANSWER: e   TYPE: M   COG: R
75. When offering advice it is important to be sure:
    a. the advice is offered in a sensitive manner.
    b. the speaker is ready to accept it.
    c. the speaker won't blame you if it doesn't work.
    d. all of the above
    e. a and b only
        ANSWER: d   TYPE: M   COG: R

Essay

76. Discuss the following quotation in terms of what you know about listening: "If you think communication is all talk, you haven't been listening." Ashleigh Brilliant
        ANSWER: TYPE: E   COG: C
77. Other than those found in the text, give examples of three counterfeit questions. Explain what makes them counterfeit rather than sincere, and then offer sincere alternatives for each.
        ANSWER: TYPE: E   COG: A
78. A friend is about to graduate and tells you that she thinks she picked the wrong major. Discuss the following four helping strategies in terms of their potential advantages and disadvantages: advising, analyzing, evaluating, and supporting.
        ANSWER: TYPE: E   COG: A
79. Imagine that you are explaining the listening unit of this course to friends or family. They want to know why it's important to be a good listener and why (since they all hear) it is possible they're not good listeners.
        ANSWER: TYPE: E   COG: C
80. Your text gives several reasons why paraphrasing assists listening. Cite three of these reasons, briefly explaining each.
        ANSWER: TYPE: E   COG: R
81. Your friend has just told you about a death in her/his family. Offer two responses that would fall into categories of nonempathizing identified in the text. Explain what makes them nonempathic; then offer and explain two empathizing alternatives.
        ANSWER: TYPE: E   COG: A

82. You and your partner are having a discussion about your relationship. Your partner says the following to you: "I don't like the way things are going between us. You don't treat me like you used to, and you embarrassed me in front of my friends last night. It seems to me like I care about you a lot more than you care about me." Explain in detail why the following responses would *not* be examples of active listening.
   a. "You're upset because you're tired. Why don't we talk about this tomorrow when I know we'll both feel a lot better?"
   b. "Don't worry. What happened last night won't happen again."
   c. "Hey, you're not the only one unhappy about this relationship."
      ANSWER: TYPE: E   COG: A
83. Respond to each of the following statements with a more reflective/less directive listening response.
   a. "You just never stop to think of me…it's just work, work, and work, as if that's all there is to life."
   b. "Frankly, I'm leaving because I'm looking for a job where my talents will be recognized and my contributions valued."
   c. "I don't know how you expect me to believe you care when you leave me waiting here for three hours."
   d. "I'm such a jerk! If I hadn't opened my big mouth, Bob and Barb would be together right now!"
      ANSWER: TYPE: E   COG: A
84. Give five different types of responses to your friend who says to you: "That professor wants me to think of him as God or something. He thinks nobody could possibly know anything prior to entering his classroom." Choose from the following: advising, analyzing, supporting, empathizing, questioning, and evaluating. Be sure to identify the style that each example illustrates.
      ANSWER: TYPE: E   COG: A
85. Explain the essential differences between "more reflective/less directive" listening responses and "less reflective/more directive" listening responses. In your answer, give two examples from each end of the listening continuum.
      ANSWER: TYPE: E   COG: A

Matching

86. Match the letter of the example that best fits the type of listening responses.

   _____ 1. Analyzing
   _____ 2. Evaluating
   _____ 3. Advising
   _____ 4. Supporting
   _____ 5. Empathizing

   a. "Wow, it sounds like you had a busy day."
   b. "I think you should go and talk to him about it."
   c. "I think she is behaving like that because she isn't feeling well."
   d. "That's a good point."
   e. "I remember when you had a similar situation, you did great."

   Answer: 1. c, 2. d, 3. b, 4. e, 5. a
                        TYPE: K   COG: A

CHAPTER 8: EMOTIONS

True/False

1. Daniel Goleman's concept of *emotional intelligence* refers to the ability to understand and manage one's own emotions and to be sensitive to others' feelings.
   ANSWER: T   TYPE: T   COG: R

2. Some researchers believe there are several "basic" or "primary" emotions.
   ANSWER: T   TYPE: T   COG: C

3. Not all physical changes that accompany emotions are universal.
   ANSWER: T   TYPE: T   COG: C

4. People tend to express their emotions nonverbally rather than verbally.
   ANSWER: T   TYPE: T   COG: C

5. Failure to express emotions plays a part in physical as well as mental health.
   ANSWER: T   TYPE: T   COG: A

6. Individuals who label themselves as *shy* tend to exhibit distinctly different behavioral patterns than those who label themselves as *not shy*.
   ANSWER: F   TYPE: T   COG: R

7. Pretending to be angry can actually make us become angry.
   ANSWER: T   TYPE: T   COG: R

8. Our interpretation of any event is a more important determinant of feelings than is the event itself.
   ANSWER: T   TYPE: T   COG: R

9. Women are consistently better than men at detecting nonverbal emotional cues.
   ANSWER: T   TYPE: T   COG: R

10. Because we talk ourselves into debilitative feelings, it is possible to talk ourselves out of feeling bad.
    ANSWER: T   TYPE: T   COG: C

11. Both men and women express anger equally, but men are less bashful about revealing their strengths and positive emotions.
    ANSWER: T   TYPE: T   COG: C

12. There are some situations in which you may (correctly) choose never to express your feelings.
    ANSWER: T   TYPE: T   COG: R

13. Many people think they're clearly expressing their feelings when in fact their statements are emotionally counterfeit.
    ANSWER: T   TYPE: T   COG: C

14. Most people find it easier to express negative emotions than positive ones.
    ANSWER: F   TYPE: T   COG: R

15. The comment "I feel as if you're trying to hurt me" is a clear statement of the speaker's feelings.
    ANSWER: F   TYPE: T   COG: A

16. Emotions that are primary in one culture may not be primary in others, with some emotions having no equivalent in other cultures.
    ANSWER: T   TYPE: T   COG: R

17. Research on emotional expression suggests that there is some truth to the cultural stereotype of the more demonstrative male and the inexpressive female.
    ANSWER: F   TYPE: T   COG: R

18. Facilitative emotions hinder or prevent effective communication.
    ANSWER: F   TYPE: T   COG: R

19. Strong emotions sharpen your thinking ability.
    ANSWER: F   TYPE: T   COG: C

20. Recent research by Bushman suggests that people who act out angry feelings actually feel worse than those who experience anger without lashing out.
    ANSWER: T   TYPE: T   COG: R

21. One of the important guidelines for expressing emotions is the ability to recognize the difference between feeling and acting.

    ANSWER: T   TYPE: T   COG: R

22. The difference between facilitative and debilitative emotions often isn't one of quality as much as of degree.

    ANSWER: T   TYPE: T   COG: R

23. In mainstream U.S. society, the unwritten rules of communication discourage the direct expression of most emotions.

    ANSWER: T   TYPE: T   COG: R

24. It is best to express our emotions spontaneously and completely in all circumstances.

    ANSWER: F   TYPE: T   COG: C

25. Being rushed, tired, or disturbed by some other matter is not adequate reason for postponing the sharing of a feeling.

    ANSWER: F   TYPE: T   COG: C

26. Physiological manifestations of fear, such as a racing heart, perspiration, tense muscles, and elevated blood pressure could also mimic excitement, which is why the physical conditions of emotions is difficult to interpret.

    ANSWER: T   TYPE: T   COG: R

27. When we feel numerous emotions at one time, we should stick to revealing only one emotion so as not to confuse others.

    ANSWER: F   TYPE: T   COG: C

28. Your friend Omar tells you about the happenings of his day, but when you ask him how he feels about one of the events, he clams up. This exemplifies that people rarely disclose how they feel, but are more comfortable sharing facts.

    ANSWER: T   TYPE: T   COG: C

29. Emotion labor means that we have to figure out what emotions to show at work.

    ANSWER: F   TYPE: T   COG: R

30. Choosing the best language to share emotions includes using single words, describing what's happening to you metaphorically, and describing what you'd like to do to the other person.

    ANSWER: F   TYPE: T   COG: R

31. Naima doesn't ever give her best friend Rita anything but positive feedback, even if it is not completely honest. She doesn't want to hurt Rita's feelings. Naima is using the fallacy of perfection.

    ANSWER: F   TYPE: T   COG: C

32. Jose says, "I can't find a girlfriend because all women just want money and I don't have a good enough job." Jose is using the fallacy of helplessness.

    ANSWER: T   TYPE: T   COG: C

33. Catastrophic thinking often takes the form of rumination.

    ANSWER: T   TYPE: T   COG: C

Multiple Choice

34. An increased heartbeat, a rise in blood pressure, and an increase in adrenaline secretions are all part of which emotional component?

    a. physiological changes
    b. nonverbal manifestations
    c. cognitive interpretations
    d. verbal expressions
    e. all of the above

    ANSWER: a   TYPE: M   COG: C

35. All of the following are guidelines for expressing emotions *except:*
    a. recognizing your feelings.
    b. recognizing the difference between feeling and acting.
    c. accepting responsibility for your feelings.
    d. choosing the best time and place to express your feelings.
    e. share only one feeling at a time.
    ANSWER: e   TYPE: M   COG: R

36. Mark and his brother, Tom, have a very difficult time expressing emotions in person but have a very close emotional relationship when e-mailing. Why might this be so?
    a. Society discourages the expression of feelings among males.
    b. Emotional self-disclosure can seem risky.
    c. Emotional honesty can be used against you.
    d. all of the above
    e. none of the above
    ANSWER: d   TYPE: M   COG: A

37. _____ is the best predictor of the ability to detect and interpret emotional expression.
    a. biological sex
    b. cultural similarity
    c. willingness to self-disclose
    d. academic background
    e. nonverbal communication
    ANSWER: a   TYPE: M   COG: C

38. Research on emotions in the workplace indicate that expressing emotions at work is:
    a. considered healthy.
    b. considered unprofessional.
    c. appropriate.
    d. appropriate only if they are happy emotions.
    e. none of the above
    ANSWER: b   TYPE: M   COG: R

39. Debilitative feelings are caused by fallacies of:
    a. perfection, repeating, and shoulds.
    b. overgeneralization and causation.
    c. helplessness and catastrophic expectation.
    d. all of the above
    e. b and c only
    ANSWER: d   TYPE: M   COG: R

40. It's been a year since Mark and Tracy broke up. Mark is still depressed and gets irate if anyone even mentions Tracy's name. Mark is experiencing:
    a. self-disclosure.
    b. self-talk.
    c. facilitative emotions.
    d. debilitative emotions.
    e. none of the above
    ANSWER: d   TYPE: M   COG: A

41. Using situational clues to label symptoms is characteristic of which emotional component?
    a. physiological changes
    b. nonverbal manifestations
    c. cognitive interpretations
    d. verbal expressions
    e. all of the above
    ANSWER: c   TYPE: M   COG: C

42. The little voice in your head that talks to you constantly is called:
   a. self-talk.
   b. cognitive performance.
   c. cognitive talk.
   d. irrational thinking.
   e. debilitative thinking.
      ANSWER: a   TYPE: M   COG: R

43. Recognizing your _____ is an important step in minimizing debilitative emotions.
   a. personality style
   b. feelings
   c. self-concept
   d. activating events
   e. none of the above
      ANSWER: d   TYPE: M   COG: R

44. If people insist that the world can operate just as they want it to, they have fallen into which fallacy?
   a. approval
   b. causation
   c. shoulds
   d. helplessness
   e. catastrophic expectations
      ANSWER: c   TYPE: M   COG: R

45. Feeling apologetic when you are not at fault is a symptom of which fallacy?
   a. approval
   b. causation
   c. shoulds
   d. helplessness
   e. catastrophic expectations
      ANSWER: a.   TYPE: M   COG: C

46. Science has established a clear relationship between _____ and the way people experience and communicate emotions.
   a. academic background
   b. personality
   c. social Status
   d. biological Sex
   e. intelligence
      ANSWER: b   TYPE: M   COG: C

47. Instead of saying "You are so boring," it is better to say _____ when your friend again talks about shopping.
   a. "I think you are boring."
   b. "I'm a little bored."
   c. "I am bored with you."
   d. "You are boring when you talk about shopping."
   e. "I get bored when you talk about shopping."
      ANSWER: e   TYPE: M   COG: A

48. "I don't have a thing to wear!" is a statement of which fallacy?
   a. causation
   b. overgeneralization
   c. shoulds
   d. helplessness
   e. catastrophic expectations
      ANSWER: b   TYPE: M   COG: A

49. If you feel you should do nothing that can hurt others because it would make them feel a particular way, you have fallen into which fallacy?
   a. causation
   b. overgeneralization
   c. shoulds
   d. helplessness
   e. catastrophic expectation
      ANSWER: a   TYPE: M   COG: A
50. If people see themselves perpetually as victims, they have fallen into which fallacy?
   a. causation
   b. overgeneralization
   c. shoulds
   d. helplessness
   e. catastrophic expectations
      ANSWER: d   TYPE: M   COG: A
51. Monitoring self-talk is a way to:
   a. recognize your feelings.
   b. share multiple emotions.
   c. accept responsibility for your feelings.
   d. choose the best time and place for expressing your feelings.
   e. speak unambiguously.
      ANSWER: a   TYPE: M   COG: R
52. The recognition that others don't cause your feelings helps you:
   a. recognize your feelings.
   b. share multiple emotions.
   c. accept responsibility for your feelings.
   d. choose the best time and place for expressing your feelings.
   e. speak unambiguously.
      ANSWER: c   TYPE: M   COG: R
53. Members of collectivist cultures are more likely to:
   a. discourage expression of negative emotions.
   b. feel comfortable revealing their feelings.
   c. speak openly abut problems.
   d. share personal ideas and feelings.
   e. b and c and d
      ANSWER: a   TYPE: M   COG: R
54. Which of the following is the most genuine expression of emotions?
   a. "It's inconvenient to be kept waiting."
   b. "We really need to get going."
   c. "I'm worried about my brother."
   d. "I feel like we've been seeing too much of each other."
   e. "I didn't get to study last night."
      ANSWER: c   TYPE: M   COG: A
55. Storming out of your bedroom to yell at your loud roommates at 3:00 am is a violation of which guideline to expressing feelings appropriately?
   a. Recognize the difference between feeling and acting.
   b. Choose the best time and place to express feelings.
   c. Share multiple feelings
   d. Recognize your feelings
   e. none of the above
      ANSWER: b   TYPE: M   COG: A

56. One result of a life spent avoiding the expression of emotion may be:
    a. a debilitating fear of self-disclosure.
    b. the limiting of behavior to stereotyped roles.
    c. the inability to recognize and act on one's emotions.
    d. failure to acknowledge strong feelings.
    e. all of the above
        ANSWER: e   TYPE: M   COG: A
57. Which of the following is a benefit of sharing feelings?
    a. an increase in the quality of problem solving
    b. a decrease in other-directedness
    c. an increase in static evaluations
    d. a need for deciding when to self-disclose
    e. none of the above
        ANSWER: a   TYPE: M   COG: R
58. Debilitative emotions can be distinguished from facilitative emotions by their:
    a. low intensity and brief duration.
    b. low intensity and extended duration.
    c. high intensity and extended duration.
    d. high intensity and brief duration.
    e. variable intensity and duration.
        ANSWER: c   TYPE: M   COG: R
59. The experience of fright, joy, or anger comes primarily from:
    a. the physical symptoms experienced.
    b. the cause of the emotion.
    c. the label we give these experiences.
    d. the situation.
    e. attribution theory
        ANSWER: c   TYPE: M   COG: C
60. Most researchers believe that there are several emotions common among people of all different
    cultures. All of the following are considered common emotions *except:*
    a. anger.
    b. joy.
    c. fear.
    d. sadness.
    e. excitement.
        ANSWER: e   TYPE: M   COG: R
61. Science has established a clear relationship between _____ and the way that people experience and
    communicate emotions.
    a. personality
    b. culture
    c. gender
    d. a. and b
    e. all of the above
        ANSWER: e   TYPE: M   COG: R
62. The fallacy of overgeneralization:
    a. confuses *is* with *might.*
    b. results from trying to obtain everyone's approval.
    c. bases a belief on a limited amount of evidence.
    d. exaggerates shortcomings.
    e. c and d
        ANSWER: e   TYPE: M   COG: R

63. "If I take chemistry, I'll probably get an 'F'." This statement is an example of the fallacy of:
    a. overgeneralization.
    b. perfection.
    c. causation.
    d. shoulds.
    e. catastrophic expectations.
    ANSWER: e   TYPE: M   COG: A

64. Ian and Zelda are in an intense fight. Zelda's heart is racing and her face feels hot with anger. Ian's palms are sweaty. Gottman calls this reaction _____, which can impede effective problem solving.
    a. frustration
    b. flooding
    c. emotional intelligence
    d. nonverbal reactions
    e. debilitative emotions
    ANSWER: b   TYPE: M   COG: A

65. _____ cultures discourage revealing emotions which could be considered hurtful to others or negative.
    a. Collective
    b. Individualistic
    c. Achieving
    d. Nurturing
    e. High power distance
    ANSWER: a   TYPE: M   COG: R

66. Quinn is trying very hard not to cry during a discussion with her boss. She doesn't want to be labeled or judged for getting so upset at work. This is an example of:
    a. emotional intelligence.
    b. facilitative emotions.
    c. debilitative emotions.
    d. self-disclosure.
    e. emotional labor.
    ANSWER: a   TYPE: M   COG: A

67. After an argument, Lyle tells his partner Paul, "I'd like to take the afternoon to myself." Lyle is demonstrating which element of expressing emotions verbally?
    a. using single words
    b. describing what's happening metaphorically
    c. describing what he'd like to do
    d. describing what he wants his partner to do
    e. none of the above
    ANSWER: c   TYPE: M   COG: A

68. Why is saying, "I feel like we're talking about the situation too much" problematic with respect to emotionally revealing vocabulary?
    a. There is no emotional content.
    b. The feeling is really a thought.
    c. The word "feel" stands for an intention.
    d. a and b only
    e. all of the above
    ANSWER: e   TYPE: M   COG: C

69. Moline says, "You never called me last night like you said you would!" What wording could Moline use to show that she accepts responsibility for her feelings?
    a. "I feel like you never call me!"
    b. "I feel like we never talk anymore."
    c. "I'm sad that I didn't hear from you."
    d. "I don't like it when some people don't call."
    e. None of the above.
        ANSWER: c   TYPE: M   COG: A

70. Tyree doesn't trust women because his last girlfriend cheated on him. When women approach him and seem romantically interested, he gets triggered, becomes distant and feels nervous. What Tyree is experiencing is an example of:
    a. emotional labor.
    b. debilitative emotions.
    c. thoughts causing feelings.
    d. facilitative emotions.
    e. emotional intelligence.
        ANSWER: c   TYPE: M   COG: A

71. If Tyree tells himself, "You know that not all women will cheat on you. This was one instance with one particular person. There are many trustworthy people out there," this is an example of:
    a. recording self-talk.
    b. noting the activating event.
    c. monitoring emotional reactions.
    d. disputing irrational beliefs.
    e. using the fallacy of causation.
        ANSWER: d   TYPE: M   COG: C

72. Liandra realizes that whenever her friends talk about weight, she starts to feel very self-conscious and upset. She decides that she will disclose her feelings to a couple of her friends and also will work on her concerns about her body. This is an example of:
    a. recording self-talk.
    b. noting the activating event.
    c. monitoring emotional reactions.
    d. disputing irrational beliefs.
    e. using the fallacy of causation.
        ANSWER: b   TYPE: M   COG: C

73. George has refused to continue to teach interpersonal communication because he sometimes has conflicts in his own relationships. George may be a victim of the fallacy of:
    a. overgeneralization.
    b. perfection.
    c. causation.
    d. shoulds.
    e. catastrophic expectations.
        ANSWER: b   TYPE: M   COG: A

Essay

74. The text states that *the fallacy of perfection* is an irrational belief that leads people to think they must perform perfectly in any situation or they are failures. Using your own experience, describe two debilitative emotions that can result from subscribing to this belief.
        ANSWER: TYPE: E   COG: A

75. Explain what is meant by the following statement: "Anger suppressed can literally 'eat away at our guts.'"
        ANSWER: TYPE: E   COG: A

76. Imagine you are a student in a class for which participating in discussions is a central requirement for a good grade. You are a relatively outgoing person, but you have always had a hard time speaking up in class to offer your comments, opinions, criticisms, and so on. In fact, you almost never do so, not even when you are completely familiar with the material. In trying to minimize this debilitative emotion, identify (1) the activating event and (2) the emotional reaction. Then offer three examples of the negative self-talk that represents the irrational belief this student is probably operating on. Finally, dispute those irrational beliefs with three coping statements.

ANSWER: TYPE: E COG: A

77. Briefly describe and provide an example of each of the four components of emotion.

ANSWER: TYPE: E COG: R

78. Briefly explain the influence of gender and culture on emotional expressiveness and sensitivity.

ANSWER: TYPE: E COG: A

79. The textbook discusses social scientists' research that people from warmer climates are more emotionally expressive than those who live in cooler spaces. Discuss whether you agree with this statement and give examples to support your views.

ANSWER: TYPE: E COG: C

80. Write a statement that includes the fallacy of should. Discuss two to three underlying messages that a receiver may hear when the word "should" is used. Rephrase the statement to avoid the fallacy.

ANSWER: TYPE: E COG: A

81. Write three statements that appear to blame others for feelings. Rewrite those statements with verbiage that indicates taking responsibility for one's feelings.

ANSWER: TYPE: E COG: A

82. The textbook mentions that women use emoticons to clarify their feelings, yet men use emoticons more likely as sarcasm. Do you agree with this statement? Why or why not?

ANSWER: TYPE: E COG: C

83. Explain "emotional labor" as it pertains to professional environments.

ANSWER: TYPE: E COG: C

84. Write three statements that a college student might say that reveal a fallacy of helplessness. Rewrite the statements to avoid the fallacy.

ANSWER: TYPE: E COG: A

85. Gottman discusses that couples in intense conflict can experience emotional "flooding", which can impede problem solving. What can couples do to avoid flooding when in conflict?

ANSWER: TYPE: E COG: A

86. With respect to emotions and personality, what do the authors mean by the statement, "While personality can be a powerful force, it doesn't have to govern your communication satisfaction"?

ANSWER: TYPE: E COG: A

87. Give an example of expressing emotions on the individualism-collectivism spectrum.

ANSWER: TYPE: E COG: C

88. Discuss two personal examples of facilitative and debilitative emotions.

ANSWER: TYPE: E COG: A

Matching

89. Match the letter of the example to the number of the reason we form relationships.

_____ 1. Disclosure
_____ 2. Complementarity
_____ 3. Rewards
_____ 4. Competency
_____ 5. Proximity

a. He's a good decorator, and I don't care where we put the couch.
b. I don't mind that she has to work some weekends, because then we can afford a nicer vacation.
c. I sometimes struggle with expressing my feelings.
d. I saw him every day in class.
e. She was really good at swimming.

1. c, 2. a, 3. b, 4. e, 5. d

90. Match the numbered descriptions with the following terms.

a. avoiding
b. bonding
c. circumscribing
d. differentiating
e. exchange theory
f. experimenting
g. expression-privacy dialectic
h. initiating

i. integrating
j. integration-separation dialectic
k. intensifying
l. metacommunication
m. stability-change dialectic
n. stagnating
o. terminating

_____ 1. Jason and Claire are in the process of a divorce. Instead of seeing one another or talking on the phone, they try to call one another at times when they will be able to use voice mail instead.

_____ 2. Jason and Claire spend more and more time together; they admit to one another that they are "in love."

_____ 3. Jason and Claire discover that they both enjoy basketball, romantic movies, and Chinese food.

_____ 4. Jason and Claire have a wedding with over 300 guests.

_____ 5. Jason and Claire confine their conversation to "safe" topics, like dinner and what's on the news.

_____ 6. Jason and Claire meet at a party. They are attracted to one another, so they both try to present as positive an image of themselves as possible.

_____ 7. Jason enjoys being able to think he knows how Claire will respond, but he also enjoys a few surprises now and then.

_____ 8. Jason and Claire's divorce is final. They decide that they will move to different cities and begin life anew.

_____ 9. Claire likes the feeling she gets from sharing her private thoughts and emotions with Jason, but there are some things that she still prefers to keep to herself.

_____ 10. Jason and Claire frequently strengthen their relationship by discussing their strengths and weaknesses in the area of communication.

_____ 11. Jason and Claire talk as little as possible. He knows that if he talks about family, she will complain about his mother. She knows that if she talks about going to see a movie, he will complain that they always have to see what she wants to see.

_____ 12. "You should really be more patient about learning how to play the piano."

_____ 13. Jason and Claire are seen as a couple. They receive joint invitations to parties and weddings.

_____ 14. Jason and Claire enjoy spending quality time with one another, but they each also value their own independence and sense of individual identity.

_____ 15. Jason and Claire begin to discover that they are not so alike after all. She loves to shop and go to the theatere, and he would rather stay home and read a book or watch a football game.

ANSWER KEY:

1. a	6. h	11. n
2. k	7. m	12. e
3. f	8. o	13. i
4. b	9. g	14. j
5. c	10. l	15. d

CHAPTER 9: DYNAMICS OF INTERPERSONAL RELATIONSHIPS

True/False

1. Your text suggests that a relationship is less a *thing* and more of a *process*.
    ANSWER: T TYPE: T COG: R
2. The relational dimension of messages makes statements about how the parties feel toward one another.
    ANSWER: T TYPE: T COG: R
3. Metacommunication is communication about communication.
    ANSWER: T TYPE: T COG: R
4. After initial impressions, average-looking people with pleasing personalities are likely to be judged as attractive.
    ANSWER: T TYPE: T COG: R
5. The *similarity thesis* proposes that it is comforting to know someone who likes the same things you like.
    ANSWER: T TYPE: T COG:R
6. Appearance is especially important in the early stages of a relationship.
    ANSWER: T TYPE: T COG: R
7. Exchange theory suggests we seek out people who can give us rewards that are greater than the costs we encounter in dealing with them.
    ANSWER: T TYPE: T COG: R
8. The best way to gain the liking of others is to be good at what you do and to deny your mistakes.
    ANSWER: F TYPE: T COG: C
9. Relational maintenance is a vital component of relational success.
    ANSWER: T TYPE: T COG: R
10. Relationships, once invented and defined, cannot be reinvented and redefined.
    ANSWER: F TYPE: T COG: R
11. In a successful relationship, it is *not* important that both partners use relational maintenance strategies.
    ANSWER: F TYPE: T COG: R
12. For adults, similarity is more important to relational happiness than even communication ability.
    ANSWER: T TYPE: T COG: C
13. Differences strengthen a relationship when they are complementary.
    ANSWER: T TYPE: T COG: R
14. When partners are radically different, the dissimilar qualities that at first appear intriguing later become cause for relational breakups.
    ANSWER: T TYPE: T COG: C
15. A chat room or an instant messaging connection constitutes virtual proximity.
    ANSWER: T TYPE: T COG: R
16. Aronson's research suggests that competent people who blunder are rated as less attractive than competent people who don't blunder.
    ANSWER: F TYPE: T COG: C
17. The relational stages described by Mark Knapp are most appropriate for describing professional rather than personal relationships.
    ANSWER: F TYPE: T COG: R
18. Telling others important information about yourself can help build liking.
    ANSWER: T TYPE: T COG: R
19. According to Knapp's theory, small talk is a meaningless pastime engaged in at initial stages of relationships.
    ANSWER: F TYPE: T COG: R
20. Dialectical tensions occur when two opposing or incompatible forces exist simultaneously.
    ANSWER: T TYPE: T COG: R

21. The dialectical tensions of stability and change involve our conflicting desires for connection and independence.

ANSWER: F   TYPE: T   COG: R

22. When we are unsure how to react to an unexpected response from an intimate friend, we are being affected by the predictability-novelty dialectic.

ANSWER: T   TYPE: T   COG: A

23. Relational messages are usually expressed nonverbally.

ANSWER: T   TYPE: T   COG: R

24. Couples in successful marriages are similar enough to satisfy each other but different enough to meet each other's needs.

ANSWER: T   TYPE: T   COG: C

25. We like to be around talented people because we hope their abilities will rub off on us, but we are uncomfortable around people who are too competent.

ANSWER: T   TYPE: T   COG: R

26. Both men and women in heterosexual relationships said the connection-autonomy dialectic was the least important factor affecting their relationship.

ANSWER: F   TYPE: T   COG: R

27. Research has indicated that the least forgivable offenses for dating partners were sexual infidelity and breaking up.

ANSWER: T   TYPE: T   COG: R

28. Forgiveness does not seem to have any relational benefits.

ANSWER: F   TYPE: T   COG: R

29. Whether a couple was friends before they became romantically involved is not a predictor of whether they will stay friends after the relationship is terminated.

ANSWER: F   TYPE: T   COG: R

30. *Proximity* is the factor that maintains that we are likely to develop strong personal feelings of either like or dislike toward others whom we encounter frequently.

ANSWER: T   TYPE: T   COG: R

Multiple Choice

31. The similarity thesis is based on which similarities between partners?
  a. educational standing
  b. race
  c. economic class
  d. likes the same things you like
  e. all of the above

ANSWER: e   TYPE: M   COG: R

32. Logical reasons for the similarity thesis include:
  a. social validation of ourselves.
  b. reduces uncertainty and anxiety.
  c. assume they like us, so we like them.
  d. all of the above
  e. a and c only

ANSWER: d   TYPE: M   COG: C

33. The old saying "Opposites attract" suggests which reason for forming relationships?
  a. appearance
  b. similarity
  c. complementarity
  d. reciprocity
  e. exchange

ANSWER: c   TYPE: M   COG: C

34. The theory that explains relationship development using an economic model is:
    a. exchange.
    b. penetration.
    c. relational dialectic.
    d. all of the above
    e. none of the above
        ANSWER: a   TYPE: M   COG: R
35. Which type of person was rated as the most attractive?
    a. superior person who did not blunder
    b. superior person who blundered
    c. average person who blundered
    d. average person who did not blunder
    e. a and d only
        ANSWER: b   TYPE: M   COG: C
36. The fact that we are likely to choose a mate with whom we frequently cross paths often points to which reason for forming relationships?
    a. appearance
    b. similarity
    c. complementarity
    d. reciprocity
    e. proximity
        ANSWER: e   TYPE: M   COG: C
37. In which stage of relational development is the communication usually brief and follows conventional formulas?
    a. initiating
    b. experimenting
    c. intensifying
    d. integrating
    e. bonding
        ANSWER: a   TYPE: M   COG: R
38. Small talk is the hallmark of which stage of relationship development?
    a. experimenting
    b. intensifying
    c. integrating
    d. bonding
    e. terminating
        ANSWER: a   TYPE: M   COG: R
39. When partners begin to refer to themselves as "we," they have moved into which relational stage?
    a. initiating
    b. experimenting
    c. intensifying
    d. integrating
    e. bonding
        ANSWER: d   TYPE: M   COG: R
40. Business contracts or marriage licenses are found in which stage of relational development?
    a. initiating
    b. experimenting
    c. intensifying
    d. integrating
    e. bonding
        ANSWER: e   TYPE: M   COG: C

41. Working late at the office could be an example of which stage of relational development?
    a. bonding
    b. differentiating
    c. circumscribing
    d. stagnation
    e. termination
        ANSWER: c   TYPE: M   COG: A
42. When your mother still calls you "my baby," even though you are in adult, she is *not* recognizing which principle about relationships?
    a. They do change.
    b. They require attention.
    c. They meet expectations of participants.
    d. They can be improved.
    e. none of the above
        ANSWER: a   TYPE: M   COG: A
43. Kahlil Gibran's statement "Let there be spaces in your togetherness. … The pillars of the temple stand apart, and the oak tree and the cypress grow not in each other's shadow" is indicative of which relational stage?
    a. bonding
    b. differentiating
    c. circumscribing
    d. stagnation
    e. avoiding
        ANSWER: b   TYPE: M   COG: A
44. Workers who have lost enthusiasm for the job reflect which relational stage?
    a. bonding
    b. differentiating
    c. circumscribing
    d. stagnation
    e. avoiding
        ANSWER: d   TYPE: M   COG: A
45. If Cal accuses Jaden of constantly interrupting him when they argue, Cal is engaging in:
    a. recalibration.
    b. reward and punishment.
    c. relational appeals.
    d. indirect appeals.
    e. metacommunication.
        ANSWER: e   TYPE: M   COG: A
46. "I've been sick lately and can't see you" is illustrative of which relational stage?
    a. bonding
    b. differentiating
    c. circumscribing
    d. stagnation
    e. avoiding
        ANSWER: e   TYPE: M   COG: A
47. Although she really loves Jon and enjoys being with him, Waynetta is beginning to feel trapped in her marriage to him. She is being pulled by the:
    a. altruistic-selfishness dialectic.
    b. integration-separation dialectic.
    c. stability-change dialectic.
    d. expression-privacy dialectic.
    e. similarity-complementarity dialectic.
        ANSWER: b   TYPE: M   COG: A

48. Self-disclosure is most related to which dialectical tension?
   a. altruistic-selfishness dialectic
   b. integration-separation dialectic
   c. stability-change dialectic
   d. expression-privacy dialectic
   e. similarity-complementarity dialectic
      ANSWER: d   TYPE: M   COG: C

49. At their marriage ceremony, Eva and Juan lit a candle to symbolize their unity. This ritual is related to the:
   a. altruistic-selfishness dialectic.
   b. integration-separation dialectic.
   c. stability-change dialectic.
   d. expression-privacy dialectic.
   e. similarity-complementarity dialectic.
      ANSWER: b   TYPE: M   COG: A

50. "Quite frankly, this relationship is getting pretty boring. I always know exactly what Bev is going to do and say about everything." The boredom of this relationship is linked to the:
   a. altruistic-selfishness dialectic.
   b. integration-separation dialectic.
   c. stability-change dialectic.
   d. expression-privacy dialectic.
   e. similarity-complementarity dialectic.
      ANSWER: c   TYPE: M   COG: A

51. It is understood that every year Bob will plan a surprise evening for Cathy's birthday. Cathy just doesn't know where the surprise will take place. Bob and Cathy are using the _____ strategy for managing the stability-change dialectic.
   a. recalibration
   b. integration
   c. segmentation
   d. alternation
   e. reaffirmation
      ANSWER: b   TYPE: M   COG: A

52. In order to manage dialectical tension in their marriage, Brianna and Enrique decide that they will dedicate certain times each week that they will spend together and other specific times to be on their own. They are using the strategy of:
   a. disorientation.
   b. denial.
   c. segmentation.
   d. alternation.
   e. balance.
      ANSWER: d   TYPE: M   COG: A

53. Cecelia enjoys romantic movies, whereas Eddie prefers action films. They explain away their differences by saying that they both love movies. They are using the strategy of:
   a. disorientation.
   b. integration.
   c. recalibration.
   d. reaffirmation.
   e. denial.
      ANSWER: a   TYPE: M   COG: A

54. Which label could be used to describe the communication when one partner in a relationship exclaims, "I can never discuss anything with you"?
    a. metacommunication
    b. responsiveness
    c. paralanguage
    d. other delegation
    e. none of the above
        ANSWER: a   TYPE: M   COG: A

55. Anna, who is a counselor at a women's crisis center, says the reason she most often hears from battered wives for returning to their husbands is "I don't have any other place to go." Which explanation of why people perform relationships best predicts this relationship?
    a. the similarity thesis, which suggests we like people whom we perceive are like us
    b. the reciprocity thesis, which suggests being liked by others is a strong source of attraction
    c. the competency thesis, which suggests we are attracted to people we believe are competent
    d. exchange theory, which suggests we form relationships through assessment of potential rewards and costs
    e. disclosure theory, which suggests we are attracted to those who use disclosure appropriately
        ANSWER: d   TYPE: M   COG: A

56. Which is not a strategy outlined by Hess for gaining distance from a relational partner?
    a. mentally dissociating
    b. showing antagonism
    c. name-calling
    d. avoiding involvement
    e. expressing detachment
        ANSWER: c   TYPE: M   COG: R

57. Terminating a relationship can be a learning experience. Some of the positive things learned include:
    a. gaining personal self-confidence.
    b. learning how to communicate better.
    c. learning more about what is desired in a partner.
    d. not jumping into a relationship too quickly.
    e. all of the above
        ANSWER: e   TYPE: M   COG: R

58. When you send someone a birthday card because she or he sent you one, you are complying with the norm of:
    a. equality.
    b. reciprocity.
    c. regularity.
    d. collegiality.
    e. familiarity.
        ANSWER: b   TYPE: M   COG: A

59. Albert Camus said, "Charm is a way of getting the answer yes without asking a clear question." This quotation refers to:
    a. a balance of power.
    b. exchange and reciprocity.
    c. an indirect appeal.
    d. face maintenance.
    e. a relational appeal.
        ANSWER: c   TYPE: M   COG: A

60. The fact that two people both like the same kind of books is most important during which relationship stage?
    a. experimenting
    b. integrating
    c. bonding
    d. circumscribing
    e. terminating
        ANSWER: a   TYPE: M   COG: A

61. Although she has a boyfriend, Kim realizes she may be happier if she is single when she goes away to college. Kim is rating her relationship according to her:
    a. reward level.
    b. cost level of alternatives.
    c. comparison level.
    d. comparison level of alternatives.
    e. social exchange level.
        ANSWER: d   TYPE: M   COG: A

62. Distancing yourself from a friend because you notice that the friend never reciprocates her/his thoughts and feelings like you do reflects which of the reasons we choose relationships?
    a. competency
    b. proximity
    c. disclosure
    d. complementarity
    e. appearance
        ANSWER: c   TYPE: M   COG: C

63. Differentiation is often a part of normal relational maintenance because:
    a. people who are different are complementary.
    b. uniqueness is a part of attraction.
    c. it marks an important turning point in the relationship.
    d. people need to be individuals as well as part of a relationship.
    e. none of the above
        ANSWER: d   TYPE: M   COG: R

64. When a family is torn between going on vacation by themselves or spending their vacation with another family what are they are experiencing?
    a. avoidance
    b. bonding
    c. internal dialectical tensions
    d. external dialectical tensions
    e. none of the above
        ANSWER: d   TYPE: M   COG: A

65. Which of the following opening lines was judged by both male and female college students to be most appropriate in initiating a conversation?
    a. a direct introduction
    b. an introduction by a friend
    c. a compliment
    d. an attempt at humor
    e. a flippant cliché
        ANSWER: b   TYPE: M   COG: R

66. Research indicates that _____ is more important in relational happiness than communication ability.
    a. appearance
    b. similarity
    c. complementarity
    d. rewards
    e. competency
       ANSWER: b   TYPE: M   COG: R

67. When a newly wed couple keeps getting asked when they are going to start having children they are experiencing what dialectical tension?
    a. expression-privacy
    b. openness-closedness
    c. integration-separation
    d. conventionality-uniqueness
    e. connection-autonomy
       ANSWER: d   TYPE: M   COG: A

68. When forgiveness is difficult, research shows that one way to improve your ability to forgive is to:
    a. practice forgiving in a mirror.
    b. get your mind off the problem by distracting yourself.
    c. remind yourself that you have wronged others and needed forgiveness.
    d. remind the other person that they have wronged you.
    e. none of the above
       ANSWER: d   TYPE: M   COG: R

69. Which of the following is not an example of metacommunication?
    a. We need to pay these bills.
    b. You're so good at small talk.
    c. When we raise our voices it scares me.
    d. I love it that you say hi to me in the morning.
    e. I'm sorry that I interrupted you.
       ANSWER: a   TYPE: M   COG: A

70. Behaving in a positive way, being open, and assuring your partner that you're committed to the relationship are examples of:
    a. avoiding.
    b. small talk.
    c. experimenting.
    d. initiating.
    e. relational maintenance.
       ANSWER: e   TYPE: M   COG: C

Essay

71. Explain how exchange theory applies to relationships. Provide an example of how comparison level and comparison level of alternatives exist within a relationship.
       ANSWER: TYPE: E   COG: A

72. Using Knapp's model of stages, identify the stage of a relationship in which you are currently involved. Briefly discuss how your communication pattern reflects the present relationship stage.
       ANSWER: TYPE: E   COG: A

73. Describe each of Knapp's five phases of coming together and five phases of coming apart. Illustrate them by tracing a real or imaginary relationship from initial formation to final dissolution, providing examples of communication at each phase.
       ANSWER: TYPE: E   COG: A

74. Defining each term, identify a dialectical tension in one of your significant relationships. Describe the problem that this tension has created (or could create) in the relationship. Describe which strategy or strategies you have used (or could use) to manage this tension.

      ANSWER: TYPE: E   COG: A

75. Using specific examples, describe the ways content and relational messages are communicated in interpersonal relationships.

      ANSWER: TYPE: E   COG: A

76. Give examples (other than the ones found in the book) of the four types of relational transgressions. For instance, give an example of a minor and significant transgression, an example of a social and a relational transgression, etc.

      ANSWER: TYPE: E   COG: A

77. Write about a time where you had to forgive someone. What was difficult about forgiving this person? What was easy about it? What strategies did you (or will you) use to forgive this person?

      ANSWER: TYPE: E   COG: A

78. Think about a current relationship that you have. Choosing four of the seven reasons we form relationships, explain how they manifested themselves in different stages of your relationship.

      ANSWER: TYPE: E   COG: A

79. Which seems more accurate: Knapp's Model of Relational Development or the idea of Dialectics? Give reasons and specific evidence for your choice.

      ANSWER: TYPE: E   COG: C

80. Explain the reasons why people choose others as potential relational partners.

      ANSWER: TYPE: E   COG: C

Matching

81. Match the letter of the example to the number of the reason we form relationships.

    _____ 1. Disclosure
    _____ 2. Complementarity
    _____ 3. Rewards
    _____ 4. Competency
    _____ 5. Proximity

a. He's a good decorator, and I don't care where we put the couch.
b. I don't mind that she has to work some weekends, because then we can afford a nicer vacation.
c. I sometimes struggle with expressing my feelings.
d. I saw him everyday in class.
    e. She was really good at swimming.

1. c, 2. a, 3. b, 4. e, 5. d

                TYPE: K   COG: A

CHAPTER 10: COMMUNICATION CLIMATE

True/False

1. The kinds of messages that affirm the value of others have been called *confirming communication*.
    ANSWER: T   TYPE: T   COG: R
2. *Communication climate* refers to the social tone of a relationship.
    ANSWER: T   TYPE: T   COG: R
3. It isn't *what* we communicate about that shapes a relational climate as much as *how* we speak and act toward one another.
    ANSWER: T   TYPE: T   COG: R
4. Some research indicates that messages that threaten or save another's face may be more powerful than culture.
    ANSWER: T   TYPE: T   COG: R
5. Communication researchers use the term *argumentativeness* to describe vicious and destructive interaction.
    ANSWER: F   TYPE: T   COG: R
6. When you have a gripe with someone, you can send a face-honoring message by being aggressive, not assertive.
    ANSWER: F   TYPE: T   COG: R
7. Separate research by Clark, Veroff, and others has identified positive climate as the best predictor of marital satisfaction.
    ANSWER: T   TYPE: T   COG: R
8. Communication climate is determined by the degree to which people see themselves as valued.
    ANSWER: T   TYPE: T   COG: R
9. Communication spirals may be either positive or negative.
    ANSWER: T   TYPE: T   COG: R
10. When we don't look at our communication partner, we are denying recognition and are probably sending a negative, disconfirming message.
    ANSWER: T   TYPE: T   COG: C
11. *Argumentativeness* is defined as presenting and defending positions on issues while attacking positions taken by others.
    ANSWER: T   TYPE: T   COG: R
12. *Defensiveness* is the attempt to protect a presented image that we perceive is bring attacked.
    ANSWER: T   TYPE: T   COG: R
13. The ability to "rebound" from negative spirals and turn them in a positive direction is a hallmark of a successful relationship.
    ANSWER: T   TYPE: T   COG: R
14. Recognition, acknowledgment, and endorsement are three increasingly positive types of messages that have the best chance of being perceived as confirming.
    ANSWER: T   TYPE: T   COG: R
15. When satisfied couples complain, they usually offer complaints about behaviors rather than complaints about personal characteristics.
    ANSWER: T   TYPE: T   COG: C
16. Your text indicates that the most negative and destructive way to disagree with someone is by engaging in complaining.
    ANSWER: F   TYPE: T   COG: R
17. Paraphrasing is effective both in helping others handle their problems and as a way of responding to their criticisms of us.
    ANSWER: T   TYPE: T   COG: R

18. Even the best descriptive statements may trigger defensive responses, because you can't control the other person's reaction.

        ANSWER: T   TYPE: T   COG: R

19. The strongest type of confirming message is acknowledgment.

        ANSWER: F   TYPE: T   COG: R

20. Gibb regards neutrality as supportive because it involves being objective and rational.

        ANSWER: F   TYPE: T   COG: R

21. *Certainty* and *control* are both defensive components in Gibb's model.

        ANSWER: T   TYPE: T   COG: R

22. Supportive communication can be used for ulterior motives to restrict and control others.

        ANSWER: T   TYPE: T   COG: C

23. "We" language is usually associated with controlling communication.

        ANSWER: F   TYPE: T   COG: C

24. Gibb's notion of spontaneity means sharing whatever you're thinking as soon as it crosses your mind.

        ANSWER: F   TYPE: T   COG: R

25. Agreeing with a critic can be a good strategy.

        ANSWER: T   TYPE: T   COG: R

26. In order to give an endorsing response, it is necessary to agree with everything that the speaker is saying.

        ANSWER: F   TYPE: T   COG: R

27. The decision about whether a message is confirming or disconfirming is in the eyes of the beholder.

        ANSWER: T   TYPE: T   COG: R

28. You walk into the doctor's office. The receptionist looks down at folders and says, "What's the name?" The receptionist is giving a confirming message since she asked for your name.

        ANSWER: F   TYPE: T   COG: A

29. Endorsement communicates the lowest form of valuing.

        ANSWER: F   TYPE: T   COG: R

30. A student sits in a professor's office crying about her grade. The professor doesn't acknowledge her emotions, but rather asks her what she plans to do about the class. This is an example of an irrelevant response.

        ANSWER: F   TYPE: T   COG: A

31. A child shows his mother a picture he drew at school. The mother says, "That's nice, sweetie. Now go clean your room." This is an example of a tangential response.

        ANSWER: T   TYPE: T   COG: A

32. When a person's words don't match their nonverbal behavior, it is known as an incongruous response.

        ANSWER: T   TYPE: T   COG: A

33. Roy asks Victor what he's doing next Saturday, rather than asking him if he'd lend a hand moving some furniture in his home. This is an example of spontaneity.

        ANSWER: F   TYPE: T   COG: A

34. Saying, "You win some, you lose some!" is an example of neutrality.

        ANSWER: T   TYPE: T   COG: C

35. One approach for offering constructive criticism is known as the "sandwich method."

        ANSWER: T   TYPE: T   COG: R

36. It is easiest to identify disconfirming communication by observing responses to others' messages.

        ANSWER: T   TYPE: T   COG: R

Multiple Choice

37. Communication climates:
    a. are a function of the way people feel about one another.
    b. refer to the tone of a relationship.
    c. can change over time.
    d. all of the above
    e. a and b only
        ANSWER: d   TYPE: M   COG: R

38. Quietly listening while someone describes his/her latest problems or asking follow-up questions about what you have heard are examples of which level of confirming response?
    a. recognition
    b. acknowledgment
    c. endorsement
    d. all of the above
    e. none of the above
        ANSWER: b   TYPE: M   COG: A

39. When an instructor listens carefully to your question in class, he or she is using which level of confirming message?
    a. recognition
    b. acknowledgment
    c. endorsement
    d. neutrality
    e. all of the above
        ANSWER: b   TYPE: M   COG: A

40. All of the following are types of defense-arousing communication identified by Jack Gibb *except:*
    a. evaluation.
    b. control.
    c. strategy.
    d. neutrality.
    e. spontaneity.
        ANSWER: e   TYPE: M   COG: R

41. Researchers who study argumentativeness:
    a. regard it as synonymous with aggressiveness.
    b. regard it as an attacking of issues, not an attacking of people.
    c. regard it as a negative trait.
    d. all of the above
    e. none of the above
        ANSWER: b   TYPE: M   COG: R

42. The decision whether a message is perceived as confirming or disconfirming is:
    a. all in the way a message is delivered.
    b. dependent on the context of a situation.
    c. not dependent on the receiver.
    d. in the eye of the beholder.
    e. none of the above
        ANSWER: d   TYPE: M   COG: C

43. All of the following are types of supportive communication identified by Jack Gibb *except:*
    a. description.
    b. problem orientation.
    c. empathy.
    d. certainty.
    e. equality.
        ANSWER: d   TYPE: M   COG: R

44. If someone used one of Gibb's attacking behaviors on you, it is best to:
    a. use defensive strategy tactics.
    b. seek more information.
    c. use certainty tactics.
    d. respond with neutrality.
    e. evaluate the situation.
        ANSWER: b   TYPE: M   COG: C

45. Research shows that aggressiveness is associated with:
    a. physical violence in marriages.
    b. juvenile delinquency.
    c. depression.
    d. all of the above
    e. none of the above
        ANSWER: d   TYPE: M   COG: R

46. Acting as though you don't hear someone and not making any response is which type of disconfirming response?
    a. impervious
    b. ambiguous
    c. tangential
    d. impersonal
    e. incongruous
        ANSWER: a   TYPE: M   COG: A

47. A monologue of intellectual, generalized statements is considered which type of disconfirming response?
    a. impervious
    b. ambiguous
    c. tangential
    d. impersonal
    e. incongruous
        ANSWER: d   TYPE: M   COG: A

48. The tendency to attack the self-concepts of other people in order to inflict psychological pain is referred to as:
    a. aggressiveness.
    b. assertiveness.
    c. argumentativeness.
    d. ambiguousness.
    e. acknowledgment.
        ANSWER: a   TYPE: M   COG: R

49. Customer: "The amount of time I've been on hold is ridiculous. I'm going to cancel my service." Customer Service Representative: "It sounds like you're angry. Can you tell me about your problem?" The listener's response is an example of:
    a. paraphrasing the speaker's ideas.
    b. agreeing with the truth.
    c. agreeing with the odds.
    d. agreeing in principle.
    e. none of the above
        ANSWER: a   TYPE: M   COG: A

50. Satisfied couples have a _____ ratio of positive to negative statements.

a. 10:1

b. 5:2

c. 10:2

d. 4:1

e. 5:1

ANSWER: e   TYPE: M   COG: R

51. Messages that communicate "I know what's best for you, and if you do as I say, we'll get along" are associated with which Gibb component?

a. control

b. spontaneity

c. neutrality

d. strategy

e. problem-orientation

ANSWER: a   TYPE: M   COG: R

52. "You never take out the garbage unless I nag you" is an example of which type of disagreeing message?

a. complaining

b. argumentativeness

c. aggressiveness

d. disconfirmation

e. irrelevant response

ANSWER: a   TYPE: M   COG: A

53. Shawn: "Did you enjoy the movie?"

Katie: "Yeah, I loved it (rolling eyes)."

Katie's response is an example of:

a. irrelevant response.

b. tangential response.

c. impersonal response.

d. ambiguous response.

e. incongruous response.

ANSWER: e   TYPE: M   COG: A

54. Generally, people respond with _____ when they are confronted with face-threatening acts.

a. empathy

b. an impervious response

c. defensiveness

d. ambiguity

e. none of the above

ANSWER: c   TYPE: M   COG: C

55. Counterfeit questions are associated with which Gibb component?

a. description

b. spontaneity

c. neutrality

d. strategy

e. problem-orientation

ANSWER: d   TYPE: M   COG: R

56. "What do I do that's unfair?" is which way to seek additional information from your critics?

a. Ask for specifics.

b. Guess about specifics.

c. Paraphrase the speaker's ideas.

d. Ask about the consequences of your behavior.

e. Ask what else is wrong.

ANSWER: a   TYPE: M   COG: A

57. Research suggests that men tend to be more defensive than women about messages regarding:

a. their mental or physical errors.
b. their weight.
c. their clothes and hair.
d. their personality.
e. a and c
ANSWER: a   TYPE: M   COG: C

58. One format for constructing an assertive message consists of five elements. Which of the following is not one of the five elements?
a. a description of the observable behavior that prompted your message
b. your interpretation of the behavior
c. your critique of what is wrong with the behavior
d. the feelings that arise from your interpretation
e. the consequences of the information you have shared
ANSWER: c   TYPE: M   COG: C

59. In order to create a confirming climate, a person needs to:
a. agree with the other's position.
b. acknowledge the other's position.
c. praise the other's position.
d. investigate the other's position.
e. do none of the above.
ANSWER: b   TYPE: M   COG: R

60. Which of the following is *not* a level of confirming communication?
a. recognition
b. acknowledgment
c. compliment
d. endorsement
e. all four are levels
ANSWER: c   TYPE: M   COG: R

61. Hugging a good friend while saying, "I think that you did well!" is an example of what level of confirming response?
a. recognition
b. acknowledgment
c. endorsement
d. all of the above
e. none of the above
ANSWER: c   TYPE: M   COG: C

62. Speaker: Lorinda makes me so mad when she's late.
Listener: Lorinda? Yeah, but she's great. We went to a party together and had a fantastic time.
The listener's response is an example of:
a. verbal aggression.
b. a tangential response.
c. an irrelevant response.
d. an ambiguous response.
e. an impersonal response.
ANSWER: b   TYPE: M   COG: A

63. Speaker: I'm really worried about trying to meet all of my obligations this semester. There's just SO much to do!

Listener: Yeah, I guess we're all overwhelmed. I had to work every day last weekend.
The listener's response is an example of:
   a. verbal aggression.
   b. a tangential response.
   c. am irrelevant response.
   d. an ambiguous response.
   e. an impersonal response.
      ANSWER: e   TYPE: M   COG: A

64. An instructor tells you, "The topic of your speech was very appealing to many in the audience. The thesis statement needed to be a single statement and less broad. Your hand gestures were energetic and well used." This constructive criticism strategy is called:
   a. harsh start-up.
   b. sandwich method.
   c. provisionalism.
   d. strategy.
   e. neutrality.
      ANSWER: b   TYPE: M   COG: A

65. Validating another person's feelings or offering direct praise is an example of:
   a. recognition.
   b. confirming communication.
   c. empathy.
   d. provisionalism.
   e. endorsement.
      ANSWER: e   TYPE: M   COG: R

66. Gottman claims that _____ is not the sign of a troubled relationship.
   a. complaining
   b. harsh start-up
   c. certainty
   d. neutrality
   e. none of the above
      ANSWER: a   TYPE: M   COG: R

67. _____ acknowledges the other person's communication, but shifts the conversation to a new direction.
   a. Incongruous response
   b. Ambiguous response
   c. Impersonal response
   d. Impervious response
   e. Tangential response
      ANSWER: e   TYPE: M   COG: R

68. Allie asks her friend Stella, "Do you like your new haircut?" instead of saying, "I don't think your new haircut is very flattering." This is an example of:
   a. confirming statement.
   b. defensiveness.
   c. face-saving.
   d. strategy.
   e. neutrality.
      ANSWER: c   TYPE: M   COG: A

69. Tia tells her partner daily how much she appreciates all the hard work she does. In turn, Tia's partner, Nelly, shares that she knows Tia is also working hard. When Tia hears this, she is motivated to share other kind thoughts. This is an example of:

a. kind start-up.
b. positive communication spiral.
c. negative communication spiral.
d. confirming statements.
e. none of the above
ANSWER: b   TYPE: M   COG: A

70. Problem orientation is consistent with what type of conflict management style?
a. compromise
b. defensiveness
c. win-win
d. lose-win
e. competition
ANSWER: c   TYPE: M   COG: R

71. Becks' research observed that _____ is put to the test when a person doesn't have superior skills, yet is in a position of authority.
a. superiority
b. equality
c. indifference
d. strategy
e. spontaneity
ANSWER: b   TYPE: M   COG: R

72. Yasmine says, "I get that you can't put into words what I did to upset you. Was it that I didn't call? Was it that I got here a little late?" Yasmine is _____ to seek more information.
a. asking for specifics
b. using defensiveness
c. guessing about specifics
d. paraphrasing the speaker's idea
e. all of the above
ANSWER: c   TYPE: M   COG: A

73. Mark says to Shannon, "So what I hear you saying is that you feel overwhelmed with all the housework that you have to do when I'm on business trips. And you feel that you're making decisions about the kids by yourself." This is an example of:
a. asking for specifics.
b. using defensiveness.
c. guessing about specifics.
d. paraphrasing the speaker's idea.
e. all of the above
ANSWER: d   TYPE: M   COG: A

74. After you "agree with the truth," what is your next step?
a. Tell the other person that you agree, but they are still wrong.
b. Discuss what you intend to do about your behavior.
c. Walk away.
d. Say, "I don't know what you expect from me."
e. Apologize, but continue to behave as you did before.
ANSWER: b   TYPE: M   COG: C

75. Agreeing with the odds has benefits that include:
a. seeing solutions that you may not have previously realized.
b. not putting the receiver on the defensive.

c.   the other person feels like their side has been heard.

d.   hidden agendas come into the open for resolution.

e.   all of the above

       ANSWER: e   TYPE: M   COG: R

76. Attacks against our presenting self are called:

a.   face-threatening acts.

b.   face-saving acts.

c.   defensive communication.

d.   offensive communication.

e.   focused communication.

       ANSWER: a   TYPE: M   COG: R

Essay

77. What are the implications of using the term *communication climate* (rather than *communication situation*, for instance)?

       ANSWER: TYPE: E   COG: C

78. Thoreau claims we should treat one another tenderly. How can your knowledge of communication climates help you to do this?

       ANSWER: TYPE: E   COG: C

79. An employee for whom you are responsible has a tendency to neglect assignments he is given at your weekly staff meetings. As a result, his projects often go uncompleted. Offer two comments about this problem that you could make during an annual review with this person; then explain how each comment reflects one of Gibb's supportive climate components.

       ANSWER: TYPE: E   COG: A

80. Despite your attempts to create a supportive climate in the preceding question, your employee gets defensive and starts criticizing you. Cite and give examples of two methods you could use to transform this negative climate into a positive one.

       ANSWER: TYPE: E   COG: A

81. Rewrite the following statements to decrease their defense-provoking potential by changing them from evaluations to descriptions.

"You are so insensitive."

"You're just not committed enough for a serious relationship."

       ANSWER: TYPE: E   COG: A

82. Respond to the following criticisms by drawing on two strategies from the "seeking more information" element and two strategies from the "agree with critic" element of the textbook's model for coping with criticism. Create the situational details from your own experience.

"You're so callous in the way you deal with people."

"You're so inflexible; it's impossible to discuss things with you."

       ANSWER: TYPE: E   COG: A

83. Give an example of choosing a poor time to discuss a problem with someone and the potential impact on communication climate, based on that decision. Discuss a better time to discuss the problem and the type of "start-up" that could be effectively used.

       ANSWER: TYPE: E   COG: A

84. Describe how you, an employer, or a professor could use the constructive criticism technique known as the "sandwich method."

       ANSWER: TYPE: E   COG: C

85. Why does Gottman say that complaining is *not* the sign of a troubled relationship? Explain and discuss whether you agree or disagree.

       ANSWER: TYPE: E   COG: C

86. Write three aggressive statements and then rewrite those statements with an assertive message.

ANSWER: TYPE: E COG: A

87. What benefits are there to "agreeing with the truth?" Explain.

  ANSWER: TYPE: E COG: C

88. Give examples of the statement, "Competent communicators protect others' face needs, as well as their own."

  ANSWER: TYPE: E COG: C

89. Discuss what a negative communication spiral may look like in either a romantic relationship or in a parent-child relationship.

  ANSWER: TYPE: E COG: C

90. Describe what the authors mean when they say, "The poor effects of neutrality become apparent when you consider the hostility that most people have for the large, impersonal organizations with which they have to deal."

  ANSWER: TYPE: E COG: C

91. Provide three messages to correspond with each of the message types: confirming, disagreeing, and disconfirming.

  ANSWER: TYPE: E COG: A

Matching

92. Match the terms in the left column with their category from the right column. (NOTE: Categories may be used more than once.)

_____ 1. recognition	a.	confirming messages
_____ 2. interrupting	b.	disagreeing messages
_____ 3. imperviousness	c.	disconfirming messages
_____ 4. endorsement		
_____ 5. argumentativeness		
_____ 6. aggressiveness		
_____ 7. acknowledgment		

  ANSWER: a, c, c, a, b, b, a TYPE: K COG: R

93. Match the letter of the defensive or supportive Gibb category with its numbered description of behaviors. Pay particular attention to the words that have been underlined.

  a. evaluation   g. description

b. controlling communication	h. problem orientation
c. strategy	i. spontaneity
d. neutrality	j. empathy
e. superiority	k. equality
f. certainly	l. provisionalism

_____ 1. Gerry insists he has all the facts and needs to hear no more information.

_____ 2. Richard has a strong opinion but will listen to another's position.

_____ 3. Linda kept looking at the clock as she was listening to Nan, so Nan thought Linda *didn't consider her comments as very important.*

_____ 4. "I know Janice doesn't agree with me," Mary said, "but she knows how strongly I feel about this, and *I think she can put herself in my position.*"

_____ 5. "Even though my professor has a Ph.D.," Rosa pointed out, "she doesn't act like she's the only one who knows something; she is really interested in me as a person."

_____ 6. "Bob tricked me into thinking his proposal was my idea so that I'd support it."

_____ 7. "Even though we **all** wait tables here, Evanne *thinks she's better than any of us*—just look at the way she prances around!"

_____ 8. Clara *sincerely and honesty* told Georgia about her reservations concerning Georgia's party.

_____ 9. The coworkers *attempted to find a solution* to the scheduling issue that would *satisfy both of their needs.*

_____ 10. "Its seems my father's favorite phrase is 'I know what's best for you; just let me tell you what to do,' and that really gripes me."

_____ 11. "You drink too much!"

_____ 12. "I was embarrassed when you slurred your speech in front of my boss."

_____ 13. "The flowers and presents are just an attempt to get me to go to bed with him."

_____ 14. She looked down her nose at me when I told her I didn't exercise regularly."

_____ 15. "Well, if you need more money and I need more help around here, what could we do to make us both happy?"

ANSWER KEY:

1. f	6. c	11. a
2. l	7. e	12. g
3. d	8. i	13. c
4. j	9. h	14. e
5. k	10. b	15. h

CHAPTER 11: MANAGING CONFLICT

True/False

1. Although it is impossible to eliminate conflict, there are ways to manage it effectively.
   ANSWER: T   TYPE: T   COG: R
2. Avoidance reflects a pessimistic attitude about conflict.
   ANSWER: T   TYPE: T   COG: R
3. Reasonable people are usually able to see mutually satisfying answers to their problems.
   ANSWER: F   TYPE: T   COG: R
4. Conflict is an expressed struggle between at least two interdependent parties who perceive incompatible goals, scarce rewards, and interference from the other party in achieving their goals.
   ANSWER: T   TYPE: T   COG: A
5. People most likely to find themselves in a conflict are independent of each other.
   ANSWER: F   TYPE: T   COG: R
6. Your text maintains that conflict is inevitable.
   ANSWER: T   TYPE: T   COG: R
7. Communication scholars usually describe beneficial conflicts as dysfunctional and harmful ones as functional.
   ANSWER: F   TYPE: T   COG: R
8. For functional problem solving to occur, it is wise to multitask, that is, to work on multiple problems simultaneously.
   ANSWER: F   TYPE: T   COG: R
9. In sharing our needs with another person, we should avoid the use of "I" language so as not to polarize the conflict.
   ANSWER: F   TYPE: T   COG: R
10. People from a high-context, collectivist backgrounds are likely to regard avoidance as a face-saving way to handle conflict.
    ANSWER: T   TYPE: T   COG: R
11. A student who dislikes a teacher but does not show it fits the textbook's definition of conflict.
    ANSWER: F   TYPE: T   COG: A
12. *Pushover*, *yes-man*, *doormat*, and *spineless* are all terms used in the United States to describe people who have a tendency to avoid or accommodate during conflict.
    ANSWER: T   TYPE: T   COG: R
13. All conflict styles have value in certain situations, and culture plays a significant role in determining how each style is valued.
    ANSWER: T   TYPE: T   COG: R
14. Partners who use different but mutually reinforcing behaviors to manage their conflicts have a conflict style called *symmetrical.*
    ANSWER: F   TYPE: T   COG: R
15. Conflict rituals prevent successful conflict management.
    ANSWER: F   TYPE: T   COG: R
16. Passive aggression occurs when a communicator expresses dissatisfaction in a disguised manner.
    ANSWER: T   TYPE: T   COG: R
17. Avoidance is never an advisable conflict-resolution style.
    ANSWER: F   TYPE: T   COG: R
18. A personal conflict style is similar to a personality trait, in that it carries across most all situations.
    ANSWER: F   TYPE: T   COG: R
19. Assertive individuals can respect and seek to satisfy their own needs and still respect and seek to satisfy the needs of others.
    ANSWER: T   TYPE: T   COG: R

20. Research suggests there is a significant connection between verbal aggression and physical aggression.
    ANSWER: T   TYPE: T   COG: R

21. Many people from the United States default to a competitive conflict style because they live in a competitive society and it's ingrained in their culture.
    ANSWER: T   TYPE: T   COG: R

22. Recent research shows that the differences in how men and women approach conflict are rather small and not at all representative of the stereotypical picture of the aggressive male and the passive female.
    ANSWER: T   TYPE: T   COG: R

23. Compared to females, males use more competing behaviors with same-sex peers and more avoiding behaviors with opposite-sex peers.
    ANSWER: T   TYPE: T   COG: R

24. Estimates are that the Japanese only have one lawyer for every 10,000 people, while in the United States there is one lawyer for every 50 people.
    ANSWER: T   TYPE: T   COG: R

25. One Chinese proverb states, "The first person to raise his voice wins the argument."
    ANSWER: F   TYPE: T   COG: R

26. Conflicts with a win-lose orientation are always destructive.
    ANSWER: F   TYPE: T   COG: R

27. Assertive approaches to conflict are likely to seem rude to members of collectivist cultures.
    ANSWER: T   TYPE: T   COG: R

28. John Gottman defines criticism as an attack on a person's character.
    ANSWER: T   TYPE: T   COG: R

29. Most research suggests that the differences in conflict styles between genders are very prominent.
    ANSWER: F   TYPE: T   COG: R

30. High-context cultures place a premium on being direct during conflict.
    ANSWER: F   TYPE: T   COG: R

Multiple Choice

31. Partners in interpersonal relationships can use which of the following styles to manage their conflicts?
    a.   complementary conflict style
    b.   symmetrical conflict style
    c.   parallel conflict style
    d.   all of the above
    e.   none of the above
       ANSWER: d   TYPE: M   COG: R

32. All of the following are elements of conflict *except:*
    a.   perceived incompatible goals.
    b.   perceived scarce rewards.
    c.   independence.
    d.   expressed struggle.
    e.   inevitability.
       ANSWER: c   TYPE: M   COG: R

33. Which element of conflict is reflected in the statement "Conflict is an inescapable fact of life"?
    a.   expressed struggle
    b.   perceived incompatible goals
    c.   inevitability
    d.   interdependence
    e.   perceived scarce rewards
       ANSWER: c.   TYPE: M   COG: R

34. Avoidance may be the best course:
    a. if the risk of speaking up is too great.
    b. if the issue is generally minor.
    c. if the conflict occurs in an unimportant relationship.
    d. all of the above
    e. none of the above
        ANSWER: d   TYPE: M   COG: R

35. Which of the following is (are) characteristic of dysfunctional conflict?
    a. Participants see each other as opponents.
    b. Participants rely heavily on coercion to get what they want.
    c. Problems seem to grow larger instead of smaller.
    d. all of the above
    e. a and c only
        ANSWER: d   TYPE: M   COG: R

36. _____ occurs when people nonassertively ignore or stay away from conflict.
    a. competition
    b. avoidance
    c. compromise
    d. collaboration
    e. accommodation
        ANSWER: b.   TYPE: M   COG: R

37. The style of handling conflict that involves a high degree of concern for both parties is:
    a. avoidance.
    b. accommodation.
    c. competition.
    d. compromise.
    e. collaboration.
        ANSWER: e   TYPE: M   COG: R

38. If two coworkers are seeking promotion to the same job, they would likely fall into which method of resolving disputes?
    a. win-lose
    b. lose-lose
    c. win-win
    d. avoidance
    e. accommodation
        ANSWER: a   TYPE: M   COG: R

39. Which kind of power can be used in problem solving based on competition (win-lose)?
    a. character attacks
    b. verbal threats
    c. ridicule
    d. passive aggression
    e. all of the above
        ANSWER: e   TYPE: M   COG: R

40. All of the following are components of Hocker and Wilmot's definition of conflict *except:*
    a. perception of incompatible goals.
    b. interdependence.
    c. surplus rewards.
    d. expressed struggle.
    e. none of the above
        ANSWER: c   TYPE: M   COG: R

41. Which of the following is typical of boys (rather than girls) in conflict?
    a. proposals beginning with the word *Let's*
    b. joint proposals
    c. assigning roles to others in pretend play
    d. giving reasons for suggestions
    e. none of the above
    　　　　ANSWER: c　　　　TYPE: M　　　　COG: R
42. Which of the following is a win-win strategy?
    a. Avoid arguments that might lead to anger and hurt feelings.
    b. Know what you are willing to give up if the other person agrees to give up something.
    c. Determine what both parties need to get out of a negotiation.
    d. Vote and abide by majority decision.
    e. None of the above is a win-win strategy.
    　　　　ANSWER: c　　　　TYPE: M　　　　COG: R
43. The attitude of "We're all in this together" reflects the quality of:
    a. expressed struggle.
    b. interdependence.
    c. individuality.
    d. caring.
    e. nonassertion.
    　　　　ANSWER: b　　　　TYPE: M　　　　COG: R
44. Which of the following factors govern the selection and use of conflict style?
    a. the situation
    b. the other person
    c. your goals
    d. all of the above
    e. none of the above
    　　　　ANSWER: d　　　　TYPE: M　　　　COG: R
45. Accommodators deal with conflict by:
    a. putting the other's needs ahead of their own.
    b. putting their needs ahead of the other's.
    c. ignoring the needs of others.
    d. ignoring their own needs.
    e. a and d
    　　　　ANSWER: a　　　　TYPE: M　　　　COG: R
46. Rolando and Laura had a fight last week about his working weekends. Today Laura is careful not to mention the coming weekend. She is using:
    a. assertive behavior.
    b. aggressive behavior.
    c. accommodation.
    d. addressing their needs.
    e. a complementary conflict style.
    　　　　ANSWER: d　　　　TYPE: M　　　　COG: A
47. Which of the following would be the most likely form of refusal in the Japanese culture?
    a. No.
    b. No, not now.
    c. I don't think so.
    d. Maybe.
    e. I will consider it and let you know.
    　　　　ANSWER: e　　　　TYPE: M　　　　COG: A

48. Studies show that among Chinese college students (in both the People's Republic and Taiwan) the most common methods of persuasion used are
    a. saying no
    b. hinting
    c. setting an example by one's own action
    d. strategically agreeing to whatever pleases others
    e. b, c, and d only
    ANSWER: e   TYPE: M   COG: R

49. Partners who use different but mutually reinforcing behaviors have a conflict style labeled:
    a. complementary.
    b. symmetrical.
    c. parallel.
    d. aggressive.
    e. assertive.
    ANSWER: a   TYPE: M   COG: R

50. When one partner says, "I want to talk about your treatment of me" and the other partner leaves, the conflict would be labeled:
    a. flight-fight.
    b. skewed.
    c. symmetrical.
    d. fight-flight.
    e. pointless.
    ANSWER: d   TYPE: M   COG: A

51. Which of the following statements best summarizes the attitude expressed toward conflict by the text?
    a. Conflict is natural and inevitable.
    b. Conflict can lead to stronger, healthier relationships.
    c. Negative attitudes about conflict are a result of socialization and lack of resolution skills.
    d. Conflict provides an outlet for feelings of frustration and aggression.
    e. All of the above reflect the text's approach to conflict.
    ANSWER: e   TYPE: M   COG: R

52. "I have tried everything in my power to make this relationship work, but it's impossible. It'll never work because you don't make any effort; you don't try at all." This statement is an example of which type of dysfunctional conflict?
    a. shortsightedness
    b. losing sight of the original issue
    c. unwillingness to cooperate
    d. polarization
    e. personalization
    ANSWER: d   TYPE: M   COG: A

53. Functional conflict is characterized by:
    a. cooperation.
    b. integration.
    c. focusing on the original problem.
    d. coercion.
    e. a, b, and c only
    ANSWER: e   TYPE: M   COG: R

54. Whenever Bridget and Tony fight, Tony always brings up additional issues until the original issue gets lost. This is an example of:
    a. escalation.
    b. "kitchen sink fighting."
    c. integration.
    d. foresight.
    e. shortsightedness.
        ANSWER: b   TYPE: M   COG: A

55. When Karen tries to talk about going to visit her family for the holidays, John changes the subject. This is an example of which conflict style?
    a. compromise
    b. competition
    c. collaboration
    d. avoidance
    e. accommodation
        ANSWER: d   TYPE: M   COG: A

56. Jack wants to limit their spending and Sandy wants to try a new restaurant. Which of the following would be an example of the competitive conflict style?
    a. "I think we should forget your stupid budget and go out to eat for once."
    b. "It's been so long since I've been in a restaurant I don't even think I'd know how to act."
    c. "That new restaurant looks good—I think you'd like their menu."
    d. "What would you like for dinner?"
    e. none of the above
        ANSWER: a   TYPE: M   COG: A

57. After much discussion, Chad finally agrees to go to the opera with his wife. As they are finding their seats he says, sarcastically, "Yeah, this is going to be a lot of fun." This is an example of which conflict style?
    a. avoidance
    b. assertion
    c. accommodation
    d. direct aggression
    e. passive aggression
        ANSWER: e   TYPE: M   COG: A

58. Paul and Stacy have a very volatile conflict style. They both are very forceful and inevitably end up hurling insults at each other until they both withdraw exhausted. This is an example of which conflict style?
    a. complementary
    b. parallel
    c. symmetrical
    d. assertive
    e. none of the above
        ANSWER: c   TYPE: M   COG: A

59. Couples with a parallel conflict style:
    a. use complementary styles.
    b. use symmetrical styles.
    c. shift back and forth between complementary and symmetrical styles.
    d. always agree with each other.
    e. none of the above
        ANSWER: c   TYPE: M   COG: R

60. Dave tells his girlfriend he wants to see a new action movie but goes along when she replies that she would rather see a romantic comedy. This is an example of:
    a. avoidance.
    b. accommodation.
    c. compromise.
    d. collaboration.
    e. competition.
        ANSWER: b   TYPE: M   COG: A

61. When someone thinks that there will be a clear winner and a clear loser in an interpersonal conflict this is an example of which type of dysfunctional conflict?
    a. polarization
    b. opposition
    c. coercion
    d. escalation
    e. drifting
        ANSWER: b   TYPE: M   COG: R

62. When an original issue gets lost because the conflict has expanded to include a number of other issues which type of dysfunctional conflict is occurring?
    a. polarization
    b. opposition
    c. coercion
    d. escalation
    e. drifting
        ANSWER: e   TYPE: M   COG: R

63. Research has shown that partners with a _____ used stonewalling more often than partners with a _____.
    a. low level of commitment/high level of commitment
    b. high level of commitment/low level of commitment
    c. parallel conflict style/symmetrical conflict style
    d. symmetrical conflict style/parallel conflict style
    e. none of the above
        ANSWER: a   TYPE: M   COG: R

64. You want to go out for Chinese, but your significant other wants Italian. You say, "That's fine, let's do Italian." You are demonstrating what conflict style?
    a. avoidance
    b. accommodation
    c. competition
    d. compromise
    e. collaboration
        ANSWER: b   TYPE: M   COG: A

65. Making a critical joke at another person's expense and then excusing the joke by saying "I was only kidding" is an example of what kind of conflict style?
    a. passive aggression
    b. direct aggression
    c. accommodation
    d. avoidance
    e. none of the above
        ANSWER: a   TYPE: M   COG: A

66. When both people use the same tactics in an interpersonal conflict they are demonstrating which type of conflict style?
    a. complementary
    b. symmetrical
    c. parallel
    d. all of the above
    e. none of the above
        ANSWER: b   TYPE: M   COG: R

67. Which of the following is NOT one of the "Four Horsemen" of toxic conflict?
    a. stonewalling
    b. defensiveness
    c. unreasonable
    d. criticism
    e. contempt
        ANSWER: c   TYPE: M   COG: R

68. A married couple has a fight. They stop talking. Eventually, the husband goes to the wife and apologizes. This pattern is repeated throughout their marriage. This example is demonstrating:
    a. variables in conflict styles.
    b. defensiveness.
    c. a compromise.
    d. a conflict ritual.
    e. an analysis.
        ANSWER: d   TYPE: M   COG: A

69. Which of the following contributes to our conflict style?
    a. culture
    b. biological makeup
    c. emotional intelligence
    d. self-concept
    e. all of the above
        ANSWER: e   TYPE: M   COG: R

70. Sherell and Monique have a disagreement about how to spend their end-of-the-year bonus. Sherell wants to go on a trip, and Monique wants to spend it on the house. Instead, they decide to buy a fishing boat. This is probably an example of:
    a. avoidance.
    b. compromise.
    c. collaboration.
    d. competing.
    e. accommodating.
        ANSWER: b   TYPE: M   COG: A

Essay

71. Suggest a possible mutually satisfying solution to the following conflicts:
        A teenager likes to wear makeup, and her parents don't want her to.
        A little boy likes to pop his gum, and the sound annoys his mother.
        A secretary likes to take her lunch hour from 11 to 12, but her boss finds this inconvenient.
        A man likes horror movies, and his wife likes comedies.
        ANSWER: TYPE: E   COG: A

72. Define a *conflict ritual*. Give an example of one, and discuss what effect it might have on a conflict.
        ANSWER: TYPE: E   COG: A

73. Define *escalatory* and *de-escalatory spirals,* and explain how they relate to complementary and symmetrical styles.
        ANSWER: TYPE: E   COG: C

74. "Partners married 40 years or more report having fewer conflicts than earlier in their relationships, since many contested issues (such as children, in-laws, and money) are no longer present." Discuss this statement in relation to the common characteristics of the definition of conflict reviewed at the beginning of this chapter.

        ANSWER: TYPE: E   COG: C

75. Is a win-lose orientation always destructive? Explain your answer.

        ANSWER: TYPE: E   COG: C

76. Does compromising create win-win or lose-lose outcomes? Explain.

        ANSWER: TYPE: E   COG: C

77. People from high-context, collectivist backgrounds (such as many Asian cultures) are likely to regard avoidance and accommodation as face-saving and noble ways to handle conflict, yet for people from low-context, individualist cultures (such as the United States), avoidance and accommodation are often viewed less positively. What important points should you consider when negotiating intercultural conflict?

        ANSWER: TYPE: E   COG: A

78. Each of the stages of the win-win problem-solving model requires the implementation of one or another of the repertoire of communication skills presented throughout the text. Given here are the seven steps. Identify at least one of the communication skills necessary to negotiate each step successfully.

    Step 1. Define your needs.
    Step 2. Share your needs with the other person.
    Step 3. Listen to the other person's needs.
    Step 4. Generate possible solutions
    Step 5. Evaluate the possible solutions and choose the best one.
    Step 6. Implement the best solution.
    Step 7. Follow up on your solution.

        ANSWER: TYPE: E   COG: C

79. Dysfunctional conflict typically has two consequences. Name each, as labeled in the text, and, in one or two sentences, explain the "why" behind each.

        ANSWER: TYPE: E   COG: C

80. The text discusses five styles of conflict behavior:

    a. avoidance
    b. accommodation
    c. competition
    d. compromise
    e. collaboration

Pick three styles. Describe the basic characteristics for each, present at least one communication behavior for each style, and present an advantage and disadvantage for each.

        ANSWER: TYPE: E   COG: C

Matching

81. Match the phrase with the type of conflict style they typify.

_____	1. "I don't want to talk about it."	a. compromise
_____	2. "We do it my way or no way."	b. accommodation
_____	3. "We can solve this problem together."	c. avoidance
_____	4. "I give up; you decide."	d. competition
_____	5. "My choice today, your choice tomorrow."	e. collaboration

    ANSWER: c, d, e, b, a TYPE: K   COG: A

82. Label the following as characteristic of functional (F) or dysfunctional (D) conflict resolution.

_____ 1. Integration
_____ 2. Isolation
_____ 3. Coercion
_____ 4. Cooperation
_____ 5. Agreement
_____ 6. De-escalation

_____ 7. Drifting
_____ 8. Focusing
_____ 9. Polarization
_____ 10. Shortsightedness
_____ 11. Escalation
_____ 12. Foresight

ANSWER: 1-F, 2-D, 3-D, 4-F, 5-F, 6-F, 7-D, 8-F, 9-D, 10-D, 11-D, 12-F
TYPE: K   COG: R

CHAPTER 12: COMMUNICATION IN FAMILIES AND AT WORK

True/False

1. A *family* is defined as "a system with two or more interdependent people who have a common past history and a present reality and who expect to influence each other in the future."
   ANSWER: T   TYPE: T   COG: R

2. Family members are interdependent. Each event is a reaction to the family's history, and each event shapes future interaction.
   ANSWER: T   TYPE: T   COG: R

3. Family systems are "closed" systems.
   ANSWER: F   TYPE: T   COG: R

4. Families that interact freely, frequently, and spontaneously, without many limitations regarding topic or time spent interacting, are said to have a high conversation orientation.
   ANSWER: T   TYPE: T   COG: R

5. *Conformity orientation* refers to the degree to which family communication stresses uniformity of attitudes, values, and beliefs.
   ANSWER: T   TYPE: T   COG: R

6. Families low in both conversation orientation and conformity orientation are pluralistic.
   ANSWER: F   TYPE: T   COG: R

7. Social scientists label families with too little cohesion as *enmeshed*.
   ANSWER: F   TYPE: T   COG: R

8. Although the Internet is meant to keep people in touch, some friendships falter or fail without face-to-face contact.
   ANSWER: T   TYPE: T   COG: R

9. You are friends with Johan because he is on your bowling team. This is an example of maintenance-oriented friendship.
   ANSWER: F   TYPE: T   COG: C

10. Men are more likely to create closeness by talking about personal matters.
    ANSWER: F   TYPE: T   COG: R

11. Women tend to disclose more personal information than men, both face-to-face and online.
    ANSWER: T   TYPE: T   COG: R

12. Guerrero and Chavez found that a friend who is not interested in romantic involvement from a platonic friend will maintain the same amount of contact and activity with that person.
    ANSWER: F   TYPE: T   COG: R

13. Many heterosexual women value their friendships with gay men because they feel more attractive.
    ANSWER: T   TYPE: T   COG: R

14. Liam did not call Brenna on her 25th birthday. Brenna believes a friend should always call you on your birthday, or at least leave a message. This is an example of expectancy violation.
    ANSWER: T   TYPE: T   COG: C

15. Social exchange theory indicates that the rewards of friendship can be the same as the cost.
    ANSWER: F   TYPE: T   COG: R

16. A good apology includes sincerely expressing remorse, admitting wrongdoing, promising to behave better, and requesting forgiveness.
    ANSWER: T   TYPE: T   COG: R

17. Shared narratives have a tendency to disconnect families.
    ANSWER: F   TYPE: T   COG: R

18. Your mother says that everyone has to be home by 10 p.m. on a weeknight. This is an example of communication rules.
    ANSWER: T   TYPE: T   COG: C

19. You know your friend Avery extremely well and believe you also know her brother Holden quite well, too. However, when you went to a birthday party at their aunt's house and the whole family was there, they behaved very differently. This is an example that a family is more than the sum of its parts.
    ANSWER: T   TYPE: T   COG: C
20. Helms' research suggests that the lowest levels of love and satisfaction are between stereotypically feminine wives and docile husbands.
    ANSWER: F   TYPE: T   COG: R
21. When children ask themselves the question, "Who am I?", they often challenge family rules and beliefs.
    ANSWER: T   TYPE: T   COG: R
22. Three dimensions of interaction explain a great deal of sibling-sibling communication: affection, rivalry, and humility.
    ANSWER: T   TYPE: T   COG: R
23. Franklin and his wife, Zelda, each take on parenting duties, make decisions on a whim, and can't decide who will pay the bills. This is known as a chaotic family.
    ANSWER: T   TYPE: T   COG: C
24. Intimacy includes emotional, financial, physical, intellectual, and shared activities.
    ANSWER: T   TYPE: T   COG: R
25. Morman and Floyd's research indicates that fathers are becoming less affectionate with their sons.
    ANSWER: F   TYPE: T   COG: R
26. Studies show that relationships mediated channels can be more effective than face-to-face communication in improving the quality of a relationship.
    ANSWER: T   TYPE: T   COG: R
27. Research shows that social networks are key in maintaining romantic relationships.
    ANSWER: T   TYPE: T   COG: R
28. Cultural notions of intimacy that were formerly seen as "American" and not followed by other cultures are fast disappearing.
    ANSWER: T   TYPE: T   COG: R
29. A woman wants to be told, "I love you." Her partner wants to show love by doing chores around the house. This is an example of men and women having similar perceptions about communicating intimacy.
    ANSWER: F   TYPE: T   COG: R
30. Boundaries must always be openly negotiated if family members are going to accept them.
    ANSWER: F   TYPE: T   COG: C

Multiple Choice

31. Which of the following is not a characteristic of how families are like systems?
    a. Family members are interdependent.
    b. A family is more than the sum of its parts.
    c. Families have systems within the larger system.
    d. Family systems are affected by their environment.
    e. All of the above are characteristics.
    ANSWER: e   TYPE: M   COG: R
32. The degree to which families favor an open climate of discussion on a wide array of topics is termed:
    a. conversation conformity.
    b. conversation orientation.
    c. communication orientation.
    d. communication conformity.
    e. none of the above
    ANSWER: b   TYPE: M   COG: R

33. Families high in both conversation orientation and conformity are:
    a. consensual.
    b. pluralistic.
    c. protective.
    d. laissez-faire.
    e. none of the above

    ANSWER: a   TYPE: M   COG: R

34. Families high on conversation orientation and low in conformity orientation are:
    a. consensual.
    b. pluralistic.
    c. protective.
    d. laissez-faire.
    e. none of the above

    ANSWER: b   TYPE: M   COG: R

35. Families low in conversation orientation and high in conformity orientation are:
    a. consensual.
    b. pluralistic.
    c. protective.
    d. laissez-faire.
    e. none of the above

    ANSWER: c   TYPE: M   COG: R

36. Families low in both conversation orientation and conformity orientation are:
    a. consensual.
    b. pluralistic.
    c. protective.
    d. laissez-faire.
    e. none of the above

    ANSWER: d   TYPE: M   COG: R

37. Friendships are created, managed, and maintained through:
    a. communication.
    b. perception.
    c. paralanguage.
    d. conflict.
    e. love.

    ANSWER: a   TYPE: M   COG: R

38. The following are all types of friendships EXCEPT:
    a. short-term vs. long-term.
    b. achievement vs. nurturing.
    c. low disclosure vs. high disclosure.
    d. low obligation vs. high obligation.
    e. task-oriented vs. maintenance-oriented.

    ANSWER: b   TYPE: M   COG: R

39. Long-time friends Grace and Kishia had little in common when Grace got married and Kishia was still single. Once Kishia got married, she found herself talking to Grace all the time again. This is an example of:
    a. communication within a friendship only works when both parties have everything in common.
    b. communication within a friendship always decreases when someone's lifestyle changes.
    c. communication within a friendship changes over time.
    d. communication within a friendship should happen every day.
    e. none of the above

    ANSWER: c   TYPE: M   COG: R

281

40. In one study, more than _____ of men said their most meaningful experiences with friends came from shared activities.
    a. 20%
    b. 45%
    c. 50%
    d. 75%
    e. 90%
        ANSWER: d   TYPE: M   COG: R
41. The biggest challenge in male-female friendship is:
    a. women talk more often than men.
    b. the potential for sexual attraction.
    c. women require more intimacy than men.
    d. men are less emotional than women.
    e. none of the above
        ANSWER: b   TYPE: M   COG: R
42. Nayib said he would call his friend Sharif when he got home from work. Sharif expects that if Nayib says he will call that he will follow through. When Nayib doesn't call, Sharif gets angry. This is an example of:
    a. miscommunication.
    b. expectancy violation.
    c. social exchange theory.
    d. autonomy.
    e. balanced exchange.
        ANSWER: b   TYPE: M   COG: A
43. _____ is/are a factor in keeping family relationships operating harmoniously.
    a. Communication
    b. Boundaries
    c. Rituals
    d. Shared narratives
    e. Rules
        ANSWER: d   TYPE: M   COG: R
44. Your family always has karaoke at family functions. This is known as a:
    a. rule.
    b. boundary.
    c. festivity.
    d. ritual.
    e. none of the above
        ANSWER: d   TYPE: M   COG: R
45. One factor affecting the comfort level in stepfamily communication is the type of _____ used by step-parents.
    a. communication
    b. conflict
    c. parenting style
    d. discipline
    e. encouragement
        ANSWER: c   TYPE: M   COG: R
46. Families are run as a _____ where members interact with one another to form a whole.
    a. clan
    b. system
    c. dictatorship
    d. democracy
    e. partnership
        ANSWER: b   TYPE: M   COG: R

47. Brian and Ilse became a couple and then became very different than when they were single. This is an example that:
    a. a family is more than the sum of its parts.
    b. family members are interdependent.
    c. family members take on each other's characteristics and behaviors.
    d. a and b only
    e. all of the above
        ANSWER: a   TYPE: M   COG: C
48. Mother-father, mother-son, mother-daughter, father-son, father-daughter, daughter-son are an example of:
    a. pairs.
    b. family members.
    c. roles.
    d. relationships.
    e. family subsystems.
        ANSWER: e   TYPE: M   COG: R
49. Daria's mother and uncle got into an argument. Daria's father was also angry about the situation. Before the situation became too tense, the three of them sat down and openly discussed the problem, which is an example of a family who uses:
    a. high conformity orientation.
    b. high conversion orientation.
    c. low interdependent orientation.
    d. low systematic orientation.
    e. high ritualistic orientation.
        ANSWER: b   TYPE: M   COG: A
50. Brennan's parents are very supportive of he and his brother finding careers that they love, expressing their individuality by dressing in ways that are comfortable to them, and by helping to make decisions about the household. This is an example of a family who uses:
    a. high conformity orientation.
    b. low conformity orientation.
    c. high conversion orientation.
    d. low conversion orientation.
    e. medium conversion orientation.
        ANSWER: b   TYPE: M   COG: R
51. When children are raised in a household where there is little discussion about private thoughts, this is known as a _____ family.
    a. high conformity orientation
    b. low conformity orientation
    c. high conversion orientation
    d. low conversion orientation
    e. medium conversion orientation
        ANSWER: d   TYPE: M   COG: R
52. The following are examples of which gender-related communication: communication that emphasizes instrumental, task-related topics and is low in expressive emotional content?
    a. stereotypical masculine
    b. stereotypical feminine
    c. androgynous
    d. undifferentiated
    e. none of the above
        ANSWER: a   TYPE: M   COG: R

53. Which of the following gender-type communication pairings in couples did research indicate had the lowest level of love and satisfaction?
    a. androgynous husbands and stereotypical feminine wives
    b. undifferentiated husbands and undifferentiated wives
    c. stereotypical masculine husbands and undifferentiated wives
    d. stereotypical masculine husbands and androgynous wives
    e. stereotypical masculine husbands and stereotypical feminine wives
        ANSWER: e   TYPE: M   COG: R

54. A blended family is:
    a. a family of mixed heritage.
    b. people who marry and have children from a prior marriage.
    c. a family where the parents are divorced but living together.
    d. people who are not married but raising children together.
    e. none of the above
        ANSWER: b   TYPE: M   COG: R

55. Families who are most successful at negotiating adolescence tend to be:
    a. undifferentiated.
    b. blended.
    c. flexible.
    d. intimate.
    e. none of the above
        ANSWER: c   TYPE: M   COG: R

56. Which of the dimensions of interaction identified in the Stocker and McHale research had the highest level of reciprocity?
    a. affection
    b. hostility
    c. rivalry
    d. contention
    e. they were all the same
        ANSWER: a   TYPE: M   COG: R

57. Staying out of the kitchen when mom is cooking a big family meal is an example of
    a. cohesion
    b. boundaries
    c. expression
    d. privacy
    e. none of the above
        ANSWER: b   TYPE: M   COG: R

58. Which of the following is NOT a characteristic of a chaotic family?
    a. impulsive decision-making
    b. dramatic shifts in roles
    c. erratic leadership
    d. extreme adaptability
    e. unclear roles
        ANSWER: d   TYPE: M   COG: R

59. Research shows that which of the following are highly confirming behaviors that parents can offer to children?
    a. telling their children they are valued
    b. genuinely listening to their children
    c. telling their children they are unique
    d. all of the above
    e. none of the above
        ANSWER: d   TYPE: M   COG: R

60. Gottman's research indicates what ratio of positive-to-negative communication is present in satisfied couples' (including couples who fight) marriages?
    a. 1:1
    b. 2:1
    c. 3:1
    d. 4:1
    e. 5:1
        ANSWER: e   TYPE: M   COG: R
61. Conflict in families _____ than in other relationships.
    a. is less violent
    b. occurs less often
    c. occurs more often
    d. is more constructive
    e. none of the above
        ANSWER: c   TYPE: M   COG: R
62. Which of the following behaviors caused both husbands and wives to feel less understood and less satisfied with their marriages?
    a. withdrawing
    b. raising voices
    c. combativeness
    d. passive aggression
    e. none of the above
        ANSWER: a   TYPE: M   COG: R
63. Talking with a friend about whether or not God exists and if there is order in the universe constitutes what type of intimacy?
    a. emotional
    b. physical
    c. intellectual
    d. shared activities
    e. all of the above
        ANSWER: c   TYPE: M   COG: A
64. Teasing one another is an example of what kind of intimacy?
    a. emotional
    b. physical
    c. intellectual
    d. shared activities
    e. all of the above
        ANSWER: d   TYPE: M   COG: R
65. Recent scholarship indicates that in terms of gender and the meaning of intimacy women and men are more _____ than _____.
    a. similar/different
    b. different/similar
    c. positive/negative
    d. negative/positive
    e. none of the above
        ANSWER: a   TYPE: M   COG: R

66. Many women think of sex as a way to _____ intimacy, while men are more likely to see it as a way to _____ intimacy.
    a.   prolong/curtail
    b.   curtail/prolong
    c.   express/create
    d.   create/express
    e.   none of the above
        ANSWER: c   TYPE: M   COG: R

67. When one partner says, "I get worried when you haven't shown me affection n a few days," it is an example of which of the strategies for maintaining romantic relationships?
    a.   positivity
    b.   openness
    c.   assurances
    d.   sharing tasks
    e.   social networks
        ANSWER: b   TYPE: M   COG: A

68. When one partner in a relationship says, "My mom and dad said we make a really good couple," it is an example of which of the strategies for maintaining romantic relationships?
    a.   positivity
    b.   openness
    c.   assurances
    d.   sharing tasks
    e.   social networks
        ANSWER: e   TYPE: M   COG: A

69. A family rule prohibiting entering a bedroom without knocking first is an example of a:
    a.   conformity.
    b.   pluralism.
    c.   boundary.
    d.   laissez-faire.
    e.   none of the above
        ANSWER: c   TYPE: M   COG: A

Essay

70. Discuss the idea that families are "systems."
        ANSWER: TYPE: E   COG: C
71. Discuss the idea that a family is "more than the sum of its parts."
        ANSWER: TYPE: E   COG: C
72. Discuss how *family narratives* can affect family communication.
        ANSWER: TYPE: E   COG: A
73. Describe the difference between task-oriented and maintenance-oriented friendships.
        ANSWER: TYPE: E   COG: C
74. Explain how the social penetration model impacts low disclosure versus high disclosure in friendships.
        ANSWER: TYPE: E   COG: C
75. Describe stages in a person's life where communication may change within the course of a friendship.
        ANSWER: TYPE: E   COG: A
76. Explain why heterosexual women say they feel more attractive around gay men.
        ANSWER: TYPE: E   COG: A
77. Give examples of families who represent high and low conversion orientation.
        ANSWER: TYPE: E   COG: C
78. Give examples of families who represent high and low conformity orientation.
        ANSWER: TYPE: E   COG: C

79. Explain the concept of "boundaries" as it pertains to families. Give examples of the three types of boundaries that exist within families.

     ANSWER: TYPE: E   COG: C

80. What are benefits and drawbacks of a chaotic or rigid family? Explain.

     ANSWER: TYPE: E   COG: A

81. Do you agree that the large differences in intimacy behaviors that once existed between Western and Eastern cultures may be fast disappearing? Why or why not?

     ANSWER: TYPE: E   COG: A

82. The textbook indicates that recent scholarship shows that emotional expression is not the only way to develop close relationships. What other ways can you think of?

     ANSWER: TYPE: E   COG: A

83. Do you agree that mediated communication is more effective than face-to-face interaction in improving the quality of a relationship? Explain.

     ANSWER: TYPE: E   COG: A

84. What role do *boundaries* play in family interaction?

     ANSWER: TYPE: E   COG: R

Matching

85. Match the lettered examples to the numbered types of friendship.

     1. Short-Term vs. Long-Term
     2. Task-Oriented vs. Maintenance-Oriented
     3. Low Disclosure vs. High Disclosure
     4. Low Obligation vs. High Obligation
     5. Infrequent Contact vs. Frequent Contact

a. Susan and Neelam's friendship primarily revolves around going to see the big new movie that has just come out.
b. Marco confides in Tim about how things at work are going.
c. Annette and Joan have been friends for years: since they were both young mothers.
d. Elise and Robert only talk about once or twice a year, but both feel that they pick up right where they left off.
e. John asks Uli to take golf lessons with him, but Uli isn't so sure.

Answer: 1. c, 2. a, 3. b, 4. e, 5. D

86. Match the lettered examples to the numbered vocabulary terms from the textbook.

_____ 1. expectancy violations
_____ 2. enmeshed
_____ 3. chaotic family
_____ 4. conformity orientation
_____ 5. intimacy

a. Oftentimes Stephen, the eldest of three children, has to pick up his little brother from daycare with little warning from his mother. His father has just decided to go back to school, despite starting a new and stressful job. School starts this week.
b. Yaping was hurt when her best friend Joy announced on Facebook that she was getting married, without telling Yaping first.
c. Tabitha's father gave her a clear curfew. When Tabitha questioned it her father said, "I will not debate this; you know I expect your compliance."
d. Martina loves to hold and rock her new baby. As she feeds him she kisses the top of his head.
e. Clay feels that he must vote the same way his family does, attend the same church and often feels guilt if he criticizes a member of his family.

1. b, 2. e, 3. a, 4. c, 5. d